The Renaissance

PROBLEMS IN
EUROPEAN CIVILIZATION

Under the editorial direction of
John Ratté
Amherst College

The Renaissance

Basic Interpretations

Second Edition

Edited and with an introduction by

Karl H. Dannenfeldt
Arizona State University

D. C. HEATH AND COMPANY
Lexington, Massachusetts Toronto

CONTENTS

INTRODUCTION

In 1860 in the introduction to his work on *The Civilization of the Renaissance in Italy,* Jacob Burckhardt predicted the present "problem of the Renaissance" when he wrote, "To each eye, perhaps, the outlines of a great civilization present a different picture. . . . In the wide ocean upon which we venture, the possible ways and directions are many; and the same studies which have served for this work might easily, in other hands, not only receive a wholly different treatment and application, but lead to essentially different conclusions."

To the writers of the Italian Renaissance itself, there was no serious problem. Their views of the age in which they were living furnished the basis for a long-held concept, namely, that after a period of about a thousand years of cultural darkness and ignorance, there arose a new age with a great revival in classical literature, learning, and the arts.

The humanists of the northern Renaissance continued this concept. "Out of the thick Gothic night our eyes are opened to the glorious torch of the sun," wrote Rabelais. Moreover, there was also now introduced a reforming religious element, further emphasizing the medieval barbarization of religion and culture. Protestant writers joined in this condemnation of the dark medieval period, an attack little circumscribed by the defense of the medieval church by Catholic apologists.

The system of classical education and the standards of classical art employed in the subsequent centuries meant a continuation of the concept established by the humanists. Indeed, the historical philosophy current in the Age of Reason, for purposes of its own, supported the earlier view. Rationalists like Voltaire, Condorcet, Bolingbroke, and Hume saw nothing but barbarism, ignorance, superstition, violence, irrationality, and priestly tyranny in the period of Western history between the fall of Rome and the beginning of the modern era, the Renaissance. They also gave currency to the concept of the Italian Renaissance as a period of brilliant culture and irreligion.

It was only in the late eighteenth and early nineteenth century, with the development of the intellectual revolution known as Romanticism, that a reaction took place. A new spirit led the Romanticists to see much in the past to understand and admire. There was a lively interest in historical growth and evolution, including that which took place in the Middle Ages. Human history was enthusiastically approached; the folk origins of art, language, literature, and music were patriotically idealized; and the irrational, the simple, and the emotional sympathetically sought out. The Age of Faith was discovered and peopled with chivalrous knights, beautiful ladies, pious clergy, and industrious peasants. The unity of medieval Christianity and the corporatism of medieval society was admired. Rescuing the Middle Ages from the oblivion to which the classicists and rationalists had relegated it, the Romantic writers found the Renaissance pagan, sensuous, villainous, and shocking—yet attractive.

The astonishing growth of historical research in the nineteenth century produced a great number of works influenced by such varying movements as nationalism, liberalism, Romanticism, neoclassicism, and Hegelian philosophy. The spirit expressed in the art and humanism of the Renaissance received especial consideration. A tendency toward periodization is also characteristic. In the seventh volume (1855) of his *History of France* (1833–1862), Jules Michelet, the liberal historian, examined the Renaissance of the sixteenth century in his own country. He saw in medieval civilization the destruction of freedom and the debasement of the human spirit while in the Renaissance came "the discovery of the world and the discovery of man" and the spontaneous rebirth of art and antiquity. Michelet applied the term "Renaissance" to the entire heroic period and not just to art and the classical revival as had been customary. His Renaissance was a distinct epoch, sharply contrasting in spirit with the preceding age.

Five years after Michelet's analysis Jacob Burckhardt formulated the modern traditional interpretation of the Italian Renaissance. Burckhardt's claim to fame is not due to the originality of his ideas and terms, for most of these had been current for centuries. Rather, the greatness of this Swiss historian lay in his ability to make use of the best elements at hand in producing a coherent masterpiece of synthesis in his *Civilization of the Renaissance in Italy* (1860). In his essay, drawn with the masterful hand of a literary artist, Burckhardt sought to lay bare the modern and inner spirit of the Italian Renaissance, approaching the period in a series of topical discussions centering around the civilization as a whole.

Burckhardt's concept of the Italian Renaissance was widely accepted. However, the intellectual, social, and economic phases, which he had neglected, received considerable attention, alteration, or expansion by historians. Renaissance art, also not a part of Burckhardt's essay, was now examined as a product of the spirit and culture of the age. Non-Italian writers related the Renaissance within their own nation to that described by Burckhardt.

While many of the writers of the late nineteenth and early twentieth centuries echo the decisive Burckhardtian synthesis, others began to feel that his harmonious picture of the Italian Renaissance was just too perfect and static. As specialized studies contributed greatly to the knowledge of other periods, especially that of the Middle Ages, questions began to arise in the minds of historians. Was the contrast between the Renaissance and the medieval period so great? What really brought on the Renaissance in Italy? Were the elements of individualism and modernity unknown before the Renaissance? Was the picture Burckhardt presented true in its delimitations, simplicity, harmony, and construction? Was the Renaissance as pagan and irreligious as depicted? Can science be used as a criterion for the modernity of the Renaissance? A variety of viewpoints on these and other questions are given in the selections which follow.

The marked growth of medieval studies in the twentieth century has been most responsible for attacks on Burckhardt's outline and for the creation of the "problem of the Renaissance." The readings which follow present a representative sample of the conflicting opinions on several of the most important aspects of this broad and complex problem.

The two selections which follow Burckhardt are concerned with the political aspects of the Renaissance. The first, an article by the leading authority on medieval political theory, C. H. McIlwain, stresses the medieval elements in our modern political heritage. He feels that the medieval period was not "one long, dreary epoch of stagnation, of insecurity, of lawless violence." Rather the Middle Ages saw the rise of the very important modern concepts of constitutionalism and the limitation of public authority by private right. In the next excerpt, however, the prominent Renaissance scholar, Hans Baron, reaffirms the Burckhardtian view that the rise of modern political ideas and institutions was one of the distinguishing marks of the Italian Renaissance. He emphasizes the role of the structure and activities of the Italian city-state in producing modern political theory and the pattern of modern government.

In his essay Burckhardt did not give much attention to economic factors or to their effect on the civilization of the Italian Renaissance. In the twentieth century, the relatively new methodologies of psychology, sociology, and economics opened up new approaches for an examination of the civilization of the Renaissance. Prominent among those who used the new methods was Alfred von Martin. Much influenced by the socioeconomic writings of Mannheim, Weber, and other German scholars, he sought to analyze the civilization of the Renaissance, "laying bare its roots." Von Martin accepted as essential Burckhardt's periodization, the stress on individualism, and the significance of the Italian Renaissance as the period of transition from the medieval to the modern world. The excerpt from *The Sociology of the Renaissance* makes evident his conviction that there was a causal relationship between what he describes as "the new dynamic" of capitalism and the characteristics of the Renaissance which Burckhardt had delineated.

While von Martin and others saw the flowering of the Italian Renaissance as the result of vast socioeconomic changes, further research and specialized studies in the economic conditions of the Middle Ages and the Renaissance led to qualifications about the brilliant results of economic changes and to some questions about the economic conditions themselves. In the selection by R. S. Lopez, which follows Von Martin's, the prevailing view of the Italian Renaissance as a brilliant period of dynamic economic expansion is criticized. Professor Lopez feels that the Renaissance in Italy was founded on an earlier medieval economic expansion. In fact, the period of the Renaissance was marked by economic depression, stagnation of population, and excessive taxation. W. K. Ferguson's survey of economic historiography of the Renaissance presents the more recent research and interpretive activity in the field of Renaissance economics. He notes that the more abundant statistical data on the economics of the period do not tell the whole story and that more attention must be given to the spirit and motives of the business community and the relationship of economic individualism and Renaissance culture.

Burckhardt had not included very much on science in his essay, but the twentieth-century emphasis on the importance of science as one of the most distinctive elements of modern civilization has led later scholars to attempt to evaluate the originality of the Renaissance in this field. The selection by Marie Boas furnishes an introduction to the growth of a fresh, humanistic exploration of Greek science and its close relationship to the rise of modern science. To the author, the period of 1450 to 1630 marks a break with the past due largely to the reexamination of the Greek legacy. In the Renaissance session of the American Historical Association meeting in December 1941, Professor Dana B. Durand of Mount Holyoke College presented a paper entitled "Tradition and Innovation in Fifteenth-Century Italy." Because of the length and technical complexity of Professor Durand's paper it is not included in the selections which follow, but basing his argument on the lack of evidence of advance in certain technical fields such as map-making and astronomy, he concluded that as far as science and scientific thought are concerned, "the balance of tradition and innovation in fifteenth-century Italy was not so decisively favorable as to distinguish that century radically from those that preceded it, nor to constitute the Quattrocento a unique and unrivaled moment in the history of Western thought."[1] In this same session, however, Dr. Baron presented a paper entitled "Toward a More Positive Evaluation of the Fifteenth-Century Renaissance" which is included. After a discussion of certain political aspects of the problem in Part I of his essay, Dr. Baron turned to the scientific contributions of the Quattrocento. He pointed out that the Burckhardtian thesis of a "fundamental change in man's outlook on life and the world" included the new scientific approach which has since marked modern civilization.

Professor P. O. Kristeller, in remarks also made at this same

[1] *Journal of the History of Ideas* 4 (1943): 20.

session, examined in some detail the contributions of the humanists to the development of science. He assigned to the Italian humanists an important, if indirect, part in the development of scientific thought, in that they recovered, edited, and made more accessible the body of ancient scientific literature and learning. Another participant at this session of the American Historical Association, Professor Lynn Thorndike, in contrast to both Baron and Kristeller, set forth with great vigor his antipathy toward the whole concept of the "so-called Renaissance." He stressed the unbroken continuity of medieval forms and interests and attacked the originality of the Renaissance in science as well as in other fields. His contribution concludes the group of selections dealing with the problem of science in the Renaissance.

Burckhardt, unfortunately, never wrote the comprehensive history of art which he had planned as a supplement to his crucial essay on Renaissance civilization. Yet, later historians of art and music could not ignore the Burckhardtian interpretation and the impact of the spirit of the times on human artistic expression. In the first selection of this group, Rudolf Wittkower concludes that the modern type of artist, a personality who is certain of his importance, rose in the Renaissance. In the next brief selection, Edward Lowinsky summarizes his study of music in the Renaissance with the contention that there was a "Renaissance" in music involving an emancipation from older musical institutions and the medieval musical aesthetics and system of modes. Numerous innovations occurred along a broad front of musical activity.

Medieval historians have always been in the forefront of the attack on the Burckhardtian conception of the Renaissance, and in the next group of excerpts three prominent medieval scholars present a variety of arguments and evidence in support of this assault.

In his review of "Modern Theories of the Renaissance," Douglas Bush, a professor of literature, evidences a wide-ranging knowledge and keen understanding of the problem of the Renaissance and concludes by placing himself among those who consider that period to be essentially an extension of the Middle Ages. Also in direct opposition to Burckhardt he feels that Italian humanism was strongly Christian in character, not irreligious and pagan.

An even stronger plea for the originality and the primacy of the medieval contribution to modern culture is to be found in the selection from one of the best known works of Charles Homer Haskins, the man who was for many years the dean of American medieval historians. In this excerpt Professor Haskins points out that many elements usually thought of as distinguishing the culture of the Renaissance, such as the revival of the Latin classics, Latin literature, and Greek science and philosophy, are to be found in the twelfth century. In the concluding piece in this group another medievalist, the famous Dutch scholar, Johan Huizinga, while ready to accept the term "Renaissance" as a convenient chronological designation, nevertheless sees the period of the fourteenth and fifteenth centuries as terminating the Middle Ages. His views are presented here in an extract from his celebrated study of the cultural history of France and the Netherlands during these two centuries.

The interpretations of the Renaissance made by the authors selected for inclusion in this book furnish only a very limited glimpse of the many specialized studies of various aspects of the Renaissance and Middle Ages which have appeared in the century since the publication of Burckhardt's essay. W. K. Ferguson, who has devoted so much of his life to the problem of Renaissance interpretation, is the author of our last selection. Drawing on his knowledge of the history of interpretation, he offers a summary of past and more recent views and concludes that the Renaissance was an age of transition with a mixture of medieval and modern elements. He also suggests a broad theory of causation.

Any student who examines the period of the Renaissance is confronted with the necessity of attempting to formulate his own answer to the vexing "problem of the Renaissance." The study of the following selections should assist in this respect. It should also bring the student to the realization of the necessary caution which must be exercised in approaching the interpretations of any historical era or civilization.

Conflict of Opinion

In the character of these states, whether republics or despotism, lies, not the only, but the chief, reason for the early development of the Italian. To this it is due that he was the firstborn among the sons of modern Europe. . . .

We must insist upon it, as one of the chief propositions of this book, that it was not the revival of antiquity alone, but its union with the genius of the Italian people, which achieved the conquest of the Western world. . . .

Since, again, the Italians were the first modern people of Europe who gave themselves boldly to speculations on freedom and necessity, and since they did so under violent and lawless political circumstances, in which evil seemed often to win a splendid and lasting victory, their belief in God began to waver, and their view of the government of the world became fatalistic.

JACOB BURCKHARDT

Did Renaissance Italy produce the first modern political state?

In the field of political institutions and ideas I venture to think that what Professor Haskins has termed "the Renaissance of the twelfth century" marks a more fundamental change than the later developments to which we usually attach the word "Renaissance"; that the constitutionalism of the modern world owes as much, if not even more, to the twelfth and thirteenth centuries than to any later period of comparable length before the seventeenth.

C. H. McILWAIN

It is because of this survival of civic initiative in geographic proximity to bureaucratic-unifying absolutism that the whole range of modern political experience was traversed in the fifteenth century, and this so rapidly that by the end of the century many of the basic tenets of modern political science had matured, and had been set forth in works of European scope by Machiavelli and Guicciardini.

HANS BARON

Is there an economic basis for the Renaissance in Italy?

The center of gravity of medieval society was the land, was the soil. With the Renaissance the economic and thus the social emphasis moves into the town; from the conservative to the liberal, for the town is a changeable and changing element. . . . What was fundamentally new was the rational management of money and the investment of capital. Capital had a creative effect and put a premium on ingenuity and enterprise.

ALFRED VON MARTIN

. . . we have to take stock of the now prevalent theory that the Renaissance witnessed a deep economic crisis though not a total catastrophe (are there any total catastrophes in history?), and that in spite of many local, partial, or temporary gains it represented an anticlimax or at least a phase of slower development after the quicker progress of the medieval commercial revolution.

R. S. LOPEZ

Did the Italian Renaissance make original contributions to science?

Above all, return to the original enforced a more serious consideration of what Aristotle, Hippocrates, Galen and Ptolemy had actually said, and this in turn involved recognition of the truth, error, fruitfulness or uselessness of the contributions the great scientists of the past had made. This constituted a first step towards scientific advance.

MARIE BOAS

. . . the balance of tradition and innovation of fifteenth-century Italy was not so decisively favorable as to distinguish that century radically from those that preceded it, not to constitute the Quattrocento a unique and unrivaled moment in the history of western thought.

DANA B. DURAND

The influence of humanism on science as well as on philosophy was indirect, but powerful. The actual performance of the humanists in these fields was rather poor. But they popularized the entire body of ancient Greek learning and literature and thus made available new source materials of which the professional scientists and philosophers could not fail to take advantage.

PAUL O. KRISTELLER

Not only has it been demonstrated that the thirteenth and fourteenth centuries were more active and penetrating in natural science than was the Quattrocento, but the notion that "appreciation of natural beauty" was "introduced into modern Europe by the Italian Renaissance" must also be abandoned.

LYNN THORNDIKE

Can studies of Renaissance art and music contribute to an understanding of the period?

Let me sum up: the artists, freed from the protective bond of the guilds, faced the struggle with their environment alone. Early in the sixteenth century they emerged in Italy as an idiosyncratical professional caste with immensely strong leading individuals, who yet developed along the grooves prepared for them. The modern type of artist had come into existence.

RUDOLF WITTKOWER

. . . every musical enterprise of the Renaissance is characterized by an endless curiosity, a firm—if at times concealed—refusal to abide by authority for authority's sake, an intrepid pioneering spirit and an inexhaustible joy in theoretical speculation, personal and literary controversy and debate, and practical experimentation.

EDWARD E. LOWINSKY

Can we still retain the periodic concept of the Renaissance?

The Middle Ages exhibit life and color and change, much eager search after knowledge and beauty, much creative accomplishment in art, in literature, in institutions. The Italian Renaissance was preceded by similar, if less wide-reaching movements; indeed it came out of the Middle Ages so gradually that historians are not agreed when it began, and some would go so far as to abolish the name, and perhaps even the fact, of a renaissance in the Quattrocento.

CHARLES HOMER HASKINS

According to the celebrated Swiss historian, the quest of personal glory was the characteristic attribute of the men of the Renaissance. . . . It was in Italy, he thinks, under the influence of antique models, that the craving for individual glory originated. Here, as elsewhere, Burckhardt has exaggerated the distance separating Italy from the Western countries and the Renaissance from the Middle Ages.

JOHAN HUIZINGA

The Renaissance, it seems to me, was essentially an age of transition, containing much that was still medieval, much that was recognizably modern, and, also, much that, because of the mixture of medieval and modern elements, was peculiar to itself and was responsible for its contradictions and contrasts and its amazing vitality.

WALLACE K. FERGUSON

Jacob Burckhardt

THE CIVILIZATION OF THE RENAISSANCE IN ITALY

THE STATE AS A WORK OF ART

This work bears the title of an essay in the strictest sense of the word. No one is more conscious than the writer with what limited means and strength he has addressed himself to a task so arduous. And even if he could look with greater confidence upon his own researches he would hardly thereby feel more assured of the approval of competent judges. To each eye, perhaps, the outlines of a given civilization present a different picture; and in treating of a civilization which is the mother of our own, and whose influence is still at work among us, it is unavoidable that individual judgment and feeling should tell every moment both on the writer and on the reader. In the wide ocean upon which we venture, the possible ways and directions are many; and the same studies which have served for this work might easily, in other hands, not only receive a wholly different treatment and application, but lead also to essentially different conclusions. Such indeed is the importance of the subject, that it calls for fresh investigation, and may be studied with advantage from the most varied points of view. Meanwhile we are content if a patient hearing is granted us, and if this book be taken and judged as a whole. It is the most serious difficulty of the history of civilization that a great intellectual process must be broken up into single, and often into what seem arbitrary categories, in order to be in any way intelligible. It was formerly our intention to fill up the gaps in this book by a special work on the "Art of the Renaissance" —an intention, however, which we have been able only to fulfill in part. The struggle between the popes and the Hohenstaufen left Italy in a political condition which differed essentially from that of other countries of the West. While in France, Spain, and England the feudal system was so organized that, at the close of its existence, it was

From Jacob Burckhardt, *The Civilization of the Period of the Renaissance in Italy*, trans. S. G. C. Middlemore (London, 1878), vol. 1, pp. 3–17, 85–86, 103–120, 181–190, 191–197, 239–242, 245–246, 283–285; vol. 2, pp. 3–20, 35–37, 42–43, 46, 109–116, 246–247, 297–301, 305, 309–317, 318–320.

naturally transformed into a unified monarchy, and while in Germany it helped to maintain, at least outwardly, the unity of the empire, Italy had shaken it off almost entirely. The emperors of the fourteenth century, even in the most favorable case, were no longer received and respected as feudal lords, but as possible leaders and supporters of powers already in existence; while the papacy, with its creatures and allies, was strong enough to hinder national unity in the future, not strong enough itself to bring about that unity. Between the two lay a multitude of political units—republics and despots—in part of long standing, in part of recent origin, whose existence was founded simply on their power to maintain it. In them for the first time we detect the modern political spirit of Europe, surrendered freely to its own instincts, often displaying the worst features of an unbridled egotism, outraging every right, and killing every germ of a healthier culture. But, wherever this vicious tendency is overcome or in any way compensated, a new fact appears in history—the state as the outcome of reflection and calculation, the state as a work of art. This new life displays itself in a hundred forms, both in the republican and in the despotic states, and determines their inward constitution, no less than their foreign policy. We shall limit ourselves to the consideration of the completer and more clearly defined type, which is offered by the despotic states.

The internal condition of the despotically governed states had a memorable counterpart in the Norman Empire of Lower Italy and Sicily, after its transformation by the emperor Frederick II. Bred amid treason and peril in the neighborhood of the Saracens, Frederick, the first ruler of the modern type who sat upon a throne, had early accustomed himself, both in criticism and action, to a thoroughly objective treatment of affairs. His acquaintance with the internal condition and administration of the Saracenic states was close and intimate; and the mortal struggle in which he was engaged with the papacy compelled him, no less than his adversaries, to bring into the field all the resources at his command. Frederick's measures (especially after the year 1231) are aimed at the complete destruction of the feudal state, at the transformation of the people into a multitude destitute of will and of the means of resistance, but profitable in the utmost degree to the exchequer. He centralized, in a manner hitherto unknown in the West, the whole judicial and political administration by establishing the right of appeal from the

FIGURE 1. The Fall of Constantinople to the Turks, 1453, as described by Hartmann Schedel in his *Buch der Chroniken* (Nuremberg, 1493), reprinted by Brussel and Brussel, Inc., New York, 1966. (*Used by permission.*)

feudal courts, which he did not, however, abolish, to the imperial judges. No office was henceforth to be filled by popular election, under penalty of the devastation of the offending district and of the enslavement of its inhabitants. Excise duties were introduced; the taxes, based on a comprehensive assessment, and distributed in accordance with Mohammedan usages, were collected by those cruel and vexatious methods without which, it is true, it is impossible to obtain any money from Orientals. Here, in short, we find, not a people, but simply a disciplined multitude of subjects; who were forbidden, for example, to marry out of the country without special permission, and under no circumstances were allowed to study abroad. The University of Naples was the first we know of to restrict the freedom of study, while the East, in these respects at all events, left its youth unfettered. It was after the example of Mohammedan rulers that Frederick traded on his own account in all parts of the Mediterranean, reserving to himself the monopoly of many commodities, and restricting in various ways the commerce of his subjects. The Fatimite caliphs, with all their esoteric unbelief, were, at least in their earlier history, tolerant of all the differences in the religious faith of their people; Frederick, on the other hand, crowned his system of government by a religious inquisition, which will seem the more reprehensible when we remember that in the persons of the heretics he was persecuting the representatives of a free municipal life. Lastly, the internal police, and the kernel of the army for foreign service, was composed of Saracens who had been brought over from Sicily to Nocera and Luceria—men who were deaf to the cry of misery and careless of the ban of the Church. At a later period the subjects, by whom the use of weapons had long been forgotten, were passive witnesses of the fall of Manfred and of the seizure of the government by Charles of Anjou; the latter continued to use the system which he found already at work.

At the side of the centralizing emperor appeared an usurper of the most peculiar kind: his vicar and son-in-law, Ezzelino de Romano. He stands as the representative of no system of government or administration, for all his activity was wasted in struggles for supremacy in the eastern part of Upper Italy; but as a political type he was a figure of no less importance for the future than his imperial protector Frederick. The conquests and usurpations which had hitherto taken place in the Middle Ages rested on real or pretended inheritance and other such claims, or else were effected against unbelievers and excommunicated persons. Here for the first time the attempt was openly made to found a throne by wholesale murder and endless barbarities, by the adoption, in short, of any means with a view to nothing but the end pursued. None of his successors, not even Cesare Borgia, rivaled the colossal guilt of Ezzelino; but the example once set was not forgotten, and his fall led to no return of justice among the nations, and served as no warning to future transgressors.

It was in vain at such a time that St. Thomas Aquinas, a born subject of Frederick, set up the theory of a constitutional monarchy, in which the prince was to be supported by an upper house named by himself, and a representative body elected by the people; in vain did he concede to the people the right of revolution. Such theories found no echo outside the lecture room, and Frederick and Ezzelino were and remain for Italy the great political phenomena of the thirteenth century. Their personality, already half legendary, forms the most important subject of "The Hundred Old Tales" whose original composition falls certainly within this century. In them Frederick is already represented as possessing the right to do as he pleased with the property of his subjects, and exercises on all, even on criminals, a profound influence by the force of his personality; Ezzelino is spoken of with the awe which all mighty impressions leave behind them. His person became the center of a whole literature, from the chronicle of eyewitnesses to the half-mythical tragedy of later poets.

The Tyranny of the Fourteenth Century

The tyrannies, great and small, of the fourteenth century afford constant proof that examples such as these were not thrown away. Their crimes, which were fearful, have been fully told by historians. As states depending for existence on themselves alone, and scientifically organized with a view to this object, they present to us a higher interest than that of mere narrative.

The deliberate adaptation of means to ends, of which no prince out of Italy had at that time a conception, joined to almost absolute power within the limits of the state, produced among the despots both men and modes of life of a peculiar character. The chief secret of government in the hands of the prudent ruler lay in leaving the incidence of taxation so far as possible where he found it, or as he had first arranged it. The chief sources of income were: a land tax, based on a valuation; definite taxes on articles of consumption and duties on exported and imported goods; together with the private fortune of the ruling house. The only possible increase was derived from the growth of business and of general prosperity. Loans, such as we find in the free cities, were here unknown; a well-planned confiscation was held a preferable means of raising money, provided only that it left public credit unshaken—an end attained, for example, by the truly Oriental practice of deposing and plundering the director of the finances.

Out of this income the expenses of the little court, of the body-guard, of the mercenary troops, and of the public buildings were met, as well as of the buffoons and men of talent who belonged to the personal attendants of the prince. The illegitimacy of his rule isolated the tyrant and surrounded him with constant danger; the most honorable alliance which he could form was with intellectual merit, without regard to its origin. The liberality of the northern princes of the thirteenth century was confined to the knights, to the nobility which served and sang. It was otherwise with the Italian despot. With his thirst for fame and his passion for monumental works, it was talent, not birth, which he needed. In the company of the poet and the scholar he felt himself in a new position, almost, indeed, in possession of a new legitimacy.

No prince was more famous in this respect than the ruler of Verona, Can Grande della Scala, who numbered among the illustrious exiles whom he entertained at his court representatives of the whole of Italy. The men of letters were not ungrateful. Petrarch, whose visits at the courts of such men have been so severely censured, sketched an ideal picture of a prince of the fourteenth century. He demands great things from his patron, the lord of Padua, but in a manner which shows that he holds him capable of them. "Thou must not be the master but the father of thy subjects, and must love them as thy children; yea, as members of thy body. Weapons, guards, and soldiers thou mayest employ against the enemy—with thy subjects goodwill is sufficient. By citizens, of course, I mean those who love the existing order; for those who daily desire change are rebels and traitors, and against such a stern justice may take its course."

Here follows, worked out in detail, the purely modern fiction of the omnipotence of the State. The prince is to be independent of his courtiers, but at the same time to govern with simplicity and modesty; he is to take everything into his charge, to maintain and restore churches and public buildings, to keep up the municipal police, to drain the marshes, to look after the supply of wine and corn; he is to exercise a strict justice, so to distribute the taxes that the people can recognize their necessity and the regret of the ruler to put his hands into the pockets of others; he is to support the sick and the helpless, and to give his protection and society to distinguished scholars, on whom his fame in after ages will depend.

But whatever might be the brighter sides of the system, and the merits of individual rulers, yet the men of the fourteenth century were not without a more or less distinct consciousness of the brief and uncertain tenure of most of these despotisms. Inasmuch as political institutions like these are naturally secure in proportion to the size of the territory in which they exist, the larger principalities were constantly tempted to swallow up the smaller. Whole hecatombs of petty rulers were sacrificed at this time to the Visconti alone. As a result of this outward danger an inward ferment was in ceaseless activity; and the effect of the situation on the character of the ruler was generally of the most sinister kind. Absolute power, with its temptations to luxury and unbridled selfishness, and the perils to which he was exposed from enemies and conspirators, turned him almost inevitably into a tyrant in the worst sense of the word. Well for him if he could trust his nearest relations! But where all was illegitimate, there could be no regular law of inheritance, either with regard to the succession or to the division of the ruler's property; and consequently the heir, if incompetent or a minor, was liable in the interest of the family itself to be supplanted by an uncle or cousin of more resolute character. The acknowledgement or exclusion of the bastards was a fruitful source of contest; and most of these families in consequence were plagued with a crowd of discontented and vindictive kinsmen. This circumstance gave rise to continual outbreaks of treason and to frightful scenes of domestic bloodshed. Sometimes the pretenders lived abroad in exile, and like the Visconti, who practiced the fisherman's craft on the Lake of Garda, viewed the situation with patient indifference. When asked by a messenger of his rival when and how he thought of returning to Milan, he gave the reply, "By the same means as those by which I was expelled, but not till his crimes have outweighed my own." Sometimes, too, the despot was sacrificed by his relations, with the view of saving the family, to the public conscience which he had too grossly outraged. In a few cases the government was in the hands of the whole family, or at least the ruler was bound to take their advice; and here, too, the distribution of property and influence led to bitter disputes.

The whole of this system excited the deep and persistent hatred

of the Florentine writers of that epoch. Even the pomp and display
with which the despot was perhaps less anxious to gratify his own
vanity than to impress the popular imagination, awakened their
keenest sarcasm. Woe to an adventurer if he fell into their hands,
like the upstart Doge Aguello of Pisa (1364), who used to ride out
with a golden scepter, and show himself at the window of his house,
"as relics are shown," reclining on embroidered drapery and cush-
ions, served like a pope or emperor, by kneeling attendants. More
often, however, the old Florentines speak on this subject in a tone of
lofty seriousness. Dante saw and characterized well the vulgarity
and commonplace which mark the ambition of the new princes.
"What mean their trumpets and their bells, their horns and their
flutes; but come, hangman—come, vultures?" The castle of the
tyrant, as pictured by the popular mind, is a lofty and solitary building, full of dungeons and listening tubes, the home of cruelty and
misery. Misfortune is foretold to all who enter the service of the
despot, who even becomes at last himself an object of pity: he must
needs be the enemy of all good and honest men; he can trust no
one, and can read in the faces of his subjects the expectation of his
fall. "As despotisms rise, grow, and are consolidated, so grows in
their midst the hidden element which must produce their dissolution
and ruin." But the deepest ground of dislike has not been stated;
Florence was then the scene of the richest development of human
individuality, while for the despots no other individuality could be
suffered to live and thrive but their own and that of their nearest
dependents. The control of the individual was rigorously carried out,
even down to the establishment of a system of passports.

The astrological superstitions and the religious unbelief of many
of the tyrants gave, in the minds of their contemporaries, a peculiar
color to this awful and Godforsaken existence. When the last Carrara
could no longer defend the walls and gates of the plague-stricken
Padua, hemmed in on all sides by the Venetians (1405), the soldiers
of the guard heard him cry to the devil "to come and kill him." . . .

The Republics: Venice and Florence

The Italian municipalities had, in earlier days, given signal proof of
that force which transforms the city into the state. It remained only
that these cities should combine in a great confederation; and this

idea was constantly recurring to Italian statesmen, whatever differences of form it might from time to time display. In fact, during the struggles of the twelfth and thirteenth centuries, great and formidable leagues actually were formed by the cities; and Sismondi is of opinion that the time of the final armaments of the Lombard confederation against Barbarossa [from 1168 on] was the moment when a universal Italian league was possible. But the more powerful states had already developed characteristic features which made any such scheme impracticable. In their commercial dealings they shrank from no measures, however extreme, which might damage their competitors; they held their weaker neighbors in a condition of helpless dependence—in short, they each fancied they could get on by themselves without the assistance of the rest, and thus paved the way for future usurpation. The usurper was forthcoming when long conflicts between the nobility and the people, and between the different factions of the nobility, had awakened the desire for a strong government, and when bands of mercenaries ready and willing to sell their aid to the highest bidder had superseded the general levy of the citizens which party leaders now found unsuited to their purposes. The tyrants destroyed the freedom of most of the cities; here and there they were expelled, but not thoroughly, or only for a short time; and they were always restored, since the inward conditions were favorable to them, and the opposing forces were exhausted.

Among the cities which maintained their independence are two of deep significance for the history of the human race: Florence, the city of incessant movement, which has left us a record of the thoughts and aspirants of each and all who, for three centuries, took part in this movement, and Venice, the city of apparent stagnation and political secrecy. No contrast can be imagined stronger than that which is offered us by these two, and neither can be compared to anything else which the world has hitherto produced. . . .

The most elevated political thought and the most varied forms of human development are found united in the history of Florence, which in this sense deserves the name of the first modern state in the world. Here the whole people are busied with what in the despotic cities is the affair of a single family. That wondrous Florentine spirit, at once keenly critical and artistically creative, was incessantly transforming the social and political condition of the state, and as

incessantly describing and judging the change. Florence thus became the home of political doctrines and theories, of experiments
and sudden changes, but also, like Venice, the home of statistical
science, and alone and above all other states in the world, the
home of historical representation in the modern sense of the phrase.
The spectacle of ancient Rome and a familiarity with its leading
writers were not without influence; Giovanni Villani confesses that
he received the first impulse to his great work at the jubilee of the
year 1300, and began it immediately on his return home. Yet how
many among the 200,000 pilgrims of that year may have been like
him in gifts and tendencies, and still did not write the history of
their native cities! For not all of them could encourage themselves
with the thought: "Rome is sinking; my native city is rising, and
ready to achieve great things and therefore I wish to relate its past
history, and hope to continue the story of the present time, and as
long as my life shall last." And besides the witness to its past,
Florence obtained through its historians something further—a
greater fame than fell to the lot of any other city of Italy.

Our present task is not to write the history of this remarkable
state, but merely to give a few indications of the intellectual freedom and independence for which the Florentines were indebted to
this history.

In no other city of Italy were the struggles of political parties so
bitter, of such early origin, and so permanent. The descriptions of
them, which belong, it is true, to a somewhat later period, give clear
evidence of the superiority of Florentine criticism.

And what a politician is the great victim of these crises, Dante
Alighieri, matured alike by home and by exile! He uttered his scorn
of the incessant changes and experiments in the constitution of his
native city in verses of adamant, which will remain proverbial so long
as political events of the same kind recur; he addressed his home in
words of defiance and yearning which must have stirred the hearts
of his countrymen. But his thoughts ranged over Italy and the whole
world; and if his passion for the empire, as he conceived it, was no
more than an illusion, it must yet be admitted that the youthful
dreams of a newborn political speculation are in his case not without a poetical grandeur. He is proud to be the first who trod this
path, certainly in the footsteps of Aristotle, but in his own way independently. His ideal emperor is a just and humane judge, dependent

on God only, the heir of the universal sway of Rome to which belonged the sanction of nature, of right and of the will of God. The conquest of the world was, according to this view, rightful, resting on a divine judgment between Rome and the other nations of the earth, and God gave his approval to this empire, since under it he became Man, submitting at his birth to the census of the emperor Augustus, and at his death to the judgment of Pontius Pilate. We may find it hard to appreciate these and other arguments of the same kind, but Dante's passion never fails to carry us with him. In his letters he appears as one of the earliest publicists, and is perhaps the first layman to publish political tracts in this form. He began early. Soon after the death of Beatrice he addressed a pamphlet on the state of Florence "to the Great ones of the Earth," and the public utterances of his later years, dating from the time of his banishment, are all directed to emperors, princes, and cardinals. In these letters and in his book *De vulgari eloquentia* the feeling, bought with such bitter pains, is constantly recurring that the exile may find elsewhere than in his native place an intellectual home in language and culture, which cannot be taken from him. On this point we shall have more to say in the sequel.

To the two Villani, Giovanni as well as Matteo, we owe not so much deep political reflection as fresh and practical observations, together with the elements of Florentine statistics and important notices of other states. Here too trade and commerce had given the impulse to economical as well as political science. Nowhere else in the world was such accurate information to be had on financial affairs. The wealth of the papal court at Avignon, which at the death of John XXII amounted to 25 millions of gold florins, would be incredible on any less trustworthy authority. Here only, at Florence, do we meet with colossal loans like that which the king of England contracted from the Florentine houses of Bardi and Peruzzi, who lost to his Majesty the sum of 1,365,000 gold florins (1338)—their own money and that of their partners—and nevertheless recovered from the shock. Most important facts are here recorded as to the condition of Florence at this time; the public income (over 300,000 gold florins) and expenditure; the population of the city, here only roughly estimated, according to the consumption of bread, in *bocche,* i.e. mouths, put at 90,000, and the population of the whole territory; the excess of 300 to 5C0 male children among the 5,800 to 6,000 annually baptised; the schoolchildren, of whom 8,000 to 10,000 learned reading, 1,000 to 1,200 in six schools arithmetic; and besides these, 600 scholars who were taught Latin grammar and logic in four schools. Then follow the statistics of the churches and monasteries; of the hospitals, which held more than a thousand beds; of the wool trade, with most valuable details; of the mint, the provisioning of the city, the public officials, and so on. Incidentally we learn many curious facts; how, for instance, when the public funds (*monte*) were first established, in the year 1353, the Franciscans spoke from the pulpit in favor of the measure, the Dominicans and Augustinians against it. The economical results of the Black Death were and could be observed and described nowhere else in all Europe as in this city. Only a Florentine could have left it on record how it was expected that the scanty population would have made everything cheap, and how instead of that labor and commodities doubled in price; how the common people at first would do no work at all, but simply give themselves up to enjoyment; how in the city itself servants and maids were not to be had except at extravagant wages; how the peasants would only till the best lands, and left the rest uncultivated; and how the enormous legacies bequeathed to the poor at the time of the plague seemed afterwards useless, since the poor had either died or had ceased to be poor. Lastly, on the occasion of a great bequest, by which a childless philantropist left six *danari* to every beggar in the city, the attempt is made to give a comprehensive statistical account of Florentine mendicancy.

This statistical view of things was at a later time still more highly cultivated at Florence. The noteworthy point about it is that, as a rule, we can perceive its connection with the higher aspects of history, with art, and with culture in general. An inventory of the year 1422 mentions, within the compass of the same document, the seventy-two exchange offices which surrounded the Mercato Nuovo; the amount of coined money in circulation (2 million golden florins); the then new industry of gold spinning; the silk wares; Filippo Brunellescchi, then busy in digging classical architecture from its grave; and Leonardo Aretino, secretary of the republic, at work at the revival of ancient literature and eloquence; lastly, it speaks of the general prosperity of the city, then free from political conflicts, and of the good fortune of Italy, which had rid itself of foreign mercenaries. The Venetian statistics quoted above which date from about the same year, certainly give evidence of larger property and profits and of a more extensive scene of action; Venice had long been mistress of the seas before Florence sent out its first galleys (1422) to Alexandria. But no reader can fail to recognize the higher spirit of the Florentine documents. These and similar lists recur at intervals of ten years, systematically arranged and tabulated, while elsewhere we find at best occasional notices. We can form an approximate estimate of the property and the business of the first Medici; they paid for charities, public buildings, and taxes from 1434 to 1471 no less than 663,755 gold florins, of which more than 400,000 fell on Cosimo alone, and Lorenzo Magnifico was delighted that the money had been so well spent. In 1472 we have again a most important and in its way complete view of the commerce and trades of this city, some of which may be wholly or partly reckoned among the fine arts—such as those which had to do with damasks and gold or silver embroidery, with wood-carving and *intarsia,* with the sculpture of arabesques in marble and sandstone, with portraits in wax, and with jewelry and work in gold. The inborn talent of the Florentines for the systematization of outward life is shown by their books on agriculture, business, and domestic economy, which are markedly superior to those of other European people in the fifteenth century. It has been rightly decided to publish selections of these works, although no little study will be needed to extract clear and definite results from them. At all events, we have no difficulty in recognizing the city, where dying parents begged the government in their wills to fine their sons 1,000 florins if they declined to practice a regular profession.

For the first half of the sixteenth century probably no state in the world possesses a document like the magnificent description of Florence by Varchi. In descriptive statistics, as in so many things besides, yet another model is left to us, before the freedom and greatness of the city sank into the grave.

This statistical estimate of outward life is, however, uniformly accompanied by the narrative of political events to which we have already referred.

Florence not only existed under political forms more varied than those of the free states of Italy and of Europe generally, but it reflected upon them far more deeply. It is a faithful mirror of the relations of individuals and classes to a variable whole. The pictures of the great civic democracies in France and in Flanders, as they are delineated in Froissart, and the narratives of the German chroniclers of the fourteenth century, are in truth of high importance; but in comprehensiveness of thought and in the rational development of the story, none will bear comparison with the Florentines. The rule of the nobility, the tyrannies, the struggles of the middle class with the proletariat, limited and unlimited democracy, pseudodemocracy, the primacy of a single house, the theocracy of Savonarola, and the mixed forms of government which prepared the way for the Medicean despotism—all are so described that the inmost motives of the actors are laid bare to the light. At length Machiavelli in his Florentine history (down to 1492) represents his native city as a living organism and its development as a natural and individual process; he is the first of the moderns who has risen to such a conception. It lies without our province to determine whether and in what points Machiavelli may have done violence to history, as is notoriously the case in his life of Castruccio Castracani—a fancy picture of the typical despot. We might find something to say against every line of the *Istorie Fiorentine,* and yet the great and unique value of the whole would remain unaffected. And his contemporaries and successors, Jacopo Pitti, Guicciardini, Segni, Varchi, Vettori, what a circle of illustrious names! And what a story it is which these masters tell us! The great and memorable drama of the last decades of the Florentine republic is here unfolded. The voluminous record of the collapse of the highest and most original life which the world could then show may appear to one but as a collection of curiosities, may awaken in another a devilish delight at the shipwreck of so much nobility and grandeur, to a third may seem like a great historical assize; for all it will be an object of thought and study to the end of time. The evil, which was forever troubling the peace of the city, was its rule over once powerful and now conquered rivals like Pisa— a rule of which the necessary consequence was a chronic state of violence. The only remedy, certainly an extreme one and which none but Savonarola could have persuaded Florence to accept, and that only with the help of favorable chances, would have been the well-timed resolution of Tuscany into a federal union of free cities. At a later period this scheme, then no more than the dream of a past age, brought (1548) a patriotic citizen of Lucca to the scaffold. From this evil and from the ill-starred Guelph sympathies of Florence for a foreign prince, which familiarized it with foreign intervention, came all the disasters which followed. But who does not admire the people, which was wrought up by its venerated preacher to a mood of such sustained loftiness, that for the first time in Italy it set the example of sparing a conquered foe, while the whole history of its past taught nothing but vengeance and extermination? The glow which melted patriotism into one with moral regeneration may seem, when looked at from a distance, to have soon passed away; but its best results shine forth again in the memorable siege of 1529–1530. They were "fools," as Guicciardini then wrote, who drew down this storm upon Florence, but he confesses himself that they achieved things which seemed incredible; and when he declares that sensible people would have got out of the way of the danger, he means no more than that Florence ought to have yielded itself silently and ingloriously into the hands of its enemies. It would no doubt have preserved its splendid suburbs and gardens, and the lives and prosperity of countless citizens; but it would have been the poorer by one of its greatest and most ennobling memories.

In many of their chief merits the Florentines are the pattern and the earliest type of Italians and modern Europeans generally; they are so also in many of their defects. When Dante compares the city which was always mending its constitution with the sick man who is continually changing his posture to escape from pain, he touches with the comparison a permanent feature of the political life of Florence. The great modern fallacy that a constitution can be made, can be manufactured by a combination of existing forces and tendencies, was constantly cropping up in stormy times; even Machiavelli is not wholly free from it. Constitutional artists were never wanting who by an ingenious distribution and division of political power, by indirect elections of the most complicated kind, by the establishment of nominal offices, sought to found a lasting order of things, and to satisfy or to deceive the rich and the poor alike. They naively fetch their examples from classical antiquity, and borrow the party names *Ottimati, Aristocrazia,* as a matter of course. The world since then has become used to these expressions and given them a conventional European sense, whereas all former party names were purely national, and either characterized the cause at issue or sprang from the caprice of accident. But how a name colors or discolors a political cause!

But of all who thought it possible to construct a state, the greatest beyond all comparison was Machiavelli. He treats existing forces as living and active, takes a large and an accurate view of alternative possibilities, and seeks to mislead neither himself nor others. No man could be freer from vanity or ostentation; indeed, he does not write for the public but either for princes and administrators or for personal friends. The danger for him does not lie in an affectation of genius or in a false order of ideas, but rather in a powerful imagination which he evidently controls with difficulty. The objectivity of his political judgment is sometimes appalling in its sincerity; but it is the sign of a time of no ordinary need and peril, when it was a hard matter to believe in right, or to credit others with just dealing. Virtuous indignation at his expense is thrown away upon us who have seen in what sense political morality is understood by the statesmen of our own century. Machiavelli was at all events able to forget himself in his cause. In truth, although his writings, with the exception of very few words, are altogether destitute of enthusiasm, and although the Florentines themselves treated him at last as a criminal, he was a patriot in the fullest meaning of the word. But free as he was, like most of his contemporaries, in speech and morals, the welfare of the state was yet his first and last thought.

His most complete program for the construction of a new political system at Florence is set forth in the memorial to Leo X, composed after the death of the younger Lorenzo de' Medici, duke of Urbino (d. 1519), to whom he had dedicated his *The Prince.* The state was by that time in extremities and utterly corrupt, and the remedies proposed are not always morally justifiable; but it is most interesting to see how he hopes to set up the republic in the form of a moderate democracy, as heiress to the Medici. A more ingenious scheme of concessions to the pope, to the pope's various adherents, and to the different Florentine interests, cannot be imagined; we might fancy ourselves looking into the works of a clock. Principles, observations, comparisons, political forecasts, and the like are to be found in numbers in the *Discorsi,* among them flashes of wonderful insight. He recognizes, for example, the law of a continuous though not uniform development in republican institutions, and requires the constitution to be flexible and capable of change, as the only means of dispensing with bloodshed and banishments. For a like reason, in order to guard against private violence and foreign interference—

"the death of all freedom"—he wishes to see introduced a judicial procedure (*accusa*) against hated citizens, in place of which Florence had hitherto had nothing but the court of scandal. With a masterly hand the tardy and involuntary decisions are characterized, which at critical moments play so important a part in republican states. Once, it is true, he is misled by his imagination and the pressure of events into unqualified praise of the people, which chooses its officers, he says, better than any prince, and which can be cured of its errors by "good advice." With regard to the government of Tuscany, he has no doubt that it belongs to his native city, and maintains, in a special *Discorso* that the reconquest of Pisa is a question of life or death; he deplores that Arezzo, after the rebellion of 1502, was not razed to the ground; he admits in general that Italian republics must be allowed to expand freely and add to their territory in order to enjoy peace at home, and not to be themselves attacked by others, but declares that Florence had always begun at the wrong end, and from the first made deadly enemies of Pisa, Lucca, and Siena, while Pistoia, "treated like a brother," had voluntarily submitted to her. . . .

THE DEVELOPMENT OF THE INDIVIDUAL

The Italian State and the Individual

In the character of these states, whether republics or despotisms, lies, not the only, but the chief, reason for the early development of the Italian. To this it is due that he was the firstborn among the sons of modern Europe.

In the Middle Ages both sides of human consciousness—that which was turned within as that which was turned without—lay dreaming or half-awake beneath a common veil. The veil was woven of faith, illusion, and childish prepossession, through which the world and history were seen clad in strange hues. Man was conscious of himself only as a member of a race, people, party, family, or corporation—only through some general category. In Italy this veil first melted into air; an *objective* treatment and consideration of the state and of all the things of this world became possible. The *subjective* side at the same time asserted itself with corresponding emphasis; man became a spiritual *individual,* and recognized himself as such.

In the same way the Greek had once distinguished himself from the barbarian, and the Arabian had felt himself an individual at a time when other Asiatics knew themselves only as members of a race. It will not be difficult to show that this result was owing above all to the political circumstances of Italy.

In far earlier times we can here and there detect a development of free personality which in northern Europe either did not occur at all, or could not display itself in the same manner. The band of audacious wrongdoers in the tenth century described to us by Luidprand, some of the contemporaries of Gregory VII, and a few of the opponents of the first Hohenstaufen, show us characters of this kind, but at the close of the thirteenth century Italy began to swarm with individuality; the charm laid upon human personality was dissolved; and a thousand figures meet us each in its own special shape and dress. Dante's great poem would have been impossible in any other country of Europe, if only for the reason that they all still lay under the spell of race. For Italy the august poet, through the wealth of individuality which he set forth, was the most national herald of his time. But this unfolding of the treasures of human nature in literature and art—this many-sided representation and criticism—will be discussed in separate chapters; here we have to deal only with the psychological fact itself. This fact appears in the most decisive and unmistakable form. The Italians of the four-teenth century knew little of false modesty or of hypocrisy in any shape; not one of them was afraid of singularity, of being and seem-ing unlike his neighbors.

Despotism, as we have already seen, fostered in the highest degree the individuality not only of the tyrant or condottiere himself, but also of the men whom he protected or used as his tools—the secre-tary, minister, poet, and companion. These people were forced to know all the inward resources of their own nature, passing or perma-nent; and their enjoyment of life was enhanced and concentrated by the desire to obtain the greatest satisfaction from a possibly very brief period of power and influence.

But even the subjects whom they ruled over were not free from the same impulse. Leaving out of account those who wasted their lives in secret opposition and conspiracies, we speak of the majority who were content with a strictly private station, like most of the urban population of the Byzantine Empire and the Mohammedan states. No doubt it was often hard for the subjects of a Visconti to maintain the dignity of their persons and families, and multitudes must have lost in moral character through the servitude they lived under. But this was not the case with regard to individuality; for political impotence does not hinder the different tendencies and manifestations of private life from thriving in the fullest vigor and variety. Wealth and culture, so far as display and rivalry were not forbidden to them, a municipal freedom which did not cease to be considerable, and a church which, unlike that of the Byzantine or of the Mohammedan world, was not identical with the state—all these conditions undoubtedly favored the growth of individual thought, for which the necessary leisure was furnished by the cessation of party conflicts. The private man, indifferent to politics, and busied partly with serious pursuits, partly with the interests of a dilettante, seems to have been first fully formed in these despotisms of the fourteenth century. Documentary evidence cannot, of course, be required on such a point. The novelists, from whom we might expect information, describe to us oddities in plenty, but only from one point of view and in so far as the needs of the story demand. Their scene, too, lies chiefly in the republican cities.

In the latter, circumstances were also, but in another way, favorable to the growth of individual character. The more frequently the governing party was changed, the more the individual was led to make the utmost of the exercise and enjoyment of power. The statesmen and popular leaders, especially in Florentine history, acquired so marked a personal character, that we can scarcely find, even exceptionally, a parallel to them in contemporary history, hardly even in Jacob von Arteveldt.

The members of the defeated parties, on the other hand, often came into a position like that of the subjects of the despotic states, with the difference that the freedom or power already enjoyed, and in some cases the hope of recovering them, gave a higher energy to their individuality. Among these men of involuntary leisure we find, for instance, an Agnolo Pandolfini (d. 1446), whose work on domestic economy is the first complete program of a developed private life. His estimate of the duties of the individual as against the dangers and thanklessness of public life is in its way a true monument of the age.

Banishment, too, has this effect above all, that it either wears the exile out or develops whatever is greatest in him. "In all our more populous cities," says Geoviano Pontano, "we see a crowd of people who have left their homes of their own free will; but a man takes his virtues with him wherever he goes." And, in fact, they were by no means only men who had been actually exiled, but thousands left their native place voluntarily, because they found its political or economical condition intolerable. The Florentine emigrants at Ferrara and the Lucchese in Venice formed whole colonies by themselves.

The cosmopolitanism which grew up in the most gifted circles is in itself a high stage of individualism. Dante, as we have already said, finds a new home in the language and culture of Italy, but goes beyond even this in the words, "My country is the whole world." And when his recall to Florence was offered him on unworthy conditions, he wrote back: "Can I not everywhere behold the light of the sun and the stars; everywhere meditate on the noblest truths, without appearing ingloriously and shamefully before the city and the people. Even my bread will not fail me." The artists exult no less defiantly in their freedom from the constraints of fixed residence. "Only he who has learned everything," says Ghiberti, "is nowhere a stranger; robbed of his fortune and without friends, he is yet the citizen of every country, and can fearlessly despise the changes of fortune." In the same strain an exiled humanist writes: "Wherever a learned man fixes his seat, there is home."

The Perfecting of the Individual

An acute and practiced eye might be able to trace, step by step, the increase in the number of complete men during the fifteenth century. Whether they had before them as a conscious object the harmonious development of their spiritual and material existence, is hard to say; but several of them attained it, so far as is consistent with the imperfection of all that is earthly. It may be better to renounce the attempt at an estimate of the share which fortune, character, and talent had in the life of Lorenzo Magnifico. But look at a personality like that of Ariosto, especially as shown in his satires. In what harmony are there expressed the pride of the man and the poet, the irony with which he treats his own enjoyments, the most delicate satire, and the deepest goodwill!

When this impulse to the highest individual development was

combined with a powerful and varied nature, which had mastered all the elements of the culture of the age, then arose the "all-sided man" —*l'uomo universale*—who belonged to Italy alone. Men there were of encyclopedic knowledge in many countries during the Middle Ages, for this knowledge was confined within narrow limits; and even in the twelfth century there were universal artists, but the problems of architecture were comparatively simple and uniform, and in sculpture and painting the matter was of more importance than the form. But in Italy at the time of the Renaissance, we find artists who in every branch created new and perfect works, and who also made the greatest impression as men. Others, outside the arts they practiced, were masters of a vast circle of spiritual interests. . . .

The fifteenth century is, above all, that of the many-sided men. There is no biography which does not, besides the chief work of its hero, speak of other pursuits all passing beyond the limits of dilettantism. The Florentine merchant and statesman was often learned in both the classical languages; the most famous humanists read the ethics and politics of Aristotle to him and his sons; even the daughters of the house were highly educated. It is in these circles that private education was first treated seriously. The humanist, on his side, was compelled to the most varied attainments, since his philological learning was not limited, as it now is, to the theoretical knowledge of classical antiquity, but had to serve the practical needs of daily life. While studying Pliny, he made collections of natural history; the geography of the ancients was his guide in treating of modern geography, their history was his pattern in writing contemporary chronicles, even when composed in Italian; he not only translated the comedies of Plautus, but acted as manager when they were put on the stage; every effective form of ancient literature down to the dialogues of Lucian he did his best to imitate; and besides all this, he acted as magistrate, secretary, and diplomatist—not always to his own advantage.

But among these many-sided men, some who may truly be called all-sided, tower above the rest. Before analyzing the general phases of life and culture of this period, we may here, on the threshold of the fifteenth century, consider for a moment the figure of one of these giants—Leon Battista Alberti (b. 1404? d. 1472). His biography, which is only a fragment, speaks of him but little as an artist, and makes no mention at all of his great significance in the history of architecture. We shall now see what he was, apart from these special claims to distinction.

In all by which praise is won, Leon Battista was from his childhood the first. Of his various gymnastic feats and exercises we read with astonishment how, with his feet together, he could spring over a man's head; how, in the cathedral, he threw a coin in the air till it was heard to ring against the distant roof; how the wildest horses trembled under him. In three things he desired to appear faultless to others, in walking, in riding, and in speaking. He learned music without a master, and yet his compositions were admired by professional judges. Under the pressure of poverty, he studied both civil and canonical law for many years, till exhaustion brought on a severe illness. In his twenty-fourth year, finding his memory for words weakened, but his sense of facts unimpaired, he set to work at physics and mathematics. And all the while he acquired every sort of accomplishment and dexterity, cross-examining artists, scholars, and artisans of all descriptions, down to the cobblers, about the secrets and peculiarities of their craft. Painting and modeling he practiced by the way, and especially excelled in admirable likenesses from memory. Great admiration was excited by his mysterious *camera obscura,* in which he showed at one time the stars and the moon rising over rocky hills, at another wide landscapes with mountains and gulfs receding into dim perspective, and with fleets advancing on the waters in shade or sunshine. And that which others created he welcomed joyfully, and held every human achievement which followed the laws of beauty for something almost divine. To all this must be added his literary works, first of all those on art, which are landmarks and authorities of the first order for the Renaissance of Form, especially in architecture; then his Latin prose writings—novels and other works—of which some have been taken for productions of antiquity; his elegies, eclogues, and humorous dinner-speeches. He also wrote an Italian treatise on domestic life in four books; various moral, philosophical, and historical works; and many speeches and poems, including a funeral oration on his dog. . . . His serious and witty sayings were thought worth collecting, and specimens of them, many columns long, are quoted in his biography. And all that he had and knew he imparted, as rich natures always do, without the least reserve, giving away his chief discoveries for nothing. But the deepest spring of his nature has yet to be spoken of—the sympathetic intensity with which he entered into the whole life around him. At the sight of noble trees and waving corn-fields he shed tears; handsome and dignified old men he honored as "a delight of nature," and could never look at them enough. Perfectly formed animals won his goodwill as being specially favored by nature; and more than once, when he was ill, the sight of a beautiful landscape cured him. No wonder that those who saw him in this close and mysterious communion with the world ascribed to him the gift of prophecy. He was said to have foretold a bloody catastrophe in the family of Este, the fate of Florence, and the death of the popes years before they happened, and to be able to read into the countenances and the hearts of men. It need not be added that an iron will pervaded and sustained his whole personality; like all the great men of the Renaissance, he said, "Men can do all things if they will."

And Leonardo da Vinci was to Alberti as the finisher to the beginner, as the master to the dilettante. Would only that Vasari's work were here supplemented by a description like that of Alberti! The colossal outlines of Leonardo's nature can never be more than dimly and distantly conceived.

The Modern Idea of Fame

To this inward development of the individual corresponds a new sort of outward distinction—the modern form of glory.

In other countries of Europe the different classes of society lived apart, each with its own medieval caste sense of honor. The poetical fame of the troubadours and minnesinger was peculiar to the knightly order. But in Italy social equality had appeared before the time of the tyrannies or the democracies. We there find early traces of a general society, having, as will be shown more fully later on, a common ground in Latin and Italian literature; and such a ground was needed for this new element in life to grow in. To this must be added that the Roman authors, who were now zealously studied, and especially Cicero, the most read and admired of all, are filled and saturated with the conception of fame, and that their subject itself—the universal empire of Rome—stood as a permanent ideal before the minds of Italians. From henceforth all the aspirations and achievements of the people were governed by a moral postulate, which was still unknown elsewhere in Europe. . . .

THE REVIVAL OF ANTIQUITY

Now that this point in our historical view of Italian civilization has been reached, it is time to speak of the influence of antiquity, the "new birth" of which has been one-sidedly chosen as the name to sum up the whole period. The conditions which have been hitherto described would have sufficed, apart from antiquity, to upturn and to mature the national mind; and most of the intellectual tendencies which yet remain to be noticed would be conceivable without it. But both what has gone before and what we have still to discuss are colored in a thousand ways by the influence of the ancient world; and though the essence of the phenomena might still have been the same without the classical revival, it is only with and through this revival that they are actually manifested to us. The Renaissance would not have been the process of worldwide significance which it is, if its elements could be so easily separated from one another. We must insist upon it, as one of the chief propositions of this book, that it was not the revival of antiquity alone, but its union with the genius of the Italian people, which achieved the conquest of the Western world. The amount of independence which the national spirit maintained in this union varied according to circumstances. In the modern Latin literature of the period, it is very small, while in plastic art, as well as in other spheres, it is remarkably great; and hence the alliance between two distant epochs in the civilization of the same people, because concluded on equal terms, proved justifiable and fruitful. The rest of Europe was free either to repel or else partly or wholly to accept the mighty impulse which came forth from Italy. Where the latter was the case we may as well be spared the complaints over the early decay of medieval faith and civilization. Had these been strong enough to hold their ground, they would be alive to this day. If those elegiac natures which long to see them return could pass but one hour in the midst of them, they would gasp to be back in the modern air. That in a great historical process of this kind flowers of exquisite beauty may perish, without being made immortal in poetry or tradition, is undoubtedly true; nevertheless, we cannot wish the process undone. The general result of it consists in this—that by the side of the church which had hitherto held the countries of the West together (though it was unable to do so much longer) there arose a new spiritual influence which, spreading itself abroad from Italy, became the breath of life for all the more instructed minds in Europe. The worst that can be said of the movement is that it was antipopular, that through it Europe became for the first time sharply divided into the cultivated and uncultivated classes. The reproach will appear groundless when we reflect that even now the fact, though clearly recognized, cannot be altered. The separation, too, is by no means so cruel and absolute in Italy as elsewhere. The most artistic of her poets, Tasso, is in the hands of even the poorest.

The civilization of Greece and Rome, which, ever since the fourteenth century, obtained so powerful a hold on Italian life, as the source and basis of culture, as the object and ideal of existence, partly also as an avowed reaction against preceding tendencies— this civilization had long been exerting a partial influence on medieval Europe, even beyond the boundaries of Italy. The culture of which Charles the Great was a representative was, in the face of the barbarism of the seventh and eighth centuries, essentially a Renaissance, and could appear under no other form. Just as in the Romanesque architecture of the North, beside the general outlines inherited from antiquity, remarkable direct imitations of the antique also occur, so too monastic scholarship had not only gradually absorbed an immense mass of materials from Roman writers, but the style of it, from the days of Eginhard onwards, shows traces of conscious imitations.

But the resuscitation of antiquity took a different form in Italy from that which it assumed in the North. The wave of barbarism had scarcely gone by before the people, in whom the former life was but half effaced, showed a consciousness of its past and a wish to reproduce it. Elsewhere in Europe men deliberately and with reflection borrowed this or the other element of classical civilization; in Italy the sympathies both of the learned and of the people were naturally engaged on the side of antiquity as a whole, which stood to them as a symbol of past greatness. The Latin language, too, was easy to an Italian, and the numerous monuments and documents in which the country abounded facilitated a return to the past. With this tendency other elements—the popular character which time had now greatly modified, the political institutions imported by the Lombards from Germany, chivalry and other northern forms of civilization, and the influence of religion and the church—

combined to produce the modern Italian spirit, which was destined
to serve as the model and ideal for the whole Western world. . . .

But the great and general enthusiasm of the Italians for classical
antiquity did not display itself before the fourteenth century. For
this a development of civic life was required, which took place only
in Italy, and there not till then. It was needful that noble and burgher
should first learn to dwell together on equal terms, and that a social
world should arise which felt the want of culture, and had the leisure
and the means to obtain it. But culture, as soon as it freed itself
from the fantastic bonds of the Middle Ages, could not at once and
without help find its way to the understanding of the physical and
intellectual world. It needed a guide, and found one in the ancient
civilization, with its wealth of truth and knowledge in every spiritual
interest. Both the form and the substance of this civilization were
adopted with admiring gratitude; it became the chief part of the
culture of the age. The general condition of the country was favorable to this transformation. The medieval empire, since the fall of
the Hohenstaufen, had either renounced, or was unable to make good,
its claims on Italy. The popes had migrated to Avignon. Most of
the political powers actually in existence owed their origin to violent
and illegitimate means. The spirit of the people, now awakened to
self-consciousness, sought for some new and stable ideal on which
to rest. And thus the vision of the worldwide empire of Italy and
Rome so possessed the popular mind, that Cola di Rienzi could
actually attempt to put it in practice. The conception he formed of
his task, particularly when tribune for the first time, could only end
in some extravagant comedy; nevertheless, the memory of ancient
Rome was no slight support to the national sentiment. Armed afresh
with its culture, the Italian soon felt himself in truth citizen of the
most advanced nation in the world. . . .

Humanism in the Fourteenth Century

Who now were those who acted as mediators between their own age
and a venerated antiquity, and made the latter a chief element in the
culture of the former?

They were a crowd of the most miscellaneous sort, wearing one
face today and another tomorrow; but they clearly felt themselves,
and it was fully recognized by their time, that they formed a wholly

new element in society. The *clerici vagantes* of the twelfth century, whose poetry we have already referred to, may perhaps be taken as their forerunners—the same unstable existence, the same free and more than free views of life, and the germs at all events of the same pagan tendencies in their poetry. But now, as competitor with the whole culture of the Middle Ages, which was essentially clerical and was fostered by the church, there appeared a new civilization, founding itself on that which lay on the other side of the Middle Ages. Its active representatives became influential because they knew what the ancients knew, because they tried to write as the ancients wrote, because they began to think, and soon to feel, as the ancients thought and felt. The traditions to which they devoted themselves passed at a thousand points into genuine reproduction.

Some modern writers deplore the fact that the germs of a far more independent and essentially national culture, such as appeared in Florence about the year 1300, were afterwards so completely swamped by the humanists. There was then, we are told, nobody in Florence who could not read; even the donkeyman sang the verses of Dante; the best Italian manuscripts which we possess belonged originally to Florentine artisans; the publication of a popular encyclopedia, like the *Tesoro* of Brunetto Latini, was then possible; and all this was founded on a strength and soundness of character due to the universal participation in public affairs, to commerce and travel, and to the systematic reprobation of idleness. The Florentines, it is urged, were at that time respected and influential throughout the whole world, and were called in that year, not without reason, by Pope Boniface VIII, "the fifth element." The rapid progress of humanism after the year 1400 paralyzed native impulses. Henceforth men looked to antiquity only for the solution of every problem, and consequently allowed literature to sink into mere quotation. Nay, the very fall of civil freedom is partly to be ascribed to all this, since the new learning rested on obedience to authority, sacrificed municipal rights to Roman law, and thereby both sought and found the favor of the despots.

These charges will occupy us now and then at a later stage of our inquiry, when we shall attempt to reduce them to their true value, and to weigh the losses against the gains of this movement. For the present we must confine ourselves to showing how the civilization even of the vigorous fourteenth century necessarily prepared the way for the complete victory of humanism, and how precisely the greatest representatives of the national Italian spirit were themselves the men who opened wide the gate for the measureless devotion to antiquity in the fifteenth century. . . .

THE DISCOVERY OF THE WORLD AND OF MAN

Journeys of the Italians

Freed from the countless bonds which elsewhere in Europe checked progress, having reached a high degree of individual development and been schooled by the teachings of antiquity, the Italian mind now turned to the discovery of the outward universe, and to the representation of it in speech and in form.

On the journeys of the Italians to distant parts of the world, we can here make but a few general observations. The Crusades had opened unknown distances to the European mind, and awakened in all the passion for travel and adventure. It may be hard to indicate precisely the point where this passion allied itself with, or became the servant of, the thirst for knowledge; but it was in Italy that this was first and most completely the case. Even in the Crusades the interest of the Italians was wider than that of other nations, since they already were a naval power and had commercial relations with the East. From time immemorial the Mediterranean Sea had given to the nations that dwelt on its shores mental impulses different from those which governed the peoples of the North; and never, from the very structure of their character, could the Italians be adventurers in the sense which the word bore among the Teutons. After they were once at home in all the eastern harbors of the Mediterranean, it was natural that the most enterprising among them should be led to join that vast international movement of the Mohammedans which there found its outlet. A new half of the world lay, as it were, freshly discovered before them. Or, like Polo of Venice, they were caught in the current of the Mongolian peoples, and carried on to the steps of the throne of the Great Khan. At an early period, we find Italians sharing in the discoveries made in the Atlantic Ocean; it was the Genoese who, in the thirteenth century, found the Canary Islands. In the same year, 1291, when Ptolemais, the last remnant of the Christian East, was lost, it was again the Genoese who made the first known attempt to find a sea-passage to the East Indies. Columbus himself is but the greatest of a long list of Italians who, in the service of the Western nations, sailed into distant seas. The true discoverer, however, is not the man who first chances to stumble upon anything, but the man who finds what he has sought. Such a one alone stands in a link with the thoughts and interests of his predecessors, and this relationship will also determine the account he gives of his search. For which reason the Italians, although their claim to be the first comers on this or that shore may be disputed, will yet retain their title to be preeminently the nation of discoverers for the whole latter part of the Middle Ages. The fuller proof of this assertion belongs to the special history of discoveries. Yet ever and again we turn with admiration to the august figure of the great Genoese, by whom a new continent beyond the ocean was demanded, sought, and found; and who was the first to be able to say: "il mondo è poco"—the world is not so large as men have thought. At the time when Spain gave Alexander VI to the Italians, Italy gave Columbus to the Spaniards. Only a few weeks before the death of that pope (July 7, 1503), Columbus wrote from Jamaica his noble letter to the thankless Catholic kings, which the ages to come can never read without profound emotion. In a codicil to his will, dated Valladolid, May 4, 1506, he bequeathed to "his beloved home, the Republic of Genoa, the prayer-book which Pope Alexander had given him, and which in prison, in conflict, and in every kind of adversity had been to him the greatest of comforts." It seems as if these words cast upon the abhorred name of Borgia one last gleam of grace and mercy.

The development of geographical and the allied sciences among the Italians must, like the history of their voyages, be touched upon but very briefly. A superficial comparison of their achievements with those of other nations shows an early and striking superiority on their part. Where, in the middle of the fifteenth century, could be found, anywhere but in Italy, such a union of geographical, statistical, and historical knowledge as was found in Aeneas Sylvius? Not only in his great geographical work, but in his letters and commentaries, he describes with equal mastery landscapes, cities, manners, industries and products, political conditions and constitutions, wherever he can use his own observation or the evidence of eyewitnesses. What he takes from books is naturally of less moment. Even the short sketch of that valley in the Tyrolese Alps, where Frederick III had given him a benefice, and still more his description of Scotland, leaves untouched none of the relations of human life, and displays a power and method of unbiased observation and comparison impossible in any but a countryman of Columbus, trained in the school of the ancients. Thousands saw and, in part, knew what he did, but they felt no impulse to draw a picture of it, and were unconscious that the world desired such pictures.

In geography as in other matters, it is vain to attempt to distinguish how much is to be attributed to the study of the ancients, and how much to the special genius of the Italians. They saw and treated the things of this world from an objective point of view, even before they were familiar with the ancient literature, partly because they were themselves a half-ancient people, and partly because their political circumstances predisposed them to it; but they would not so rapidly have attained to such perfection had not the old geographers showed them the way. The influence of the existing Italian geographies on the spirit and tendencies of the travelers and discoverers was also inestimable. Even the simple dilettante of a science—if in the present case we should assign to Aeneas Sylvius so low a rank—can diffuse just that sort of general interest in the subject which prepares for new pioneers the indispensable groundwork of a favorable predisposition in the public mind. True discoverers in any science know well what they owe to such mediation.

Natural Science in Italy

For the position of the Italians in the sphere of the natural sciences, we must refer the reader to the special treatises on the subject, of which the only one with which we are familiar is the superficial and depreciatory work of Libri. The dispute as to the priority of particular discoveries concerns us all the less, since we hold that, at any time, and among any civilized people, a man may appear who, starting with very scanty preparation, is driven by an irresistible impulse into the path of scientific investigation, and through his native gifts achieves the most astonishing success. Such men were Gerbert of Rheims and Roger Bacon. That they were masters of the whole knowledge of the age in their several departments was a natural consequence of the spirit in which they worked. When once the veil of illusion was torn asunder, when once the dread of nature and the slavery to books and tradition were overcome, countless problems lay before them for solution. It is another matter when a whole people takes a natural delight in the study and investigation of nature, at a time when other nations are indifferent, that is to say, when the discoverer is not threatened or wholly ignored, but can count on the friendly support of congenial spirits. That this was the case in Italy is unquestionable. The Italian students of nature trace with pride in the *Divine Comedy* the hints and proofs of Dante's scientific interest in nature. On his claim to priority in this or that discovery or reference, we must leave the men of science to decide; but every layman must be struck by the wealth of his observations on the external world, shown merely in his pictures and comparisons. He, more than any other modern poet, takes them from reality, whether in nature or human life, and uses them, never as mere ornament, but in order to give the reader the fullest and most adequate sense of his meaning. It is in astronomy that he appears chiefly as a scientific specialist, though it must not be forgotten that many astronomical allusions in his great poem, which now appear to us learned, must then have been intelligible to the general reader. Dante, learning apart, appeals to a popular knowledge of the heavens, which the Italians of his day, from the mere fact that they were nautical people, had in common with the ancients. This knowledge of the rising and setting of the constellations has been rendered superfluous to the modern world by calendars and clocks, and with it has gone whatever interest in astronomy the people may once have had. Nowadays, with our schools and handbooks, every child knows —what Dante did not know—that the earth moves round the sun; but the interest once taken in the subject itself has given place, except in the case of astronomical specialists, to the most absolute indifference.

The pseudoscience, which also dealt with the stars, proves nothing against the inductive spirit of the Italians of that day. That spirit was but crossed, and at times overcome, by the passionate desire to penetrate the future. We shall recur to the subject of astrology when we come to speak of the moral and religious character of the people.

The church treated this and other pseudosciences nearly always with toleration; and showed itself actually hostile even to genuine science only when a charge of heresy together with necromancy was also in question—which certainly was often the case. A point which it would be interesting to decide is this: whether, and in what cases, the Dominican (and also the Franciscan) Inquisitors in Italy were conscious of the falsehood of the charges, and yet condemned the accused, either to oblige some enemy of the prisoner or from hatred to natural science, and particularly to experiments. The latter doubtless occurred, but it is not easy to prove the fact. What helped to cause such persecutions in the North, namely, the opposition made to the innovators by the upholders of the received official, scholastic system of nature, was of little or no weight in Italy. Pietro of Albano, at the beginning of the fourteenth century, is well known to have fallen a victim to the envy of another physician, who accused him before the Inquisition of heresy and magic; and something of the same kind may have happened in the case of his Paduan contemporary, Giovannino Sanguinacci, who was known as an innovator in medical practice. He escaped, however, with banishment. Nor must it be forgotten that the inquisitorial power of the Dominicans was exercised less uniformly in Italy than in the North. Tyrants and free cities in the fourteenth century treated the clergy at times with such sovereign contempt that very different matters from natural science went unpunished. But when, with the fifteenth century, antiquity became the leading power in Italy, the breach it made in the old system was turned to account by every branch of secular science. Humanism, nevertheless, attracted to itself the best strength of the nation, and thereby, no doubt, did injury to the inductive investigation of nature. Here and there the Inquisition suddenly started into life, and punished or burned physicians as blasphemers or magicians. In such cases it is hard to discover what was the true motive underlying the condemnation. And after all, Italy, at the close of the fifteenth century, with Paolo Toscanelli, Luca Pacciolo and Leonardo da Vinci, held incomparably the highest place among European nations in mathematics and the natural sciences, and the learned men of every country, even Regiomontanus and Copernicus, confessed themselves its pupils.

A significant proof of the widespread interest in natural history is found in the zeal which showed itself at an early period for the collection and comparative study of plants and animals. Italy claims to be the first creator of botanical gardens, though possibly they may have served a chiefly practical end, and the claim to priority may be itself disputed. It is of far greater importance that princes and wealthy men, in laying out their pleasure gardens, instinctively made a point of collecting the greatest possible number of different plants in all their species and varieties. Thus in the fifteenth century the noble grounds of the Medicean Villa Careggi appear from the descriptions we have of them to have been almost a botanical garden, with countless specimens of different trees and shrubs. Of the same kind was a villa of the Cardinal Trivulzio, at the beginning of the sixteenth century, in the Roman Campagna towards Tivoli, with hedges made up of various species of roses, with trees of every description—the fruit trees especially showing an astonishing variety—with twenty different sorts of vines and a large kitchen garden. This is evidently something very different from the score or two of familiar medicinal plants, which were to be found in the garden of any castle or monastery in western Europe. Along with a careful cultivation of fruit for the purposes of the table, we find an interest in the plant for its own sake, on account of the pleasure it gives to the eye. We learn from the history of art at how late a period this passion for botanical collections was laid aside, and gave place to what was considered the picturesque style of landscape gardening.

The collections, too, of foreign animals not only gratified curiosity, but served also the higher purposes of observation. The facility of transport from the southern and eastern harbors of the Mediterranean, and the mildness of the Italian climate, made it practicable to buy the largest animals of the south, or to accept them as presents from the sultans. The cities and princes were especially anxious to keep live lions, even when the lion was not, as in Florence, the emblem of the state. The lions' den was generally in or near the government palace, as in Perugia and Florence; in Rome, it lay on the slope of the Capitol. The beasts sometimes served as executioners of political judgments, and no doubt, apart from this, they kept alive a certain terror in the popular mind. Their condition was also held to be ominous of good or evil. Their fertility, especially, was considered a sign of public prosperity, and no less a man than Giovanni Villani thought it worth recording that he was present at the delivery of a lioness. The cubs were often given to allied states and princes, or to condottieri, as a reward of valor. In addition to the lions, the Florentines began very early to keep leopards, for which a special keeper was appointed. Borso of Ferrara used to set his lions to fight with bulls, bears, and wild boars.

By the end of the fifteenth century, however, true menageries (*serragli*), now reckoned part of the suitable appointments of a court, were kept by many of the princes. "It belongs to the position of the great," says Matarazzo, "to keep horses, dogs, mules, falcons, and other birds, court jesters, singers, and foreign animals." The menagerie at Naples, in the time of Ferrante and others, contained a giraffe and a zebra, presented, it seems, by the ruler of Baghdad. Filippo Maria Visconti possessed not only horses which cost him each 500 or 1,000 pieces of gold, and valuable English dogs, but a number of leopards brought from all parts of the East; the expense of his hunting birds which were collected from the countries of northern Europe amounted to 3,000 pieces of gold a month. "The Cremonese say that the Emperor Frederick II brought an elephant into their city, sent him from India by Prester John," we read in Brunetto Latini; Petrarch records the dying out of the elephants in Italy. King Emanuel the Great of Portugal knew well what he was about when he presented Leo X with an elephant and a rhinoceros. It was under such circumstances that the foundations of a scientific zoology and botany were laid.

A practical fruit of these zoological studies was the establishment of studs, of which the Mantuan, under Francesco Gonzaga, was esteemed the first in Europe. An interest in, and knowledge of, the different breeds of horses is as old, no doubt, as riding itself, and the crossing of the European with the Asiatic must have been common from the time of the Crusades. In Italy, a special inducement to perfect the breed was offered by the prizes at the horse races held in every considerable town in the peninsula. In the Mantuan stables were found the infallible winners in these contests, as well as the best military chargers, and the horses best suited by their stately appearance for presents to great people. Gonzaga kept stallions and mares from Spain, Ireland, Africa, Thrace, and Cilicia, and for the sake of the last he cultivated the friendship of the sultan. All possible experiments were here tried, in order to produce the most perfect animals.

Even human menageries were not wanting. The famous Cardinal Ippolito Medici, bastard of Giuliano, duke of Nemours, kept at his strange court a troop of barbarians who talked no less than twenty different languages, and who were all of them perfect specimens of their races. Among them were incomparable *voltigeurs* of the best blood of the North African Moors, Tartar bowmen, Negro wrestlers, Indian divers, and Turks, who generally accompanied the cardinal on his hunting expeditions. When he was overtaken by an early death (1535), this motley band carried the corpse on their shoulders from Itri to Rome, and mingled with the general mourning for the open-handed cardinal their medley of tongues and violent gesticulations.

These scattered notices of the relations of the Italians to natural science, and their interest in the wealth and variety of the products of nature, are only fragments of a great subject. No one is more conscious than the author of the defects in his knowledge on this point. Of the multitude of special works in which the subject is adequately treated, even the names are but imperfectly known to him. . . .

The Discovery of Man

To the discovery of the outward world the Renaissance added a still greater achievement, by first discerning and bringing to light the full, whole nature of man.

This period, as we have seen, first gave the highest development to individuality, and then led the individual to the most zealous and thorough study of himself in all forms and under all conditions. Indeed, the development of personality is essentially involved in the recognition of it in oneself and in others. Between these two great processes our narrative has placed the influence of ancient literature, because the mode of conceiving and representing both the individual and human nature in general was defined and colored by that influence. But the power of conception and representation lay in the age and in the people.

The facts which we shall quote in evidence of our thesis will be few in number. Here, if anywhere in the course of this discussion, the author is conscious that he is treading on the perilous ground of conjecture, and that what seems to him a clear, if delicate and gradual, transition in the intellectual movement of the fourteenth and fifteenth centuries, may not be equally plain to others. The gradual awakening of the souls of a people is a phenomenon which may produce a different impression on each spectator. Time will judge which impression is the most faithful.

Happily the study of the intellectual side of human nature began, not with the search after a theoretical psychology—for that, Aristotle still sufficed—but with the endeavor to observe and to describe. The indispensable ballast of theory was limited to the popular doctrine of the four temperaments, in its then habitual union with the belief in the influence of the planets. Such conceptions may remain ineradicable in the minds of individuals, without hindering the general progress of the age. It certainly makes on us a singular impression, when we meet them at a time when human nature in its deepest essence and in all its characteristic expressions was not only known by exact observation, but represented by an immortal poetry and art. It sounds almost ludicrous when an otherwise competent observer considers Clement VII to be of a melancholy temperament, but defers his judgment to that of the physicians, who declare the pope of a sanguine-choleric nature; or when we read that the same Gaston de Foix, the victor of Ravenna, whom Giorgione painted and Bambaia carved, and whom all the historians describe, had the saturnine temperament. No doubt those who use these expressions mean something by them; but the terms in which they tell us their meaning are strangely out of date in the Italy of the sixteenth century. . . .

Even apart from the *Divine Comedy,* Dante would have marked by these youthful poems the boundary between medievalism and modern times. The human spirit had taken a mighty step towards the consciousness of its own secret life.

The revelations in this matter which are contained in the *Divine Comedy* itself are simply immeasurable; and it would be necessary to go through the whole poem, one canto after another, in order to do justice to its value from this point of view. Happily we have no need to do this, as it has long been a daily food of all the countries of the West. Its plan, and the ideas on which it is based, belong to the Middle Ages, and appeal to our interest only historically; but it is nevertheless the beginning of all modern poetry, through the power and richness shown in the description of human nature in every shape and attitude.

From this time forwards poetry may have experienced unequal

fortunes, and may show, for half a century together, a so-called relapse. But its nobler and more vital principle was saved forever; and whenever in the fourteenth, fifteenth, and in the beginning of the sixteenth centuries, an original mind devotes himself to it, he represents a more advanced stage than any poet out of Italy, given—what is certainly not always easy to settle satisfactorily—an equality of natural gifts to start with.

Here, as in other things in Italy, culture—to which poetry belongs—precedes the plastic arts and, in fact, gives them their chief impulse. More than a century elapsed before the spiritual element in painting and sculpture attained a power of expression in any way analogous to that of the *Divine Comedy.* How far the same rule holds good for the artistic development of other nations, and of what importance the whole question may be, does not concern us here. For Italian civilization it is of decisive weight. . . .

That the ancient poets, particularly the elegists, and Virgil, in the fourth book of the *Aeneid,* were not without influence on the Italians of this and the following generation is beyond a doubt; but the spring of sentiment within the latter was nevertheless powerful and original. If we compare them in this respect with their contemporaries in other countries, we shall find in them the earliest complete expression of modern European feeling. The question, be it remembered, is not to know whether eminent men of other nations did not feel as deeply and as nobly, but who first gave documentary proof of the widest knowledge of the movements of the human heart. . . .

SOCIETY AND FESTIVALS

The Equalization of Classes

Every period of civilization which forms a complete and consistent whole, manifests itself not only in political life, in religion, art, and science, but also sets its characteristic stamp on social life. Thus the Middle Ages had their courtly and aristocratic manners and etiquette, differing but little in the various countries of Europe, as well as their peculiar forms of middle-class life.

Italian customs at the time of the Renaissance offer in these respects the sharpest contrast to medievalism. The foundation on which they rest is wholly different. Social intercourse in its highest and most perfect form now ignored all distinctions of caste, and was based simply on the existence of an educated class as we now understand the word. Birth and origin were without influence, unless combined with leisure and inherited wealth. Yet this assertion must not be taken in an absolute and unqualified sense, since medieval distinctions still sometimes made themselves felt to a greater or less degree, if only as a means of maintaining equality with the aristocratic pretensions of the less advanced countries of Europe. But the main current of the time went steadily towards the fusion of classes in the modern sense of the phrase.

The fact was of vital importance that, from certainly the twelfth century onwards, the nobles and the burghers dwelt together within the walls of the cities. The interests and pleasures of both classes were thus identified, and the feudal lord learned to look at society from another point of view than that of his mountain castle. The church, too, in Italy never suffered itself, as in northern countries, to be used as a means of providing for the younger sons of noble families. Bishoprics, abbacies, and canonries were often given from the most unworthy motives, but still not according to the pedigrees of the applicants; and if the bishops in Italy were more numerous, poorer, and, as a rule, destitute of all sovereign rights, they still lived in the cities where their cathedrals stood, and formed, together with their chapters, an important element in the cultivated society of the place. In the age of despots and absolute princes which followed, the nobility in most of the cities had the motives and the leisure to give themselves up to a private life free from the political danger and adorned with all that was elegant and enjoyable, but at the same time hardly distinguishable from that of the wealthy burgher. And after the time of Dante, when the new poetry and literature were in the hands of all Italy, when to this was added the revival of ancient culture and the new interest in man as such, when the successful condottiere became a prince, and not only good birth, but legitimate birth, ceased to be indispensable for a throne, it might well seem that the age of equality had dawned, and the belief in nobility vanished forever.

From a theoretical point of view, when the appeal was made to antiquity, the conception of nobility could be both justified and condemned from Aristotle alone. Dante, for example, adapts from Aristotelian definition, "Nobility rests on excellence and inherited wealth," his own saying, "Nobility rests on personal excellence or on that of predecessors." But elsewhere he is not satisfied with this conclusion. He blames himself, because even in *Paradise,* while talking with his ancestor Cacciaguida, he made mention of his noble origin, which is but a mantle from which time is ever cutting something away, unless we ourselves add daily fresh worth to it. And in the *Convito* he disconnects *nobile* and *nobiltà* from every condition of birth, and identifies the idea with the capacity for moral and intellectual eminence, laying a special stress on high culture by calling *nobiltà* the sister of *filosofia.*

And as time went on, the greater the influence of humanism on the Italian mind, the firmer and more widespread became the conviction that birth decides nothing as to the goodness or badness of a man. In the fifteenth century this was the prevailing opinion. Poggio, in his dialogue *On Nobility,* agrees with his interlocutors—Niccolò Niccoli, and Lorenzo de' Medici, brother of the great Cosimo—that there is no other nobility than that of personal merit. The keenest shafts of his ridicule are directed against much of what vulgar prejudice thinks indispensable to an aristocratic life. "A man is all the farther removed from true nobility, the longer his forefathers have plied the trade of brigands. The taste for hawking and hunting savors no more of nobility than the nests and lairs of the hunted creatures of spikenard. The cultivation of the soil, as practised by the ancients, would be much nobler than this senseless wandering through the hills and woods, by which men make themselves liker to the brutes than to the reasonable creatures. It may serve well enough as a recreation, but not as the business of a lifetime." The life of the English and French chivalry in the country or in the woody fastnesses seems to him thoroughly ignoble, and worst of all the doings of the robber-knights of Germany. Lorenzo here begins to take the part of the nobility, but not—which is characteristic— appealing to any natural sentiment in its favor, but because Aristotle in the fifth book of the *Politics* recognizes the nobility as existent, and defines it as resting on excellence and inherited wealth. To this Niccoli retorts that Aristotle gives this not as his own conviction, but as the popular impression; in his *Ethics,* where he speaks as he thinks, he calls him noble who strives after that which is truly good. Lorenzo urges upon him vainly that the Greek word for nobility means good birth; Niccoli thinks the Roman word *nobilis* (i.e., remarkable)

a better one, since it makes nobility depend on a man's deeds. Together with these discussions, we find a sketch of the conditions of
the nobles in various parts of Italy. In Naples they will not work, and
busy themselves neither with their own estates nor with trade and
commerce, which they hold to be discreditable; they either loiter at
home or ride about on horseback. The Roman nobility also despise
trade, but farm their own property; the cultivation of the land even
opens the way to a title; "It is a respectable but boorish nobility."
In Lombardy the nobles live upon the rent of their inherited estates;
descent and the abstinence from any regular calling constitute
nobility. In Venice, the *nobili,* the ruling caste, were all merchants.
Similarly in Genoa the nobles and nonnobles were alike merchants
and sailors, and only separated by their birth; some few of the
former, it is true, still lurked as brigands in their mountain castles.
In Florence a part of the old nobility had devoted themselves to
trade; another, and certainly by far the smaller part, enjoyed the
satisfaction of their titles, and spent their time, either in nothing at
all, or else in hunting and hawking.

The decisive fact was that, nearly everywhere in Italy, even those
who might be disposed to pride themselves on their birth could not
make good the claims against the power of culture and of wealth,
and that their privileges in politics and at court were not sufficient
to encourage any strong feeling of caste. Venice offers only an
apparent exception to this rule, for there the *nobili* led the same life
as their fellow citizens, and were distinguished by few honorary
privileges. The case was certainly different at Naples, where the
strict isolation and the ostentatious vanity of its nobility excluded,
above all other causes, from the spiritual movement of the Renaissance. The traditions of medieval Lombardy and Normandy, and the
French aristocratic influences which followed, all tended in this
direction; and the Aragonese government, which was established by
the middle of the fifteenth century, completed the work, and accomplished in Naples what followed a hundred years later in the rest of
Italy—a social transformation in obedience to Spanish ideas, of
which the chief features were the contempt for work and the passion
for titles. The effect of this new influence was evident, even in the
smaller towns, before the year 1500. We hear complaints from La
Cava that the place had been proverbially rich, as long as it was
filled with masons and weavers; whilst now, since instead of looms

and trowels nothing but spurs, stirrups and gilded belts was to be seen, since everybody was trying to become Doctor of Laws or of Medicine, Notary, Officer or Knight, the most intolerable poverty prevailed. In Florence an analogous change appears to have taken place by the time of Cosimo, the first grand duke; he is thanked for adopting the young people, who now despise trade and commerce, as knights of his order of St. Stephen. This goes straight in the teeth of the good old Florentine custom, by which fathers left property to their children on the condition that they should have some occupation. But a mania for titles of a curious and ludicrous sort sometimes crossed and thwarted, especially among the Florentines, the leveling influence of art and culture. This was the passion for knighthood, which became one of the most striking follies of the day, at a time when the dignity itself had lost every shadow of significance.

MORALITY AND RELIGION

Morality

. . . If we now attempt to sum up the principal features in the Italian character of that time, as we know it from a study of the life of the upper classes, we shall obtain something like the following result. The fundamental vice of this character was at the same time a condition of its greatness, namely, excessive individualism. The individual first inwardly casts off the authority of a state which, as a fact, is in most cases tyrannical and illegitimate, and what he thinks and does is, rightly or wrongly, now called treason. The sight of victorious egotism in others drives him to defend his own right by his own arm. And, while thinking to restore his inward equilibrium, he falls, through the vengeance which he executes, into the hands of the powers of darkness. His love, too, turns mostly for satisfaction to another individuality equally developed, namely, to his neighbor's wife. In face of all objective facts, of laws and restraints of whatever kind, he retains the feeling of his own sovereignty, and in each single instance forms his decision independently, according as honor or interest, passion or calculation, revenge or renunciation, gain the upper hand in his own mind.

If therefore egotism in its wider as well as narrower sense is the root and fountain of all evil, the more highly developed Italian was for this reason more inclined to wickedness than the members of other nations of that time.

But this individual development did not come upon him through any fault of his own, but rather through an historical necessity. It did not come upon him alone, but also, and chiefly, by means of Italian culture, upon the other nations of Europe, and has constituted since then the higher atmosphere which they breathe. In itself it is neither good nor bad, but necessary; within it has grown up a modern standard of good and evil—a sense of moral responsibility—which is essentially different from that which was familiar to the Middle Ages.

But the Italian of the Renaissance had to bear the first mighty surging of a new age. Through his gifts and his passions, he has become the most characteristic representative of all the heights and all the depths of his time. By the side of profound corruption appeared human personalities of the noblest harmony, and an artistic splendor which shed upon the life of man a luster which neither antiquity nor medievalism either could or would bestow upon it. . . .

Religion and the Spirit of the Renaissance

But in order to reach a definite conclusion with regard to the religious sense of the men of this period, we must adopt a different method. From their intellectual attitude in general, we can infer their relation both to the Divine idea and to the existing religion of their age.

These modern men, the representatives of the culture of Italy, were born with the same religious instincts as other medieval Europeans. But their powerful individuality made them in religion, as in other matters, altogether subjective, and the intense charm which the discovery of the inner and outer universe exercised upon them rendered them markedly worldly. In the rest of Europe religion remained, till a much later period, something given from without, and in practical life egotism and sensuality alternated with devotion and repentance. The latter had no spiritual competitors, as in Italy, or only to a far smaller extent.

Further, the close and frequent relations of Italy with Byzantium and the Mohammedan peoples had produced a dispassionate tolerance which weakened the ethnographical conception of a privileged Christendom. And when classical antiquity with its men and institutions became an ideal of life, as well as the greatest of historical memories, ancient speculation and scepticism obtained in many cases a complete mastery over the minds of Italians.

Since, again, the Italians were the first modern people of Europe who gave themselves boldly to speculations on freedom and necessity, and since they did so under violent and lawless political circumstances, in which evil seemed often to win a splendid and lasting victory, their belief in God began to waver, and their view of the government of the world became fatalistic. And when their passionate natures refused to rest in the sense of uncertainty, they made a shift to help themselves out with ancient, oriental, or medieval superstition. They took to astrology and magic.

Finally, these intellectual giants, these representatives of the Renaissance, show, in respect to religion, a quality which is common in youthful natures. Distinguishing keenly between good and evil, they yet are conscious of no sin. Every disturbance of their inward harmony they feel themselves able to make good out of the plastic resources of their own nature, and therefore they feel no repentance. The need of salvation thus becomes felt more and more dimly, while the ambitions and the intellectual activity of the present either shut out altogether every thought of a world to come, or else caused it to assume a poetic instead of a dogmatic form.

When we look on all this as pervaded and often perverted by the all-powerful Italian imagination, we obtain a picture of that time which is certainly more in accordance with truth than are vague declamations against modern paganism. And closer investigation often reveals to us that underneath this outward shell much genuine religion could still survive. . . .

That religion should again become an affair of the individual and of his own personal feeling was inevitable when the church became corrupt in doctrine and tyrannous in practice, and is a proof that the European mind was still alive. It is true that this showed itself in many different ways. While the mystical and ascetical sects of the North lost no time in creating new outward forms for their new modes of thought and feeling, each individual in Italy went his own way, and thousands wandered on the sea of life without any religious guidance whatever. All the more must we admire those who attained and held fast to a personal religion. They were not to blame for being unable to have any part or lot in the old church, as she then was; nor would it be reasonable to expect that they should all of them go through that mighty spiritual labor which was appointed to the German reformers. The form and aim of this personal faith, as it showed itself in the better minds, will be set forth at the close of our work.

The worldliness, through which the Renaissance seems to offer so striking a contrast to the Middle Ages, owed its first origin to the flood of new thoughts, purposes, and views, which transformed the medieval conception of nature and man. The spirit is not in itself more hostile to religion than that "culture" which now holds its place, but which can give us only a feeble notion of the universal ferment which the discovery of a new world of greatness then called forth. This worldliness was not frivolous, but earnest, and was ennobled by art and poetry. It is a lofty necessity of the modern spirit that this attitude, once gained, can never again be lost, that an irresistible impulse forces us to the investigation of men and things, and that we must hold this inquiry to be our proper end and work. How soon and by what paths this search will lead us back to God, and in what ways the religious temper of the individual will be affected by it, are questions which cannot be met by any general answer. The Middle Ages, which spared themselves the trouble of induction and free enquiry, can have no right to impose upon us their dogmatical verdict in a matter of such vast importance. . . .

Antiquity exercised an influence of another kind than that of Islam, and this not through its religion, which was but too much like the Catholicism of this period, but through its philosophy. Ancient literature now worshiped as something incomparable, is full of the victory of philosophy over religious tradition. An endless number of systems and fragments of systems were suddenly presented to the Italian mind, not as curiosities or even as heresies, but almost with the authority of dogmas, which had now to be reconciled rather than discriminated. In nearly all these various opinions and doctrines a certain kind of belief in God was implied; but taken altogether they formed a marked contrast to the Christian faith in a Divine government of the world. . . .

The fourteenth century was chiefly stimulated by the writings of Cicero, who, though in fact an eclectic, yet, by his habit of setting forth the opinions of different schools, without coming to a decision between them, exercised the influence of a sceptic. Next in importance came Seneca, and the few works of Aristotle which had been translated into Latin. The immediate fruit of these studies was the capacity to reflect on great subjects, if not in direct opposition to the authority of the church, at all events independently of it.

In the course of the fifteenth century the works of antiquity were discovered and diffused with extraordinary rapidity. All the writings of the Greek philosophers which we ourselves possess were now, at least in the form of Latin translations, in everybody's hands. It is a curious fact that some of the most zealous apostles of this new culture were men of the strictest piety, or even ascetics. Fra Ambrogio Camaldolese, as a spiritual dignitary chiefly occupied with ecclesiastical affairs, and as a literary man with the translation of the Greek Fathers of the church, could not repress the humanistic impulse, and at the request of Cosimo de' Medici, undertook to translate Diogenes Laertius into Latin. His contemporaries, Niccolò Nocoli, Giannozzo Manetti, Donato Acciajuoli, and Pope Nicholas V, united to a many-sided humanism profound biblical scholarship and deep piety. In Vittorino da Feltre the same temper has been already noticed. The same Matthew Vegio, who added a thirteenth book to the *Aeneid,* had an enthusiasm for the memory of St. Augustine and his mother Monica which cannot have been without a deeper influence upon him. The result of all these tendencies was that the Platonic Academy at Florence deliberately chose for its object the reconciliation of the spirit of antiquity with that of Christianity. It was a remarkable oasis in the humanism of the period.

This humanism was in fact pagan, and became more and more so as its sphere widened in the fifteenth century. Its representatives, whom we have already described as the advancd guard of an unbridled individualism, display as a rule such a character that even their religion, which is sometimes professed very definitely, becomes a matter of indifference to us. They easily got the name of atheists, if they showed themselves indifferent to religion, and spoke freely against the church; but not one of them ever professed, or dared to profess, a formal, philosophical atheism. If they sought for any leading principle, it must have been a kind of superficial rationalism—a careless inference from the many and contradictory opinions of antiquity with which they busied themselves, and from the discredit into which the church and her doctrines had fallen. This was the sort of reasoning which was near bringing Galeottus Martius to the stake, had not his former pupil Pope Sixtus IV, perhaps at the request of Lorenzo de' Medici, saved him from the hands of the Inquisition. Galeotto had ventured to write that the man who walked uprightly, and acted according to the natural law born within him, would go to heaven, whatever nation he belonged to. . . .

With respect to the moral government of the world, the humanists seldom get beyond a cold and resigned consideration of the prevalent violence and misrule. In this mood the many works "On Fate," or whatever name they bear, are written. They tell of the turning of the wheel of Fortune, and on the instability of earthly, especially political, things. Providence is only brought in because the writers would still be ashamed of undisguised fatalism, of the avowal of their ignorance, or of useless complaints. Geoviano Pontano ingeniously illustrates the nature of that mysterious something which men call Fortune by a hundred incidents, most of which belonged to his own experience. The subject is treated more humorously by Aeneas Sylvius, in the form of a vision seen in a dream. The aim of Poggio, on the other hand, in a work written in his old age, is to represent the world as a vale of tears, and to fix the happiness of various classes as low as possible. This tone became in future the prevalent one. Distinguished men drew up a debit and credit of the happiness and unhappiness of their lives, and generally found that the latter outweighed the former. . . .

But the way in which resuscitated antiquity affected religion most powerfully was not through any doctrines or philosophical system, but through a general tendency which it fostered. The men, and in some respects the institutions, of antiquity were preferred to those of the Middle Ages, and in the eager attempt to imitate and reproduce them, religion was left to take care of itself. All was absorbed in the admiration for historical greatness. To this the philologians added many special follies of their own, by which they became the mark for general attention. How far Paul II was justified in calling his Abbreviators and their friends to account for their paganism is certainly a matter of great doubt, as his biographer and chief victim, Platina, has shown a masterly skill in explaining his vindictiveness on other grounds, and especially in making him play a ludicrous figure. The charges of infidelity, paganism, denial of immortality, and so forth, were not made against the accused till the charge of high treason had broken down. Paul, indeed, if we are correctly informed about him, was by no means the man to judge of intellectual things. He knew little Latin, and spoke Italian at consistories and in diplomatic negotiations. It was he who exhorted the Romans to teach their children nothing beyond reading and writing. His priestly narrowness of views reminds us of Savonarola, with the difference that Paul might fairly have been told that he and his like were in great part to blame if culture made men hostile to religion. It cannot, nevertheless, be doubted that he felt a real anxiety about the pagan tendencies which surrounded him. And what, in truth, may not the humanists have allowed themselves at the court of the profligate pagan, Sigismondo Malatesta? How far these men, destitute for the most part of fixed principle, ventured to go, depended assuredly on the sort of influences they were exposed to. Nor could they treat of Christianity without paganizing it. . . .

Charles Howard McIlwain

MEDIAEVAL INSTITUTIONS IN THE MODERN WORLD

Charles Howard McIlwain was born in 1871 and had a long and distinguished career as a political scientist and historian. Professor at Harvard University from 1911 until his death in 1968, he inspired many generations of students with his brilliant and incisive lectures in the history of political thought. Although his chief interest was in the medieval period and he had written several notable works dealing with the political thought and institutions of this era, in 1924 he was awarded the Pulitzer Prize for his book on The American Revolution: A Constitutional Interpretation. *In 1936 he was honored by being elected president of the American Historical Association.*

It is a common fault, to which I suppose we are all more or less subject, when we are asked long in advance to speak on some topic, to accept gaily without counting the cost. It was in that spirit that I welcomed the honor but incurred the obligation of speaking to you today on the subject of the Mediaeval in the Modern. But when I set to work my troubles began. For before we dare speak of the mediaeval in the modern, we must know what we mean when we use the term "mediaeval"; and it is amazing what different pictures that word calls up for different minds . . . .

. . . In the intellectual sphere, there is the view that the thirteenth century is, as it has been called, "the greatest of Christian centuries"; and, on the other hand, the notion, widespread a generation ago if not now, that the Renaissance was a "rediscovery of the world and of men." What shall we believe about that? For these two views are irreconcilable. No doubt historians as far removed from our time as we are from the Middle Ages will have somewhat the same conflicting opinions about the first half of the twentieth century. Even today we find some saying that these moving times are a great time to be alive, while others can only look back with longing to an earlier period when rights and honor and oaths were at least respected, even if not always observed.

With such a disparity of opinions about the present, how can we

From C. H. McIlwain, "Mediaeval Institutions in the Modern World," in *Speculum* 16, no. 3 (1941): 275–283. Reprinted by permission of the Mediaeval Academy of America.

be surprised to find them in regard to the Middle Ages? Our definitions of the mediaeval, like those of the present, will be affected by
our temperament, our traditions, and our peculiar studies. The best
definition we can frame will be partial, incomplete, and inadequate;
and the sum of all these defects will probably be the result of ignorance of something essential. . . .

The period that we dub mediaeval is a long one, and on that side
of it in which my own studies have lain I think we find, within the
period itself, changes as profound, if not even more profound, than
those which mark off our modern institutions from the ones we call
mediaeval. In the field of political institutions and ideas I venture
to think that what Professor Haskins has termed "the Renaissance
of the twelfth century" marks a more fundamental change than the
later developments to which we usually attach the word "Renaissance"; that the constitutionalism of the modern world owes as
much, if not even more, to the twelfth and the thirteenth centuries
than to any later period of comparable length before the seventeenth.

All this is to do little more than say that the term "Middle Ages"
in its widest extent is a term which includes institutions and ideas
as widely different from each other as the so-called mediaeval is
from the modern. If so, which of them shall we term "mediaeval"
par excellence? Or shall we give it all up, and say that all we dare
do is to term "mediaeval" anything and everything we find in the
whole millennium generally included under the phrase "Middle
Ages"? Pitfalls certainly do lie in the path of anyone who is looking
for the peculiar flavor of the Middle Ages, and many there are who
have fallen in. In my own field I am thinking particularly of historians
such as Freeman, who became so obsessed by the notion of constitutional liberty as the dominant note of mediaeval political life that
he could never see the feudalism that everywhere stared him in the
face, or, if he saw it, could only damn it as an abuse. He had a pattern
ready-made to which the institutions of the time must conform.

There have been many like patterns. Another such is the notion
that a more or less complete decentralization of government is a
characteristic necessarily inherent in the Middle Ages; and therefore,
if we find a strong monarchy somewhere in the midst of the mediaeval period, that we must not call it mediaeval; it must be an aberra-
tion. But because we find that so many of these patterns do not truly
fit the existing facts, must we conclude that after all there is nothing

whatever whose character warrants us in attaching to it the adjective "mediaeval"? Is there no distinctive mediaeval pattern at all? Or further, is there nothing in our modern culture that we may safely trace back in unbroken continuity into the mediaeval period and term a mediaeval heritage?

In the attempt to list a few things that seem at the same time mediaeval and modern, I shall not venture to touch anything but the field of political institutions and ideas, beyond which my knowledge is mainly but secondhand. And in making even such a tentative list I think we must always bear in mind the vast difference between the earlier and the later part of the long period to which we apply the word "mediaeval." As a whole, I suppose we might roughly describe the epoch generally as one in which rather primitive men gradually and progressively assimilated the more advanced institutions and ideas that antiquity had bequeathed them. It is amazing how long a period of contact is required for men at such a primitive state of culture to make their own the remains of a civilization so much higher than theirs. In western Europe one can hardly make this period of progressive assimilation shorter than seven or eight centuries. It was a long, gradual, progressive development, a slow evolution; and the term "mediaeval" is probably most fittingly applied to the culmination in its later centuries, on Aristotle's general teleological principle that the nature of any developing thing is only fully knowable in the final outcome of that development.

One of the things, probably the most important of all the things in my own particular field, that we seem to owe in largest part to these developments of the Middle Ages, is the institution of limited government, which I take to be the synonym for constitutionalism.

This constitutionalism was, of course, no new thing when the mediaeval records of it first appear. It had been a characteristic of republican Rome, had never been wholly obliterated by the growing absolutism of the empire, and it was enshrined in the Roman legal sources which the ruder successors of the Romans inherited and gradually came in course of time to assimilate, understand, and apply to their own lives. More and more I have become impressed lately with the relative importance of this Roman influence upon the mediaeval growth of our own principles of political liberty; an importance that political developments since the Middle Ages have tended to obscure, and one that it has been the usual fashion of the historians of our laws and constitutions to belittle, to ignore, or even to deny. The recent repudiation of Roman law by the Nazis in Germany because it is inconsistent with their totalitarianism makes one wonder if we have not, for a long time, been greatly over-emphasizing the despotic influence of that law in our history, and as seriously underrating the importance of Roman constitutionalism in the early development of our own.

Dyed-in-the-wool mediaevalists may object to a procedure like this which admits the possibility that events, even of today, may or should affect our interpretation of an epoch as far behind us as the Middle Ages. And yet, as Maitland says, all history is "a seamless web," and the present is a part of it as well as the past. Thus we all admit that the past should influence our ideas and ideals for the present, but if so it is hard to deny the validity of the converse of this: that the outcome of the past in the present should also have some influence upon our estimate of the past, and in fact of the whole drama of human destiny whose final dénouement no man can know. In saying this I do not, of course, wish to imply the crude transfer of modern modes of thought and action into past periods, the mechanical undiscriminating discovery of modern factors in the mediaeval world which has constituted probably the chief defect in our histories of the past development of our political institutions and ideas. It is easy enough to find the present in the past if we put the present there in this fashion before we start.

But this slipshod, unscientific method is a far cry from the one I have advocated above, in which we assume the oneness of the entire history of our institutions and insist merely that a careful and discriminating study of their outcome today may be of help toward a fuller understanding of the earlier stages through which this later stage has been reached. To do so in this way, it seems to me, is only to carry out in our historical investigations the sound general principle of Aristotle which I cited a moment ago. The best way to learn most about an acorn is to look at an oak. It is thus, and thus only, that the present should influence our views of the past. But "art is long and life is fleeting," and if we are to be good mediaevalists we must devote our main attention to the Middle Ages themselves and at the cost of some other periods.

Yet I submit that this must not lead to the narrow view that we should look at nothing else. The true nature of the Middle Ages cannot be fully understood except by some study of their outcome in the Renaissance and of their modern development. We can no more understand the true nature of this period in our history without consideration of its outcome than we could know all about a tadpole without studying the toad. As indicated above, in some things, particularly in the growth of the institutions and ideas with which I have been chiefly concerned, the so-called "Renaissance of the twelfth century" seems to me to be on the whole more significant on a perspective of the whole of history, than the later development to which we usually attach the word "Renaissance." But this is in no way to belittle that later period whose influence is undeniable, and ought to be so to the mediaevalist above all others, because he, more clearly than any others, is able to see the utter falsity of the notion that then for the first time since the ancients men rediscovered both the world and man. He knows that the Renaissance is in many ways only an extension of the Middle Ages, and this knowledge ought to heighten, not to lessen his interest in that later period, even though life is too short to study it in detail; for undoubtedly some of the best and most important elements of the culture of the Renaissance are a heritage from the period before.

It is for considerations like this that I venture to say that the events in Europe even of today or tomorrow, equally with those of the Renaissance, may legitimately influence our interpretation of things as remote as those of the twelfth or the thirteenth century, or even as far back as the seventh or the eighth. If we find, for instance, that the Nazis in Germany are now repudiating Roman law because the political principles they think it incorporates have proved to be too favorable to individual liberty to suit these promoters of totalitarianism, one is naturally led to ask whether they may not be right in so thinking, and whether we, after all, may not be wrong even in the interpretation of the Middle Ages, in our usual assumption that Roman principles are synonymous with absolutism: that the political essence of this Romanism is the maxim, "Quod principi placuit legis vigorem habet." . . .

In coming, then, at long last, to the subject I am supposed to talk about, the mediaeval in the present, this subject of Roman law furnishes one good example. In England and America at least, we have on the whole been prone to accept without enough examination the thesis that on its political side Roman law in the Middle Ages was but a prop to absolutism. We have usually taken at its face value the assertion of Sir John Fortescue, near the end of the fifteenth century, that the absolutist doctrines contained in such maxims as "quod principi placuit legis vigorem habet," or Ulpian's statement "princeps legibus solutus est" express "the chief principles among the civil laws" (*inter leges civiles praecipua sententia*), as he called them. To one who has accepted this tradition without much question it is something of a shock to look back to the thirteenth century and learn that Bracton sees nothing whatsoever of this kind in Roman law.

Once started on such an investigation, the student soon finds that thirteenth century men generally, unlike those of the fifteenth or the sixteenth, found no absolutism in the law of Rome, but rather constitutionalism. Such absolutist statements as the ones above do not for Bracton express the true central principle either of Roman or of English politics. That central principle is rather to be found in Papinian's dictum "Lex est communis sponsio rei publicae," "the common engagement of the republic," *not* "the pleasure of the prince." And in this, the mediaeval conception of the political side of Roman law is typical of mediaeval political ideas generally. To men of the thirteenth century Roman political principles and their own seemed essentially alike, not unlike; and neither the Roman nor their own were despotic. In proof of this, other passages of Roman law might easily be cited in addition to the ones we have already noted.

In our own earlier history there is, for example, the famous extract in Edward I's writ of summons to the Parliament of 1295, in which the archbishop of Canterbury is enjoined, before appearing himself, to secure the presence in person or by deputy of the lower clergy of his province:

> *Sicut lex justissima, provida circumspectione sacrorum principum stabilita, hortatur et statuit ut quod omnes tangit ab omnibus approbetur, sic et nimis evidenter, ut communis periculis per remedia provisa communiter obvietur.*

> *As a most just law, established by the far-sighted wisdom of sacred princes urges and has ordained that what touches all should be approved by all; equally and most clearly [it implies] that common dangers should be met by remedies provided in common.*

In its original use, as repeated in Justinian's *Code,* this provision has to do only with the private law, but it is here used as a maxim of state in a matter of the highest political importance. It is true that some have regarded Edward's quotation of it as of very little significance, and Professor G. B. Adams even cites its frequent use in earlier ecclesiastical documents as proof of this; but to me this repeated quotation is an indication not of its unimportance, but rather of the wide prevalence in mediaeval politics of the idea it expresses.

Modern interpretations of this famous writ have usually failed to notice its emphasis on the inference to be drawn from Justinian's words, as expressed in the added clause "that common dangers should be met by remedies provided in common." This added clause contains the kernel of the writ, and indicates the royal purpose in calling up the extraordinary number of the lower clergy. The writ is, in fact, Edward's anticipation of and answer to the principle of the papal bull *Clericis laicos* of the next year; and it is precisely the same answer, though much more politely worded, as that of Philip the Fair, expressed in the well-known document printed by Depuy, beginning with the words *Antequam essent clerici.* It was very natural and very effective, in a writ summoning the clergy to an assembly in which a large grant was to be asked for, thus to cite in justification a maxim which the clergy themselves had used so long and so often in their own provincial assemblies. The political idea underlying this maxim finds constant expression, not only in the words of the thirteenth century, in England, in France, and in many other parts of western Europe; but in the institutions as well.

It is to such institutions that I should like in the next place to turn as a further example of the mediaeval in its influence upon the modern. It is a commonplace of modern constitutional history that the power of the purse has been the principal means of securing and maintaining the liberties of the subject against the encroachments of the prince. Probably in no part of our constitutional history is the influence of the Middle Ages upon the modern world more obvious than here. For the constitutional principle just mentioned can be shown to be the outgrowth, the gradual and at times almost unperceived outgrowth, of the mediaeval principle that a feudal lord in most cases can exact no aid from his vassal save with the consent of all like vassals of the same fief. The whole principle contained in our maxim "no taxation without representation" has this feudal practice as its origin.

This is probably so obvious and so generally admitted that it needs little proof or illustration. But one aspect of it we are likely to overlook. These rights of the vassal are proprietary rights, and we are likely to give them a definition as narrow as our own modern definition of proprietary rights. This, however, is to misinterpret the nature of these limitations and vastly to lessen the importance of the principle of consent in the Middle Ages. For these rights of vassals, though protected by what we should call the land-law, included almost all of those rights which today we term "personal," such as the right to office, the right to immunities, or, as they were usually called then, to "liberties" or franchises, and even to the right to one's security in his social and personal status. A serf, for example, was protected against the abuse by his lord of rights which we call "personal" by remedies which it is difficult to distinguish from those used for the protection of the seisin of land. One might be truly said to have been "seized" of the rights securing his person as much as of those protecting his fief. It may be said of the Middle Ages generally, then, that private rights were immune from governmental encroachment under the political principles of the time. In this the Middle Ages shared the principles of Roman law, and no doubt it was this common feature of both systems that enabled Glanvil and Bracton and all the jurists in the period between to liken the English law in so many respects to the Roman.

If we are estimating the importance of the mediaeval in the modern in this field from which I have chosen to illustrate it, this constitutionalism, this limitation of governmental authority by private right, is the main tradition handed down by the Middle Ages to the modern world. It is the chief element in the political part of our mediaeval heritage. With the decay of feudal institutions, however, the sanctions by which these principles were maintained in practice tended to be greatly weakened, and no doubt it is the lawlessness of this later period of weakness following the decay of the feudal and preceding the development of the national sanctions for law, which has led to the popular impression that the Middle Ages as a whole are nothing more than one long stretch of uncontrolled violence. No doubt the violence of this later period may also be considered to be the chief cause of the increasing power of monarchy and the almost unlimited theories of obedience which we find among the chief characteristics of the period of the Renaissance. As was said then, it is better to submit to one tyrant than to a thousand. And without doubt the weakness of these sanctions of law in the later Middle Ages is a prime cause of the strength of monarchy in the period immediately following. In the reaction and revolution which in time were provoked in the period of the Renaissance or afterward by the extension and abuse of these powers of government we may find the true causes of the modern sanctions for the subjects' rights. In the early stages at least of this revolution the precedents cited in favor of liberty are largely drawn from the Middle Ages.

The particular side of the Middle Ages with which we have been dealing certainly offers little proof of either of the extreme interpretations that we find in modern times. It was both a lawful and a lawless period. At no time was law more insisted upon, but at times few of these laws were observed. When we consider this period in comparison with periods following, the same discrimination is necessary. The political theory of that time included more limitations upon governmental power than many theories of a much later time. It may indeed be said that political absolutism, at least as a theory of government, is a modern and not a mediaeval notion. In fact, the great champions of liberty against oppression, if their own words are to be trusted, have fought for the maintenance of liberties inherited from the Middle Ages. In our own day such traditional conceptions of liberty appear less seldom perhaps, for many liberals, and certainly most extreme radicals, are now frequently struggling for rights for which the Middle Ages can furnish few precedents. But this should not blind us to the all-important fact that for a long period in this historic struggle, indeed for the whole of the early part of it, it was for their mediaeval inheritance that all opponents of oppression engaged.

The lesson of it all is discrimination. If some modern elements had not been added to our mediaeval inheritance, elements nonexistent before modern times, even that inheritance could scarcely have persisted; and yet the central principle for which free men have always fought, the sanctity of law against oppressive will, is a principle recognized by our mediaeval ancestors as fully as by ourselves, and more fully, apparently, than by their successors of the sixteenth century. We cannot, therefore, truly entertain notions of the Middle Ages which make it one long, dreary epoch of stagnation, of insecurity, of lawless violence; neither can we truly consider it the Golden Age that some have pictured. What we need above all is discrimination and yet more discrimination.

Hans Baron

TOWARD A MORE POSITIVE EVALUATION OF THE FIFTEENTH-CENTURY RENAISSANCE: *Part I*

Dr. Hans Baron, born and educated in Germany, is now associated with the Newberry Library in Chicago. A very productive scholar, Dr. Baron has intensively studied the civilization of the Renaissance, especially that of Florence. His writings center on the relation and interconnection between ideas and the political and social structure of the civilization of Renaissance Italy. The following discussion of its political aspects is part of a paper given by Dr. Baron at a session of the 1941 convention of the American Historical Association which was devoted to the problem of the Renaissance. The balance of this paper which relates to science is given in a subsequent selection.

The tendency to minimize the role played by fifteenth-century Italy in the emergence of the modern world is by no means the product of conditions peculiar to the field of science. In political history, when attention is focused on such elements of the modern state as constitutionally guaranteed civil rights and parliamentary representation on a nationwide basis, it is difficult to avoid similar negative conclusions about the contribution made by the Renaissance. Bearing in mind such aspects of the modern state, Professor McIlwain in a suggestive lecture before the Mediaeval Academy recently gave it as his opinion that "what Professor Haskins has termed 'the Renaissance of the twelfth century' marks a more fundamental

From Hans Baron, "Toward a More Positive Evaluation of the Fifteenth-Century Renaissance," in the *Journal of the History of Ideas* 4 (1943): 22–27. Reprinted by permission of the editors of the *Journal of the History of Ideas*.

change" and "seems to be on the whole more significant in a perspective of the whole history, than the later development to which
we usually attach the word 'Renaissance.' " Opinions like these, more
or less pronounced, are probably held by the majority of present-
day historians of English law. They form, for instance, the keynote of
R. W. and A. J. Carlyle's six volumes on *Mediaeval Political Theory
in the West*. Again, students who place greater emphasis on the
growth of administration and on the rise of a trained, nationally
minded bureaucracy frequently trace the pedigree of the modern
state from Norman institutions or from the Sicilian monarchy of
Frederick II to the jurist-administration of fourteenth-century France,
and then to the centralized organization of the absolute monarchy of
the seventeenth and eighteenth centuries—without having recourse
to any essential contributions derived from the Renaissance.

Yet in the field of political history one can hardly say that this
new balance has been established beyond doubt. No sooner are
attempts made to reverse what is regarded as an overemphasis on
the Renaissance, than some one comes forward to enhance old
claims for some priority of fifteenth-century Italy. The way in which
discussions have developed in the present meeting reflects this
situation. In a vein very different from that of Dr. Durand's criticism
of the *"primato dell'Italia* in the field of science," Professor Nelson's
contribution from political history has been a vigorous restatement of
the thesis—which was virtually that of Ranke—that the state-system
of the fifteenth-century Italy, composed of Venice, Milan, Florence,
Naples, and the Papal State, witnessed the origin of modern balance-
of-power diplomacy. In other words, the differences of opinion that
embarrass us in our assessment of the Renaissance cut across the
border line between political and intellectual history. In every field
of study we are faced with the same problem. In cases without
number we learned to look at modern ideas and institutions as an
outgrowth of medieval conditions, which have revealed themselves
as indispensable stages in the historical continuity. But at the same
time students ask: does this view, however undisputed it may be,
force us henceforth to disclaim all that was once deemed the
"modern" face and the "precursorship" of the Italian Renaissance?
Apparently there are two sides to the picture. In order to understand their complementary truth, a brief methodological digression
seems advisable.

When Burckhardt coined the famous phrase that the Italian of the Renaissance was "the firstborn among the sons of modern Europe," he certainly was prompted by what we must today call an overestimate of the direct impact of the Italian Renaissance on the rise of the modern world. He underrated the continuity of medieval conditions in thought, in politics, and in many spheres of life. On the other hand, by the phrase "firstborn son of modern Europe" he did not mean simply that the ideas and institutions of the modern world must be traced largely to fourteenth- and fifteenth-century Italy as their historical source. If the words are taken literally, the meaning is that fifteenth-century Italy saw the coming of the first member of a family that subsequently spread throughout the Western world—the first specimen of a new species. Burckhardt was thinking of a pattern of society, education, and thought kindred in its sociological and cultural structure to the life of the later West, and therefore potentially stimulating to all subsequent generations—the *prototype* far more than the *origin* of the modern world.

The label of "historical significance" we so frequently employ is in fact made to cover two essentially different types of relationship between the past and the present. On the one hand, in our evaluation of past periods we view history as if it were a chain, in which the role of each link is merely to bridge the gap between the preceding and following links. But were this the only basis of historical evaluation, our estimate of the import of ancient Greece and Rome for the modern world would be much lower than it is. As a matter of fact, we constantly make use of a second method of historical evaluation, one based on the realization that history is more than a mere chain in which each link has contacts only with its neighbors. For instance, the political and ethical ideals of the Greek city-state may become powerless in the Hellenistic period immediately following, but be revived to historical potency whenever kindred patterns of life emerge—as in Cicero's Rome, in the fifteenth century, in Bacon's England, and possibly in our own day, or in days to come. Ideas of God, the world, space and time, conceived in a religious atmosphere, may later affect the whole fabric of culture and of thought, when kindred thought-patterns become possible in the sphere of science.

These are no doubt truisms. Yet they are easily overlooked. What they imply is that in every given case our attention must be turned both to the role of a period as a link in the chain of continuity, and to its potential affinities, in intellectual and social structure, to later periods. This balance of historical emphasis, I think, has recently been neglected in our study of the Renaissance. When it is taken into account, the present antagonism between two apparently ir-reconcilable schools of thought in the appraisal of the fifteenth century is largely explained.

In the field of political history it is comparatively easy to discern both the merits and the limitations of the two methods. From the outset it is improbable that representative government and a cen-tralized administration—institutions made to answer the specific problems of large nation-states—could have been substantially pro-moted by the conditions in the small city-republics and tyrannies of fifteenth-century Italy. There is no doubt that the medieval assem-bly of the crown vassals, giving counsel to their king, and the emergence of a new *noblesse de robe* in the national monarchies, were the chief, if not the only, roots of parliamentarism and bu-reaucracy in England and France. Yet this verdict passed from the perspective of the nation-state leaves unsolved all the questions which might reveal a *structural* kinship of fifteenth-century Italy with those patterns of political and social life which eventually emerged in the modern West.

In the case of the English constitution, increasing knowledge of its preparation throughout the Middle Ages has not removed the gap between "medieval constitutionalism" and "modern constitu-tionalism." In spite of the importance attached by Professor Mc-Ilwain to the institutions and thought of the twelfth and thirteenth centuries, no one has emphasized more strongly than he himself that to find in fifteenth-century England any ideas of republican participation by the people in the government or of active control of the administration by the nation, is to read modern concepts into the medieval context. If it is true that parliamentary institutions and the limitation of despotic monarchy were growing in feudal Europe from the twelfth century onward, it is also true that "medieval con-stitutionalism," meaning subordination of the king to the law and the imposition of restrictions upon him in matters of jurisdiction, was one thing, while the modern idea "that the members of a free state must be true citizens" by having "a part in its control" (as Professor McIlwain puts it) is another. The latter—modern—notion, which had

had its major precedent in the ancient world, played no role in England until the middle of the seventeenth century, i.e., after the cataclysm of the Civil War.

Yet in the smaller orbit of the Italian city-state the basic features of modern government by discussion and participation of the citizens in political control appeared as early as the twelfth century. In this milieu, ideas of citizenship that were destined to become, in McIlwain's words, "the commonplace of all political thought in modern times" came to the fore at once when political thought of the Scholastics was transplanted into the urban atmosphere. The fact that these ideas survived throughout the Quattrocento is fundamental for the appraisal of its political and intellectual makeup. Republican freedom and civic initiative, continuing through the "Age of the Despots," were forced to develop their full bearing on political ideals and thought in their life-or-death struggle with Renaissance tyranny. It is because of this survival of civic initiative in geographic proximity to bureaucratic-unifying absolutism that the whole range of modern political experience was traversed in the fifteenth century, and this so rapidly that by the end of the century many of the basic tenets of modern political science had matured, and been set forth in works of European scope by Machiavelli and Guicciardini.

Now Professor Nelson has recalled one of the most significant implications of these conditions, namely, that by the second half of the fifteenth century integration and interplay of the Italian states had reached a point where they produced something like a prelude to the later European power-system. One may go further and conclude that there must have been an underlying general affinity between the texture of political life in Renaissance Italy and the structure of the modern state. To refer to one example of recent date, when Professor Heckscher, in his broad study of modern mercantilism, confronted the medieval and modern economic pattern by pointing out the interrelationship between industrial "protectionism" and the modern state, he found the first appearance of the protectionist policy of the modern type in the Italian city-states and even more in the urbanized regional states which formed the power system of fifteenth-century Italy. From my own knowledge I should say that it is possible to round out such analogies for the whole orbit of political life. For instance, not only was the mechanism of modern

power-diplomacy anticipated in the time of Lorenzo de' Medici
. . , but the idea of a "balance" between equal members of a
state-system then, as later in the modern West, issued from a cycle
of events that had started with the threat by one power to transform the whole system into a single universal state—a threat followed by wars of independence, from which the individual states
emerged conscious of their identity, strengthened in national feeling, with the will to assert themselves in a balance of power. In
short, it is not alone in diplomatic technique (the feature which
immediately spread from Italy throughout Europe), but in the inherent dynamics of international relations that Renaissance Italy
foreshadowed the character of the family of modern Western nations.

Bearing these facts in mind, we shall find it hard to subscribe to
any judgment to the effect that, from the viewpoint of political ideas
and conditions, the twelfth century was more significant than the
fifteenth century. At the present stage of our knowledge, the only
fair judgment seems to be one not couched in the terms of an
alternative. As far as the political pattern of modern life is characterized by the existence of nation-states, spanning a large geographical
area by virtue of representative government, the foundation laid in
the Middle Ages looms larger indeed than any possible contribution by the Italian Renaissance. Still, when we ask what after all
distinguishes modern political life from the feudal epoch, it is of
equal significance that the *state of aggregation* of the modern world,
as it were, was first foreshadowed in the Italian Renaissance, with a
political system of smaller compass and simpler sociological conditions—albeit the nation-state and the representative system had
not yet entered into the historical compound.

Alfred von Martin
SOCIOLOGY OF THE RENAISSANCE

Alfred von Martin, born in 1882, has taught at the universities of Göttingen and Munich. His many books, dealing with sociological interpretations of the medieval, Renaissance, and modern scenes, are widely known. His book on the religion of Burckhardt was confiscated by the Gestapo in 1942.

Inertia and motion, static and dynamic, are fundamental categories with which to begin a sociological approach to history. It must be said, though, that history knows inertia in a relative sense only: the decisive question is whether inertia or change predominates.

The center of gravity of medieval society was the land, was the soil. With the Renaissance the economic and thus the social emphasis moves into the town: from the conservative to the liberal, for the town is a changeable and changing element. Medieval society was founded upon a static order of estates, sanctioned by the church. Everyone was assigned to his place by nature, i.e. by God himself, and any attempt to break away from it was a revolt against the divine order. Everyone was confined within strictly defined limits, which were imposed and enforced by the ruling estates, the clergy and the feudal nobility. The king himself was bound to rule according to definite laws: he had to carry out his reciprocal obligations towards his vassals; he had to treat the church according to the principles of *justitia*. Otherwise his vassals had a right of rebellion, and the church denounced him who had strayed from his assigned position as a *tryrannus*. The burgher could be fitted into this order by the church so long as he remained the modest middle-class man, who saw himself as a part of the established order, living in the medieval town which was still based upon a primary economy and a conservative scheme of things. Even in Renaissance Italy this petite bourgeoisie had its outlook closely circumscribed by such an order of society. But, as the burghers became a power with the rise of a money economy, as the small artisan became the great

From *Sociology of the Renaissance,* translated for the International Library of Sociology and Social Reconstruction from *Soziologie der Renaissance* (Stuttgart, 1932), pp. 1–19. Copyright 1944. Reprinted by permission of the Oxford University Press and Routledge and Kegan Paul Ltd.

merchant, we find a gradual emancipation from the traditional forms of society and the medieval outlook: there was a revolt against those sections of society which were most dependent upon this structure and upon these ways of thought, by virtue of which they exercised their authority. We find arising against the privileged clergy and the feudal nobility the bourgeoisie, which was throwing off their tutelage and emerging on the twin props of money and intellect as a bourgeoisie of "liberal" character. By revolting against the old domination they also freed themselves from the old community ties which had been interlinked with it. Blood, tradition and group feeling had been the basis of the community relationships as well as of the old domination. The democratic and urban spirit was destroying the old social forms and the "natural" and accepted divine order. It thus became necessary to order the world starting from the individual and to shape it, as it were, like a work of art. The guiding rules in this task accorded with those liberal aims set by the constructive will of the bourgeoisie.

Life in a primary community is apt to produce a conservative type of thought, a religious way of thought which orders the world in an authoritarian manner. Everything temporal is to it no more than a parable, a symbol of the metaphysical, and nature is but a reflection of the transcendental. But the bourgeois world as seen from the coolly calculating, realist point of view of the city-state is a world that has lost its magic. The liberal mode of thought of the emancipated individual attempts to control the outside world more and more consciously. Thus community becomes society, and thus arises the new domination by a new oligarchy, the capitalist domination by the moneyed great bourgeoisie, which exploits those "democratic" tendencies which had destroyed feudalism, as the best way to ensure its own domination. In the Middle Ages political power with religious sanction had prevailed: now comes the era of an intellectually supported economic power. Religion as well as politics becomes a means, just as previously commerce and secular culture had been no more than the means to an end.

The Middle Ages in their social structure as well as in their thought had a rigidly graduated system. There was a pyramid of estates as well as a pyramid of values. Now these pyramids are about to be destroyed, and "free competition" is proclaimed as the law of nature. God and blood, the traditional powers, are deposed, and though they maintain some of their importance their dominance is shattered.

The spirit of capitalism which begins to rule the modern world with the Renaissance deprives the world of the divine element in order to make it more real. But the spirit of early capitalism did not as yet dehumanize it. Reason was not as yet rated above humanity; it was not yet the be-all and end-all of all action. Riches were, as yet, no more than a means to independence, respect and fame (L. B. Alberti). Although time was beginning to become scarce, the individual could yet lead a cultured existence and see himself as a full personality. The culture of Renaissance Italy, and only Italy knew a genuine Renaissance, contained from the very beginning certain aristocratic elements and tended to emphasize them increasingly. It is significant that Italy led the way in the development of early, but by no means of full, capitalism.

Thus the typological importance of the Renaissance is that it marks the first cultural and social breach between the Middle Ages and modern times: it is a typical early stage of the modern age. And the outstanding ideal type is the Italian situation above all in Florence. Jacob Burckhardt could already write: "The Florentine was the model and prototype of the present-day Italian and of the modern European in general," and Pöhlmann said that we find in Florence "the most varied expression of the spirit of modern times to be seen anywhere at the end of the Middle Ages or within so confined an area." The reasons for this advanced position of Italy, and above all of Florence, are to be found in political, constitutional, economic, social and educational history, as well as in the relations with the church.

But for the sociologist the interest of the period lies in the fact that it presents him with a complete rhythmic progression of the ideal type of a cultural epoch dominated by the bourgeoisie. The differentiation of Early, Full, and Late Renaissance, originally devised by the art critic, finds its sociological meaning in those social changes which are expressed in the stylistic ones. The prelude to the bourgeois era which we call the Renaissance begins in the spirit of democracy and ends in the spirit of the court. The first phase represents the rise of a few above the rest. This is followed by the securing of their newly won exalted position and the attempt to establish relations with feudal aristocracy and to adopt their way of life. From the very beginning, that part of the bourgeoisie which gave its character to the period, i.e. the capitalist entrepreneurs, feels itself called upon to rule. In order to achieve this end it must first eliminate the former rulers on its "Right" by making an alliance with the "Left." But from the very beginning it has a tendency toward the Right; a tendency to intermix with the traditional ruling classes, to adopt their way of life, their attitude and their mode of thought and to attempt to become part of feudal "good" society.

The humanists—representatives of the intelligentsia—follow the same road and feel themselves tied to the new elite; whether this attachment was voluntary or not is of secondary importance here. Under the circumstances "democracy" meant no more than opposition to the privileges of the old powers, the clergy and the feudal nobility; hence the negation of those values which served to uphold their special position; it meant a new, bourgeois principle of selection according to purely individual criteria and not according to birth and rank. But liberty was not made into a revolutionary principle symbolizing an onslaught upon all and every established authority. In particular the church was respected as an authoritative institution, and the only aim of the bourgeoisie was to vindicate its right to a position of importance. "A complete self-disarmament, such as the upper Estates carried through before the Revolution in France under the influence of Rousseau, was out of the question among these utilitarian Italians" (F. G. J. von Bezold). This bourgeoisie of the Renaissance had a strong sense of what would enhance its power; its rationalism served it without ever endangering its position.

THE NEW DYNAMIC

Changes in Social Structure

"Italy, always delighting in a new thing, has lost all stability . . . ; a servant may easily become a king." It was the new power of money that made Aeneas Sylvius say this, a power which changes and sets in motion. For it is a part of the "power of money to subject all walks of life to its tempo" (Simmel). In an era of primary economy the individual was immediately dependent upon the group and the interchange of services linked him closely to the community; but now money makes the individual independent because, unlike the soil, it gives mobility. "Cash payments" are now "the tie between people" (Lujo Brentano); the relationship between employer and employed is based upon a free contract, with each party to it determined to secure the utmost advantage. At the stage of development represented by a primary economy human and personal relationships predominated; a money economy makes all these relationships more objective.

Authority and tradition were able to dominate the medieval economy because of the methods of the self-sufficient, individual undertaking; but the resulting limitations become unbearable when the economic system of segregated small or medium-sized units is replaced by capitalist enterprises pointing the way to the factory system, and when industry begins to produce for a larger market, the world market in fact.

Now competition becomes a serious factor, whereas the essence of the guild organization, with its price fixing and compulsory corporization, had been the elimination of competition. In those days the individual had been unfree but secure—as in a family. But for obvious reasons, that had been possible only in an economy designed to satisfy immediate and local needs. Even the professional trader had been able to maintain the characteristics of the artisan owing to his unchanging methods and life. As long as the horizon remained comparatively limited all this was possible, but as soon as the horizon expands, as great money fortunes are accumulated (in the Middle Ages fortunes consisted solely of land), these conditions are bound to disappear. The great merchants and moneyed men regard the rules of the guild as so many fetters, and they know how to rid themselves of them. In Florence they free themselves from the restrictions of the guilds and achieve individual freedom to carry on trade and commerce, thus freeing themselves from all the medieval barriers against the rise of a class of real entrepreneurs. The individualist spirit of early capitalism thus replaces the corporate spirit of the medieval burgher.

The Florentine development was both typical and the first in point of time. The townspeople of the Middle Ages were "essentially similar and economically independent individuals" (Doren); all this was fundamentally altered by the increasing power of mobile capital. In step with the industrial developments we find radical alterations in the social structure, for now an elite of capitalists was forming itself; it no longer took part in manual work, but was active in the sphere of organization and management, standing apart from the remainder of the middle class and the working proletariat. The wage earners—excluded from the possession of the means of production and from all political rights—were ruthlessly exploited and even deprived of the right of association. But the mercantile and industrial capitalist elements also asserted their power over the master craftsmen, the *popolo grasso* of the *arti maggiori* over the *popolo minuto* of the *arti minori*. And it was the great merchants, leading the *arti maggiori,* who in 1293 made the guild organization into the basis of the Florentine constitution. Only formally speaking was this a victory of a broad middle-class democracy (cf. Davidson). Not the "people," but the monetary power of the upper guilds defeated the feudal aristocracy, and the middle class represented by the lower guilds was for all intents and purposes excluded from power. The Florentine constitution of 1293 gave power to a selected plutocracy. The "rule of the people" remained an ideological facade, a slogan for the masses. It was designed to tie them to the new rulers, and deck out as the rule of justice the new form of government which degraded and deprived of political rights the whole feudal class. The struggle against the feudal aristocracy was the first trial of strength of the haute bourgeoisie, in which it needed the support of the middle and small bourgeoisie.

It is true to say that feudalism had never been fully established in Italy, yet even Florence had a medieval constitution which had to be destroyed. Eberhard Gothein, in his *Renaissance in Süditalien,* shows to how small an extent the legislation even of a Frederick II had destroyed feudalism in southern Italy, and how it was systematically reestablished in Renaissance Naples. But on the other hand, he also shows how largely it had become "an empty form, a lie" even there; how much a "fiction" and a "disguise" which no longer corresponded to reality. "The spirit of ruler and ruled alike had long since outgrown the ideas of feudalism"; "these forms of tenure, deprived of their pristine meaning," had become fictitious. The primacy of the old rulers had corresponded to their military importance, the importance of the heavy cavalry of the vassal and his followers. In the measure in which the infantry, the weapon of the burghers, acquired increasing and then overwhelming tactical importance, the nobility was bound to take a place of secondary rank even in its very own military sphere. But the same was true of economic and cultural trends: the nobility was no longer at home in an era of reason. Even though the nobility had—before the bourgeois—fought against the church as the sole arbiter of conscience, it was now deprived of the basis of its power—the monopoly in military matters and the link of wealth with landed property. It stood, senile and outlived, in the midst of a new era. Even its respect for "honor" was anachronistic; one remembers Vespasiano da Bisticci's story of King Alfonso's impulsive refusal to destroy the Genoese fleet by purely technical means, because it seemed unchivalrous to do so. Such scruples were bound to appear as old-fashioned, aristocratic prejudices to an era which rationally shaped its means to serve its ends, and reckoned only the chances of success. Against an ideology which bases its power upon an empty legitimacy, which is therefore felt to be false, against such an ideology the realistic bourgeois stakes the reality of power, for it alone impresses him, whereas its absence appears contemptible. But the basis of power in a money economy is twofold: (a) the possession of money and (b) an orderly management of business. Giovanni Villani believes that the disorderly management of their resources by the [Teutonic] feudal nobility forced them to satisfy their need for money by arbitrary means such as violence and faithlessness. It is part of the self-respect of the great bourgeois that he, a good merchant, has no need of such methods, for economic reason gives him a way of calculating correctly; it is here that he sees the superiority of his civilization, the civilization of the towns.

The medieval system knew in the field of economics only one type of order, the order of the small men, peasants and artisans, who by the work of their hands earned their keep, in accordance with the necessities of their rank, their traditionally fixed "needs." Apart from this static order, which applied to the vast majority, there was the static disorder in which the great lords, the rich of pre-capitalist days, led their particular lives. It did not matter whether they were secular magnates or among those priests who, according to Alberti, desired to outdo all in splendor and display, in inclination to inactivity and the absence of all economy. As a matter of fact, such an unregulated and indolent mode of life led to the economic ruin of the majority of the old noble families. In contra-

distinction to the nobleman as well as the medieval peasant or artisan, the bourgeois entrepreneur calculates; he thinks rationally, not
traditionally; he does not desire the static (i.e., he does not acquiesce
in the customary and the traditional) or the disorderly, but the dynamic (i.e., he is impelled towards something new) and the orderly.
He calculates, and his calculations take the long-term view. All sentiment (such as the peasant's love for his own or the pride that the
artisan takes in his handiwork) is foreign to him. What he values is
the drive and discipline of work, directed single-mindedly toward an
end. It is this that produces order as a human work of art.

But characteristic of the Renaissance is a far-reaching assimilation of the nobility to the new conditions and the reception of the
nobles in the towns. The country nobility, in so far as it is not destroyed by "chivalrous feuds and extravagance, settles in the town"
and takes up commercial activities. It thus wins for itself wealth, and
upon that basis a new political power; in the process it becomes
bourgeois in its nature, attitude and modes of thought, so that the
bourgeois is no longer determined by his ancestry. This type of
noble intermarries with the great patrician families and together with
them forms an exclusive aristocracy of commerce. This process is
accelerated by the inclination of those families which are not noble
to invest their industrial and commercial profits in land. This is
done in the interest of the prestige of their firm and their own social
standing, perhaps after they have ruined the original noble owners.
It leads to a complete reconstitution of "good society"; it is a new
aristocracy of talent and determination (in place of birth and rank),
which begins by combining economic with political prowess, but
whose mode of life is on the whole determined by the economic,
i.e. the bourgeois, element.

The New Individualist Entrepreneur

In acquiring power and social standing through wealth, the finan-
cially powerful bourgeoisie had thus become superior to the nobility,
even in politics. What was fundamentally new was the rational management of money and the investment of capital. Capital had a
creative effect and put a premium on ingenuity and enterprise. In
the Middle Ages, a period of predominantly agricultural production,
interest had centered upon consumption; after all, it is relatively

impossible either to lose or increase landed property, which is essentially static. Only money, in the form of productive capital, creates the unlimited openings which emphasize the problem of acquisition as against that of consumption. With this growth in scope came the desire to exploit it: the enlargement of business increased the will and the ability to overcome the problems involved. The stability of an as yet static economy was upset by a dynamic element which increasingly and fundamentally altered its whole character. A progressive and expansive force was inherent in the new type of economic man and the new economy, a force which was to break up slowly but surely the old world of small economic unit. Thus an economy of money and credit made possible the hitherto unknown spirit of enterprise in economic matters.

It became possible in quite a new sense to follow "enterprising" aims since they could be pursued by completely rational means, by the full exploitation of the possibilities inherent in a money economy. The rationally calculating foresight of the merchant served to fashion in addition to the art of trade also the arts of statecraft and of war. The bourgeois, having gained his position of power, continued to press on and, in accordance with his psychology and will to power, appeared as a freely competing capitalist entrepreneur not only in commerce but also in political matters. It might be that he combined the functions of business magnate and political leader (as did the Medici, who relied upon their wealth and their position as party leaders), or he might, by capitalist methods, secure free disposal over a military force as a condottiere or over a subdued state as *nuovo principe*.

It is one of the traits of the early capitalist civilization of the Renaissance that business and politics became so thoroughly interdependent that it is impossible to separate the interests that they represented. We can see this clearly already in the case of Giovanni Villani. Business methods served political ends, political means served economic ends. Political and economic credit were already inseparable. The fame and glory of a state (also increased by successful wars) were reflected in profits. On the other hand, we can already discern the difficulties brought about by the cosmopolitan character of the new power of money and the interlocking of international capital. Nevertheless, this obstacle to vigorous foreign policies was more than offset by the stimulus it gave to imperialist aims. The numerically small group of commercial and industrial magnates which at home had won political along with economic power, pursued in its external relations, too, a policy fashioned on broad lines—a policy of territorial expansion (such as the Florentine conquest of the ports of Pisa and Livorno, which was to benefit Florentine seaborne trade) or of winning new markets which was pursued "even at the price of internal unrest and without hesitating to conjure up war and its misery" (Doren). This may be contrasted with the more restricted policy of the petit bourgeois, the artisan, whose goal was a "bourgeois" existence and the "peaceful comfort of a small circle" (Doren). The entrepreneur, abroad as at home, was turning the state to his own ends.

But above all, the state itself was now becoming a capitalist entrepreneur; the politician began to calculate and politics were becoming rational. Political decisions were influenced by commercial motives, and politics were closely circumscribed by the categories of means and ends dictated by bourgeois aims and interests. We see politics pervaded by the spirit of reason, which had been alien to the medieval state at a time when the church had been the one rationally guided institution. It is of minor importance whether the bourgeoisie democratically controlled the state or whether the bourgeois methods were adopted by an absolutist state in the shape of mercantilism and rational statecraft. In both cases realistic policy guided by economic considerations provided the contrast, typical of the age, with the practices of the Middle Ages, which had been sustained by the privileged estates, the clergy and the feudal nobility. The attack upon these classes reveals a complete parallelism between the legislation of the first modern absolutist state, the realm of Frederick II in Lower Italy, and the Florentine *Ordinamenti della Giustizia,* where justice means, in a completely modern sense, the abolition of traditional privileges. In this way the modern monarchy and the formal democracy of a city-state fulfilled the same function: both were adequate to deal with the new social reality created by economic developments. These forms of government represented the two possible ways of adjusting the nature of the state to the nature of society. Accordingly, the Italian despotisms or signorie continued along lines laid down by the town commune: both were built upon the foundation of the new money economy, the free development of individual forces and, on the other hand, the centralization of all power which increasingly substituted administrative for constitutional principles and subjected all spheres of life to conscious and rational regulation. The unifying factor was no longer an organic and communal one (e.g., blood relationship, neighborhood or the relationships of service) but an artificial and mechanized social organization which cut adrift even from the old religious and moral power and proclaimed the *ratio status* as an expression of the secular nature of a state which was its own law. The resulting statecraft was "objective" and without prejudices, guided only by the needs of the situation and the desired end and consisting only of a pure calculation of power relationships. It was an entirely methodicized, objective and soulless craft and the system of a science and technique of state management.

The Norman state of Roger II showed already, at a very early date, the tendency towards bourgeois valuations, i.e. a spirit of sober calculation and the prominence given to ability and efficiency rather than to birth and rank. At the time of Roger's death Georgio Majo, the son of a Bari merchant who made big deals in oil, was high chancellor of the Sicilian kingdom. Roger himself had already built up a professional civil service and sponsored a conscious economic policy (cf. his foundation of industries). Using these foundations, Frederick II loosened the old ties by limiting the rights of the church and the feudal nobility in favor of a centralized organization which used fiscal and rational methods and employed a salaried bureaucracy and an army of mercenaries. Even the modern trait of basic distrust, of not trusting one's fellowmen—that characteristic of society as opposed to the community, which means traditional trust or confidence—which we later find in the urban communes, already characterized the regime of Frederick II: "The whole machinery of administration was so constructed that one section of it watched and controlled the others as much as was possible" (Ed. Winkelmann). And the enlightened despot knew how to exploit the magic position assigned to the medieval emperors as providing a prop for his rule and serving as an ideology to counter the papal theory of the two swords.

This Norman kingdom was in need of a rational basis in legislation and administration because it was a state built upon the might of the sword and the powerful personality (E. Caspar). It was for this reason that Burckhardt earlier pointed out its similarity to the condottiere states of the Quattrocento. These were "purely factual" structures relying on talent and virtuosity to assure their survival. In such an artificially created situation "only high personal ability" and carefully calculated conduct could master the perpetual menaces. In these states which lacked any traditional sanction the conception of the state as a task for conscious construction had to develop. And thus all depended upon the objective and correct attack upon this task by the proper constructor: to support this new objectivity the modern individual appeared. There was no distinction between the prince and the state: its power was his power, its weakness was his weakness. Therefore the "tyrant," himself the negation of the static medieval ideal of the *rex iustus,* has to be judged by the historical and political criterion of "greatness" disregarding the criteria of morals and religion.

The prototype of the combination of the "spirit of enterprise" and the "bourgeois spirit," the two elements that Sombart distinguishes in the capitalist spirit, was the combination of war and business. We find it, even before the Crusades, in the Italian ports. "The warlike enterprises of the Italian sea-trading towns"—Pisa, Genoa, Venice— often "had the character of shareholding ventures," the share in the loot being distributed according to the extent of participation and whether it was only in the capacity of soldier or by the provision of capital (Lujo Brentano). And as a military profession at the disposal of the highest bidder developed, war became increasingly a matter of big business for the military entrepreneur, the condottiere, who "with the shrewd sense of a modern speculator changed sides and even fixed in advance the price of an expected victory" (v. Bezold), as well as for his employer. Stefano Porcaro debated before the Signoria at Florence whether it be "more profitable" to fight one's battles with a levy of citizens or with mercenaries, and he concluded that, in spite of the cost, it was "safer and more useful" to settle the business with money.

The Curia itself had to bow to the new trends which made for clearly circumscribed sovereignties forming the basis of financial power. The Vatican "was increasingly robbed of its economic basis in the shape of the powers of taxation of the Church Universal; after the Great Schism it had to create its own state as a necessary foundation" (Clemens Bauer): thus its monetary needs involved it in the internal Italian struggles.

New Modes of Thought

The new mode of thought, evident in all these developments, naturally emanated from an upper class only. The middle-class petit bourgeois, whose attitude we see in Vespasiano da Bisticci, remained essentially conservative. He still clung to a patriarchal order divided into estates of a static nature. He regarded as "just" the existing state of affairs, with which one should moreover remain content. Honest and straightforward, he took the view of a "good Christian and a good citizen." His simple piety knew no problems; he defended his faith as an absolute truth against the modern, liberal and intellectual belief that everything may be subjected to discussion: he was indignant with the "many unbelievers" who "dispute about the immortality of the soul as though it were a matter for discussion," seeing that it was "almost madness to cast doubt on so great a matter in the face of the testimony of so many eminent men." Here we see a way of thought that was traditional and tied to authority; there is in it no individualist emancipation, so much so, in fact, that Vespasiano could regard a name as a "matter of indifference." And yet this middle class was easily impressed and it bestowed its admiration where it could not really follow. It had to pay tribute to what impressed it and thus admitted, despite itself, valuations which ran counter to its own. Of course, it demanded that glory be not immorally acquired, but it also realized that the great "quegli che governano gli stati e che vogliono essere innanzi agli altri," are not always able to keep to the rules of morality. And the church itself at once came to the rescue! What, after all, was the purpose of indulgences? Infringements of the moral code could be expiated in money. So even the middle class made money the last instance, thanks to the lead given by the church. On the other hand, almost anything, even noble descent, would impress this middle class, which had not yet won through to democratic consciousness. It felt at once the influence of a gentleman of noble birth, a "signore di nobile istirpe e sangue." It was impressed by anything outstanding, and it made no difference whether the dis-

FIGURE 2. Warfare, made more destructive with the improved use of gunpowder
and portable firearms, was a constant element in Renaissance life. Here a squad
of arquebusiers in processional dress march in parade. From the 1526 edition
of *The Triumph of Maximillian I,* translated by S. Appelbaum (New York, 1964).
(*Used by permission of Dover Publications, Inc.*)

tinction were military or literary, of ability, birth or wealth. In this
context it is worth recalling Simmel's opinion: that when for the
first time large accumulations of capital were concentrated in one
hand and when the power of capital was as yet unknown to the great
majority, "its influence was increased by the psychological effect of
the unprecedented and the inexplicable." By its very novelty, capital,
when it first appeared as a force, acted upon a set of circumstances
completely alien to it "like a magic and unpredictable power." The
lower classes were "bewildered by the acquisition of great wealth"

and regarded its owners as "uncanny personalities." Thus it was, for example, in the case of the Grimaldi and the Medici.

This admiration for the "demoniac" we also find in the cult of *virtu,* of the man who was in any way great, which was rapidly spreading everywhere: this new type could achieve greatness only by boldly setting himself above all ethical and religious traditions and relying upon himself along with frightening boldness. Traditional morality was outmoded: even a man such as Villani, though he would morally condemn those who lacked objective virtue, could admire subjective *virtu* in them, and in his appreciation of Castruccio Castracani anticipated Machiavelli himself. Christian ethics, inasmuch as they condemned *superbia,* the complete reliance upon one's own strength, though not rejected in theory, in practice lost all influence. The individual was conscious of the fact that he had to rely completely upon his own forces. And it was the superiority of *ratio* over tradition, brought about by a mercantile age, which gave him the requisite strength. Such a penetration of all activities by the cold and calculating attitude of the merchant easily achieved a demoniac character. It was well illustrated by an entry in the ledger of the Venetian Jacopo Loredano: "The Doge Foscari: my debtor for the death of my father and uncle." And when he had removed him together with his son we find the entry "paid" on the opposite page. We see the complete repression of impulse and the absolute control of the emotions by a ruthlessly calculating reason which inexorably moves to its goal. All this is the approach of a bourgeois age, an age of a money economy.

Money capital and mobile property naturally linked up with the kindred power of time for, seen from that particular point of view, time is money. Time is a great "liberal" power as opposed to the "conservative" power of space, the immobile soil. In the Middle Ages power belonged to him who owned the soil, the feudal lord; but now Alberti could say that he who knew how to exploit money and time fully could make himself the master of all things: such are the new means to power of the bourgeois. Money and time imply motion: "there is no more apt symbol than money to show the dynamic character of this world: as soon as it lies idle it ceases to be money in the specific sense of the word . . . the function of money is to facilitate motion" (Simmel). Money, because it circulates, as landed property cannot, shows how everything became more mobile. Money which can change one thing into another brought a tremendous amount of unrest into the world. The tempo of life was increased. Only now was formulated the new interpretation of time which saw it as a value, as something of utility. It was felt to be slipping away continuously—after the fourteenth century the clocks in the Italian cities struck all the twenty-four hours of the day. It was realized that time was always short and hence valuable, that one had to husband it and use it economically if one wanted to become the "master of all things." Such an attitude had been unknown to the Middle Ages; to them time was plentiful and there was no need to look upon it as something precious. It became so only when regarded from the point of view of the individual who could think in terms of the time measured out to him. It was scarce simply on account of natural limitations, and so everything from now on had to move quickly. For example, it became necessary to build quickly, as the patron was now building for himself. In the Middle Ages it was possible to spend tens and even hundreds of years on the completion of one building—a cathedral, a town hall or a castle (e.g., the Certosa di Pavia which is built in the Gothic style): for life was the life of the community in which one generation quietly succeeds another. Men lived as part of an all-embracing unity and thus life lasted long beyond its natural span. Time could be expended just as possessions or human lives themselves were. For the Middle Ages knew a hand-to-mouth economy, as was natural in an age of primary production, for agricultural produce will not keep over long periods, and the accumulation of values was thus impossible. "Where the produce of the soil is immediately consumed, a certain liberality prevails in general . . . which is less natural when money brings the desire to save" (Simmel); money will keep indefinitely. Largesse was a medieval virtue; Bisticci could still praise the giving of any amount "without counting the cost" and with a "liberal hand" for the "love and greater glory of God" and according to "conscience." But the splendid liberality of the Renaissance was of a totally different type. On principle it was bestowed only where it was "in place." Alberti said that "contributions towards the erection of churches and public buildings are a duty that we owe to the honour of the family and of our ancestors." Under such circumstances one gave no more than was necessary, though always as much as was seemly. The reputation of the family which could not be separated from the credit of the firm had a role of its own in the thought of the merchant. *Onesta* called for certain expenditures, but they had to prove useful and not superfluous. It would not do to be pettifogging, but the rule to spend as little as possible is the natural corollary to the rule to gain as much as possible; here is the real meaning of the specifically bourgeois virtues. An orderly plan was the rule. To make headway it was necessary to spend less or at any rate no more than one's earnings, one must treat "economically" the body and the mind (Alberti regarded hygiene and sports as the way to strength and comeliness) and one must be industrious in contrast to the noble loafers. It was necessary to portion out time, even ration the time spent in political affairs. The Kingdom of Naples enforced overfrequent attendance at church, and Caraccioli thought that though this might be "useful, it was most detrimental to a thorough exploitation of the day's time."

Furthermore, the merchant developed his own particular form of religiousness. The small artisan had an intimate and almost overfamiliar attitude to God. The great bourgeois, on the other hand, faced him as a business partner. Giannozzo Manetti saw God as the "maestro d'uno trafico," circumspectly organizing the world on the analogy of a big firm. One could open a kind of account with him, as was easily suggested by Roman Catholic emphasis on good works. Villani quite definitely regarded the giving of alms and the like as a way of securing almost by contract—the honoring of contracts is the highest virtue in the code of the honest merchant—the divine help, so that one may rely upon it. "Ne deo quidem sine spe remunerationis servire fas est" (Valla). Prosperity, according to Alberti, is the visible remuneration for an honest conduct of affairs pleasing to God: this is the true religious spirit of capitalism, and in a truly Roman Catholic way a kind of cooperation between grace and personal efficiency was assumed. But this "grace" was contractually due in return for one's own performance. Even religiousness became a matter for the calculation of advantages, part of a speculation designed to succeed in economic as well as political matters (cf. Villani).

The state of affairs, in fact, was that religion had ceased to be a moving force on its own and had become part of the systematized outlook of the bourgeoisie, which was primarily determined by economic considerations. The religious idea was unable fully to penetrate human life and had ceased to cause effects of any magnitude. (The success of popular preachers of repentance was transient and sporadic.) The consciousness of belonging to a family of Western, Christian peoples, which in the Middle Ages had been upheld by knights and clergy, was alien to the bourgeoisie, taken up as it was with the feeling of national and political separations. Similarly, the class-conscious proletariat cannot recognize the bourgeois concept of the nation and the state. The living regard for Christendom or Europe taken as a whole died together with the belief in a divinely ordained duty to protect it against the infidel. The concept of a supranational occidental community lost its meaning with the decline of those social groups which had upheld it. It now appeared out-moded and threadbare. Indeed, the idea was first abandoned by those who were called to uphold it more than anyone else, the popes. Gregory IX and Innocent IV solicited Mahometan help against the Christian emperor. Here too the church, the one rational institu-tion of the Middle Ages, had beaten the path which the Renaissance was to follow. The divers Italian states then grew accustomed to ally themselves with the Turk, "openly and unashamed" as Burckhardt has it, against the other Italian powers: "it seemed a political weapon like any other" (Burckhardt). Especially for the Italians the concep-tion of Christian solidarity had lost all meaning; nowhere was there less dismay at the fall of Constantinople. On the contrary, an impres-sive personality such as Mahomet II was bound to be respected: Francesco Gonzaga, marquess of Mantua, was prepared to address him as "friend and brother." If a pope was asked to give aid against the Turks it was necessary to show "what advantages might accrue and what harm would be done if he were not to move." It was a pope, Alexander VI, who did his best, in concert with Ludovico il Moro, to turn the Turks against Venice.

Religion had lost its position as a power and its function as the common bond of all to the same extent as the ruling groups of the Middle Ages had been supplanted by the bourgeoisie. Similarly national languages began to supersede Latin, the universal language of the clergy. Clerical demirationalism, i.e. the Thomist reconcilia-tion of the natural and the supernatural, of the world and God, now led to complete rationalism. Religion was increasingly formalized, becoming a matter of outward observances (cf. the growing "judi-cial" character of religious beliefs). It was, in effect, neutralized and robbed of its hold upon life and the present. One did not go as far as to deny the theoretical possibility of divine interference by way of miracles: that was left to a later antitheist enlightenment, which by the very intransigence of its protest showed its continued or renewed preoccupation with religious problems. The typical Italian of the Renaissance was already one step further: his was that genuine atheism which has eliminated the idea of divine power from the considerations governing his actions and indeed from his thoughts and writings. Men had ceased to believe that anything irrational might intentionally interfere to disturb their own systematic designs, they thought themselves able to master *fortuna* by *virtu.* This is also shown by the absolute position that humanists assigned to the free human will. It is true that the medieval church had held the doctrine of free will in matters of morality, but it deliberately maintained the theological antinomy of free will and divine grace as a religious paradox. But now in this matter too, modes of thought tending towards complete individual freedom threw off the leadership of the church.

Social conditions which had lacked a rational basis had already given way to a systematic order. Everyone had to rely upon himself in the knowledge that neither metaphysical concepts nor supra-individual forces of the community were backing him. No longer did anyone feel himself as a trustee in office or vocation. The one goal was that of being a virtuoso. . . .

Robert S. Lopez

HARD TIMES AND INVESTMENT IN CULTURE

Robert S. Lopez was born in Italy in 1910. Educated there and in the United States, he is now professor of history at Yale University. His publications mark him as an excellent scholar in the area of economic history, especially in medieval trade and banking. Professor Lopez presented the following paper at the Symposium on the Renaissance held at the New York Metropolitan Museum of Art on February 8–10, 1952.

When humanists like Michelet and Burckhardt accredited the term Renaissance, a good many years ago, economic history had hardly been born. Their lofty reconstruction of civilization in the Renaissance was unencumbered by the suspicion that the passions of Caliban might have something to do with the achievements of Ariel. Then came the followers of Marx and historical materialism, who trimmed the wings of the poet-historians and inserted literature into the digestive process. We ought to pay our deepest respects to both schools, not only to set an example to posterity when our own turn in obsolescence comes, but also because both the brain and the stomach certainly have an influence on the movements of the heart.

Historians, however, after letting the pendulum swing fully in either direction, have labored to find an equilibrium and a chain of relations between cause and effect. The easiest way to link two unfolding developments is to describe them as parallel and interlocked at every step. The notion that wherever there was an economic peak we must also find an intellectual peak, and vice versa, has long enjoyed the unquestioned authority of mathematical postulates. In an examination book of a sophomore which I graded not so long ago, the postulate entailed these deductions: Double-entry bookkeeping in the Medici Bank goaded Michelangelo to conceive and accomplish the Medici Chapel; contemplation of the Medici Chapel in turn spurred the bankers to a more muscular management of credit. But these statements, even if they were more skillfully

From Robert S. Lopez, "Hard Times and Investment in Culture," in *The Renaissance: A Symposium* (New York, 1953), pp. 19–32. Reprinted by permission of the New York Metropolitan Museum of Art and the author.

worded, are quite misleading. There is no denying that many beautiful homes of the Renaissance belonged to successful business-men—in Italy above all, then in Flanders, in southern Germany, and in other regions. Yet if bankers like the Medici and the Fuggers had been capable of conjuring up artists like Michelangelo and Dürer, then our own Rothschilds and Morgans ought to have produced bigger and better Michelangelos. And how could we explain the emergence of Goya in an impoverished Spain, or the artistic obscu-rity of the business metropolis that was Genoa? A minimum of sub-sistence is indispensable for art and a minimum of intelligence is indispensable for business. But this does not mean that great artists and great businessmen must be born in the same group and in the same generation.

What strikes us at the outset is the different relation between economy and culture in the High Middle Ages and in the Renais-sance. I must beg leave to begin by a very brief description of what we call the "commercial revolution" of the High Middle Ages. This great economic upheaval, comparable in size only to the modern industrial revolution, surged from the Dark Ages at about the same time as the *chansons de geste* and early Romanesque art. It reached its climax in the age of Dante and rayonnant Gothic, after which a great depression occurred. Like the modern industrial revolution, it was a period of great, continuous demographic growth, of steady if not spectacular technological progress, of expansion both through increased production and consumption at home and through con-quest of new markets abroad. It was an epoch of great opportunities and great hopes, of small wars for limited objectives, and of growing toleration and interchange of ideas among persons of different classes, nations, and beliefs. Its pace was, of course, slower than that of the industrial revolution, because progress traveled by horse and galley rather than by train, steamship, and airplane. The final results, however, were probably of the same order of magnitude. The medieval commercial revolution was instrumental in bringing about the momentous changes which bequeathed to the Renaissance a society not too different from our own, and was in turn influenced by all of these changes. It caused the old feudal system to crumble and the old religious structure to weaken. It all but wiped out slavery, it gave liberty to serfs over large areas, and created a new elite based upon wealth rather than birth.

A great expansion in all other fields occurred at the same time. The blossoming of a new literature and art, the revival of science and law, the beginning of political and religious individualism, the spread of education and of social consciousness to larger strata of the population were concurrent and contemporaneous with the commercial revolution of the High Middle Ages. Though not all facets of medieval literature and philosophy were such as one might expect of an economic expansion, who will deny that there was a connection between economic and intellectual progress? It is also proper to suggest that the economic and social change of the High Middle Ages was an indispensable preparation for the Renaissance, even as it is safe to state that a man must have been an adolescent before he can become a father. But we must not confuse two different ages. Probably there would have been no Renaissance—or, rather, the Renaissance would have taken another course—if the Middle Ages had not previously built the towns, humbled the knights, challenged the clergymen, and taught Latin grammar. But the towns of the Middle Ages created the civilization of the Middle Ages. Whether or not this civilization was as great as that of the Renaissance, it certainly was different.

Let us not say that the general coincidence of an exuberant civilization and an expansive economy in the High Middle Ages shows that great art and great business must always go together. Consider the different experience of different countries. Italy was to the medieval economic process what England was to that of the eighteenth and nineteenth centuries. It was the cradle and the pathfinder of the commercial revolution, which was on the move in several Italian towns long before it made its way through the rest of Europe. Like the industrial revolution, the commercial revolution did not spread evenly: here it passed by large areas or slackened its speed, there it gained impetus as it engulfed other generators of economic advance. In Flanders, for instance, the currents coming from Italy swelled a river which had sprung from local streams. But Ile de France, the home of so much glorious medieval art, literature, and philosophy, was a retarded if not quite a forgotten area. Its towns were small and sleepy in the shadow of the great cathedrals at a time when the Italian towns hummed with business activity and made great strides in the practical sciences of law, mathematics, and medicine, but had not yet produced a Dante, a Giotto, or an Aquinas.

With these three giants Italy concluded the Middle Ages in a thoroughly medieval way. Petrarch, another Italian, ushered in the intellectual Renaissance at the very moment when the economic trend was reversed. The exact span of the Renaissance is variously measured by historians of civilization. There was a lag in time between the Renaissance in Italy and that of the other countries. Moreover, the imperialism of certain lovers of the Renaissance has led them to claim as forerunners or followers men who would be better left to the Middle Ages or to Baroque. I shall assume that, chronologically speaking, the Renaissance means roughly the period between 1330 and 1530, though the economic picture would not substantially change if we added a few decades at the beginning or at the end. Now that period was not one of economic expansion. It was one of great depression followed by a moderate and incomplete recovery.

Time alone will tell whether the economy of the age in which we live is the early stage of another "Renaissance" rather than the prelude to another "Dark Age," or a mere pause before another cycle of expansion. We shall see in a moment that certain resemblances seem to bring the Renaissance closer to us than any other historical period, in the economic field as in many others. But there was no resemblance in regard to population trends. Following a great plunge in the midfourteenth century, the population of Europe tended to stagnate at a far lower level than that of the High Middle Ages. A number of epidemics, far more terrible than any medieval contagion, whittled down the population. Famines, birth control, and other causes which cannot be enumerated here even in the most summary fashion, contributed to the same end. The decline was particularly pronounced in cities—the very homes of the essentially urban civilization that was the Renaissance. The country suffered less and recovered better, but it did not escape the general pattern.

The falling curve of the population was to some extent connected with other retarding factors. Technological progress continued, but, with the notable exceptions of the insurance contract, the printing press and certain advances in metallurgy, it was represented by diffusion and improvement of medieval methods and tools rather than by the invention of new ones. True, there was Leonardo da Vinci; but his amazing inventions were of no avail to his contemporaries, who were uninformed and probably uninterested in them. Again, the Renaissance introduced a better type of humanistic schools and of education for the elite, but it made no sweeping changes in technical education and no significant advances in bringing literacy to the masses. In these respects the Renaissance was less "modern" than the High Middle Ages.

A closer resemblance to our own times lies in the fact that the gradual shrinking of political horizons frustrated the improved means of transportation and the powerful organization of international trade which the Middle Ages had bequeathed to the Renaissance. Shortly before the Renaissance began, a Florentine merchant had described the road from the Crimea to Peking as perfectly safe to Westerners—a statement which we would hesitate to make today. But, during the Renaissance, East and West were split deeply, first by the collapse of the Mongolian Empire in the Far and Middle East, then by the Turkish conquest in the Near East. A medieval advance in the opposite direction was nullified before its possibilities were grasped: the Scandinavians abandoned Vinland, Greenland, and Iceland. Within Europe each state manifested its incipient centralization by raising economic barriers against all of the others. To be sure, the twilight of the Renaissance was lighted up by the greatest geographic discoveries. But it was a long time before the beneficial effects of the new round of discoveries were felt. The first telling result was the disruptive revolution of prices through the flood of American silver and gold—and even this came when the Renaissance had already been seized by its gravediggers, the Reformation and the Counter-Reformation.

War and inflation were as familiar to the Renaissance as they are, unfortunately, to us. It is true that already in the High Middle Ages a continuous but gradual and moderate inflation of the coinage and a parallel growth of credit money had provided much needed fuel for the demographic and economic expansion of the commercial revolution. But in the Renaissance inflation was steeper and steeper. Soft money did not supply larger means of payment for a growing number of producers and consumers. It was chiefly turned out by monarchies and city-states to pay for the largest wars that had afflicted Europe since the fall of the Roman world—the largest that Europe was to witness before the Napoleonic period, or perhaps our own world wars. One thinks first of the Hundred Years' War, which, with some intermediate truces, lasted well over a century and plagued most of western Europe. The Angevin-Aragonese contest was smaller in scope, but it desolated the whole of southern Italy and Sicily for almost 200 years. The Turkish armies inflicted still greater sufferings upon southeastern and east-central Europe. In northern Italy the mercenaries may have been gentle when fighting one another, but they were a plague to private harvests and public treasuries. Germany was the theater of incessant local wars and brigandage, and Spain was hardly more peaceful. It is true that in the second half of the fifteenth century most of Europe had some respite. But then came the wars between the Hapsburgs and France, with intervention of the Turks, which involved the whole of Europe, used artillery on a large scale, and renewed atrocities that had almost disappeared in the High Middle Ages. They had not ended when the wars of religion began.

Needless to say, disease and famine were faithful companions of war. Moreover, during the fourteenth century desperate revolts of peasants and city proletarians burst out almost everywhere from England to the Balkans and from Tuscany to Flanders. They also claimed their victims. In the fifteenth century a dull resignation seemed to prevail and banditism sprouted—sometimes even in the vicinity of towns. The early sixteenth century was marred by terrible peasants' revolts in Hungary, Germany, northeastern Italy, Switzerland, and northern France.

Then, as now, inflation was not enough to support the burden of war. Taxation rose to much higher levels than during the commercial revolution, when a booming economy could have borne it more easily. It fleeced peasants and landlords, but it skinned the bourgeoisie, which had greater amounts of cash. In France and England the Renaissance marked the downfall of town autonomy, largely though not exclusively because the towns were unable to balance their budgets and because the richer bourgeois, who could have come to the assistance of their poorer fellow citizens, refused to bear even their own full share. In Italy the independent towns survived, at a price. They fell under dictators, who brought about some equalization of burdens through universal oppression; or under small oligarchies of very rich men, who could either bear or evade taxation.

Yet it would not be fair to ascribe to taxation alone the principal blame for an economic recession which was essentially caused by shrinking or dull markets. The markets had shrunk because the population had diminished or stagnated, and because the frontier had receded and had been locked up. Perhaps some compensation would have been found through a better distribution of wealth if the scattered revolts of the fourteenth century had grown into a general social revolution. They failed. The recurrence of wars and epidemics throttled whatever social ferment remained in the fifteenth century. In the general stagnation some of the rich men grew richer, many of the poor men grew poorer, and the others at best obtained security at the expense of opportunity.

The ominous signs are visible everywhere. Land prices and land-lords' profits in the Renaissance were at their lowest ebb in centuries. The great movement of land reclamation and colonization which had characterized the centuries between the tenth and the early fourteenth was arrested. As early as the thirteenth century, to be sure, many landlords in England, in Spain, in southern Italy, and in northwestern France had transformed arable land into sheep ranges. Wool was a good cash crop and sheep farming required little manpower. The process continued throughout the Renaissance, but it became less and less rewarding as the demand for wool became stagnant or declined. Great patches of marginal and even fairly good land, which had been exploited in the Middle Ages, were now returned to waste. Fertile estates were sold or rented for nominal prices. But even these low prices were too high for many hungry, landless peasants who lacked even the small capital needed to buy seeds and tools. Fortunate was the peasant whose lord was willing to advance money in return for a share in the crop.

In the High Middle Ages the towns had absorbed not only an ever increasing amount of foodstuffs and industrial raw materials, but also the surplus product of the human plant. Noblemen, yeomen, and serfs, each one according to his capacity, could then easily find occupation and advancement in town. In the Renaissance, opportunities were usually reserved for those who were citizens of the town. Yet citizens, too, had little chance to improve their lot. The guilds formerly had accepted apprentices freely and assured every apprentice of the opportunity of becoming a master. Now they became rigid hierarchies; only the son of a master could hope to succeed to the mastership. Outsiders were either rejected or kept permanently in the subordinate position of journeymen. This trend also affected the guilds of artists. Occasionally, to be sure, a town encouraged immigration of qualified groups of countrymen on condition that they carry out the humbler industrial tasks at lower salaries than those of the lowest journeymen. Again, the old practice of putting out raw materials for peasants to work at home gained some ground, but the increase of manufacturing in the country fell far short of compensating for the decrease of industrial production in towns. It was not a symptom of economic growth but merely a means of depressing wages. Luxury industries alone maintained and perhaps increased their production. This reflects the decline of production for the masses and the growing distance between the very rich and the very poor.

The growing dullness of European markets and the loss of many Eastern markets was bound to depress commerce. The leitmotif now was to offer for sale, not the greatest quantity and variety of goods, but—to quote a fifteenth-century manual of business—"only as much as one can sell in the place of destination." Nor was it always possible to buy as much as one desired. Wars and embargoes frequently interfered with trade. Increased duties in nearly every country from England to Egypt raised the cost of many wares to prohibitive heights. The age of rapid fortunes won in daring oversea and overland ventures was over. Sedentary merchants could still maintain their position if they employed many able and loyal employees and commission agents, if they planned every step carefully, and if they could wait patiently for their investments to bring hard-won profits. In Italy 5 to 8 percent was now regarded as a fair interest in commercial loans—a much lower rate than those prevailing in the High Middle Ages, although risks had not diminished. Banks improved their methods and often increased their size while diminishing in numbers. But they had to use a larger and larger proportion of their capital not for trade but for loans to the idle upper class and more frequently to belligerent states. Such investments usually brought high interest for a very short period and failure when the debtor was unable to pay the principal.

One business—insurance—boomed during the Renaissance. It bordered on gambling. Investors had no statistics to rely upon. Risky speculations on foreign exchange also drained capital away from commercial investments. Overt gambling attracted ambitious men who despaired of other gainful occupations. There were the extreme cases of scoundrels who staked their money against the life of an unknowing person and had that person murdered so that they could cash the bet. At the other extremity were many business-men who abandoned trade and invested in land, not merely a part of their capital, as merchants had always done, but everything they had. Even when bought at the lowest prices, land was not very remunerative; but it could insure some reward for the owner who sank enough money in improvements and administered the invest-ment in the spirit of business. The shift of production from butter to guns was reflected in the different fortune of merchants who exploited mines. After a long slump in mining there was a sudden boom in the late fifteenth and early sixteenth centuries. Metallurgy prospered: iron and bronze were war materials, and precious metals were the sinews of war. They also were needed to pay tributes to the Turks and increased custom duties to the Egyptians. But alum, a basic material for the declining cloth industry, was not in great demand. When the mines increased their output, the price of alum fell.

Italy, the earliest and most brilliant center of the artistic Renais-sance, felt the impact of the economic recession most heavily. Its condition resembled somewhat that of England after 1918, or that of New England after 1929. Italy fell harder because it had climbed higher. It had exploited most of its possibilities, and it could not seek recovery by opening up many new fields of enterprise. Con-versely, those countries which watered down their intellectual Renaissance with the largest proportion of medieval strains also seem to have felt the shock of the economic crisis less deeply.

Of course, we must not overstress the dark side of the picture. Contraction and stagnation had succeeded expansion, but the economic ceiling of the fifteenth century was still much higher than the top level of the twelfth, though it was lower than the peak of the thirteenth. The bourgeoisie preserved its commanding position in Italy and its influence in the western monarchies. The amazing progress of the commercial revolution in methods and techniques was not lost; indeed, the depression spurred businessmen to further rationalization and sounder management. Thanks to their accumulated experience and capital, the Italians not only defended their leading position but also quickened the recovery of other countries by investing capital and frequently establishing their residence abroad. Some countries which had formerly been retarded felt the full impact of the commercial revolution only now.

Finally, the depression and even the greatest disasters were sources of profit for some men. In many places food prices declined faster than real wages. Cheap land and cheap manpower made the fortune of many entrepreneurs. War enabled Jacques Coeur to grab fabulous riches. Inflation was a boon to the Fuggers, who controlled silver and copper mines. Southern Germany gained from the disruption of communications through France and, later, from the ruin of Venetian and Florentine banks. Barcelona inherited some of the trade which had slipped from Pisa. Antwerp fell heir to the commerce, though not to the industry, of other Flemish towns. Some of these successes were fleeting. Others lasted as long as the Renaissance. None of them, however, was as durable as had been the commercial and industrial blossoming of Italy and Belgium or the prime of English and French agriculture in the High Middle Ages. Qualitatively and quantitatively the compensations fell short of the deficiencies.

Economic historians are usually expected to back their statement with figures. These are not easily tested for a period which had not yet learned how to use statistics for the information of friends and the misinformation of enemies. Still what statistical data we have are reliable enough as indications of trends in growth or decrease, if not as absolute indexes of size. Here are some figures:

In 1348 the population of England was at least 3.7 million. In the early fifteenth century it plunged as low as 2.1 million. Then it rose slowly, but as late as 1545 it was still half a million short of the pre-Renaissance level. Yet England suffered comparatively little from war, and presumably was less affected by the economic slump than were some more advanced countries. Again, Florence in the time of Dante had more than 100,000 inhabitants, but no more than 70,000 in the time of Boccaccio, and approximately the same number in the time of Michelangelo. Zürich, a typical middle-size town, fell from 12,375 inhabitants in 1350 to 4,713 in 1468. Similar declines can be measured for the larger part of towns and countries. As for the often cited compensating factors, Antwerp, the one Belgian town whose population increased in the Renaissance while that of all the others decreased, in 1526 had 8,400 houses. There still were as many houses in Bruges, its ruined rival. Again, Catalonia, one of the few countries which continued to grow after the early fourteenth century, rose from 87,000 to 95,000 homesteads from 1359 to 1365. But it declined to 59,000 in 1497, and it was still down at 75,000 in 1553.

To turn to another kind of figures, the incoming and outgoing wares subject to tax in the port of Genoa were valued at £3,822,000 Genoese in 1293. The figure fell to £887,000 in 1424. In 1530 it was still more than 1 million short of the 1293 level, in spite of the fact that the purchasing power of the pound had greatly declined in the interval. Again, the aggregate capital of the main house and seven of the eight branches of the Medici bank in 1458 was less than 30,000 florins, whereas the capital of the Peruzzi bank in the early fourteenth century had risen above the 100,000 florin mark. Yet the Medici company in the Renaissance towered above all other Florentine companies, whereas the medieval Peruzzi company was second to that of the Bardi. Similarly, the combined fortunes of the three richest members of the Medici family in 1460 were valued at only 15 percent more than the fortune of one Alberti merchant a hundred years earlier. As for the so-called compensating factors, it is true that in 1521 Jakob Fugger the Rich obtained from Emperor Charles V an acknowledgment of debt for 600,000 florins. But in the early fourteenth century the English king owed the Bardi company an equal sum, according to English documents, which probably underestimated the debt, or 900,000 florins according to Villani, who may have overestimated it. In addition, the English king owed the Peruzzi company a sum two-thirds as large.

The woolen industry affords the best examples in regard to manufacturing because it worked chiefly for an international market. Without leaving Florence, we note that in 1378 the weavers went on strike to demand of the industrialists that they should pledge a minimum yearly output of 24,000 pieces of cloth. Forty years earlier the yearly output had been between 70,000 and 80,000 pieces. Yet the depression did not hit Florence as hard as Flanders, her greater rival. The slow growth of English woolen industry, which occurred at the same period, was far from compensating the decline of production in the other major centers. Total export figures very seldom exceeded 50,000 pieces, and usually were not higher than 30,000.

It is harder to put one's finger upon agrarian figures. But we may regard as suitable examples the contraction of cultivated areas and the falling prices of agricultural products in a time of general monetary inflation. In Prussia the price of rye fell by almost two-thirds between 1399 and 1508. In England the price of grain declined by 47 percent between 1351 and 1500, and that of cattle and animal products declined by 32 percent. "Of the 450 odd [English] manors for which the fifteenth-century accounts have been studied, over 400 show a contraction of land in the hands of tenants." In Gascony after 1453 "thirty percent of the rural villages were ravaged or seriously damaged." The plain of southern Tuscany, which had been reclaimed in the High Middle Ages, now relapsed to its previous condition of a malaria-ridden waste. In Castile the most powerful company of sheep owners in 1477 owned 2.7 million sheep, or roughly a sheep for every other inhabitant of the country. Figures of this kind, and the frequent reports about starvation and vagrancy, more than offset what information we have on agricultural progress in some parts of Lombardy and the introduction of some new plants to France.

I hope I have said enough to show that the Renaissance was neither an economic golden age nor a smooth transition from moderate medieval well-being to modern prosperity. I have fired only a small part of the available ammunition; still less would have been needed but for the fact that the newer findings of economic historians do not easily pierce the crust of preconceived impressions. Is it necessary to add that nobody should jump to the opposite conclusion and contend that the coincidence of economic depression and artistic splendor in the Renaissance proves that art is born of economic decadence? I do not think it is. We have just seen that the peak of medieval economy coincided with the zenith of medieval art.

A more insidious path would be open to straight economic determinism if someone invoked the overwrought theory of cultural lags. Cultural lags, as everybody knows, are ingenious, elastic devices to link together events which cannot be linked by any other means. Someone might suggest that a cultural lag bridged the gap between the economic high point of the thirteenth century and the intellectual high point of the fifteenth, so that the intellectual revolution of the Renaissance was a belated child of the commercial revolution of the Middle Ages. What should one answer? Personally, I doubt the paternity of children who were born 200 years after the death of their fathers. To be sure, the Renaissance utilized for its development the towns which the Middle Ages had built, the philosophy which the Greeks had elaborated, and nearly everything else that mankind had contrived ever since Neanderthal; but its way of life was conditioned by its own economy and not by the economy of the past.

There is no heap of riches and no depth of poverty that will automatically insure or forbid artistic achievement. Intellectual developments must be traced primarily to intellectual roots. But that does not at all mean that they are independent of economic conditions. The connection is not a direct and crude relation of cause and effect. It is a complicated harmony in which innumerable economic factors and innumerable cultural factors form together a still greater number of chords. That some of them are incongruous or dissonant should not surprise us. Every age is full of contradictions.

We have a unison rather than an accord when the literature and the art of the Renaissance make direct allusions to the troubled economic circumstances. Machiavelli in his *History of Florence* is well aware of the crisis, its causes and its manifestations. Martin Luther inveighs against the consequences of economic causes which he does not clearly perceive. The anonymous author of *Lazarillo de Tormes* embraces in his sympathetic irony the disinherited of all social classes. Agrippa d'Aubigné described in Biblical terms the terrible sufferings of France. Donatello and Jerome Bosch crowd their bas-reliefs and their paintings with portraits of starved persons. The enumeration could continue, but it would bring little light to the interrelation of economics and culture. What we look for is not the direct image of economic facts, but the indirect repercussions of these facts on the development of ideas.

Of the many connections that might be suggested, some are too farfetched and dubious for an earthly economic historian to take stock of them. For instance, some clever contrivance might be found to link together economic rationalization and intellectual rationalism. One might compare the clarity and symmetry of Renaissance double-entry books of accounting to the clarity and symmetry of Renaissance buildings. But the Renaissance also created such poems as that of Ariosto, which is anything but symmetrical, and such philosophies as that of Marsilio Ficino, which is anything but clear. Moreover, double-entry accounting was not a monopoly of the Renaissance. It made its first appearance in the early fourteenth century, if not earlier, and it is still used today. Perhaps we should leave these lofty comparisons to the examination book which I cited at the beginning.

More definite connections probably existed between specific economic factors and some themes or fashions in the literature, art, and thought of the Renaissance. Consider, for instance, the theme of the Wheel of Fortune, which is one of the refrains of the age. To be sure, the blind goddess at all times has exercised her influence upon all forms of human activity. But her sway has seldom been as capricious and decisive as in the Renaissance, when gambling was one of the principal means of making a fortune, and when ill fortune alone could unseat the fortunate few who were sitting pretty. Then consider the vogue of pastoral romance and the fresh interest in country life. The country always has its fans and its idealizers. Still its charm must have been particularly alluring to merchants who returned to the country after generations of rush to the city. They found there not only a better investment but also a healthier atmosphere and a more sincere way of life. Again, the list could easily be lengthened, but it might seem an anticlimax to those who are waiting for a comprehensive interpretation of the interplay of economy as a whole and culture as a whole. I shall not attempt to concoct a catch-all formula, which would only conceal the endless variety of actions and reactions. No harm is done, however, if the discordant details are grouped in tentative generalizations.

We have seen that the essential phases of Renaissance economy were first a depression, then stabilization at a lower level than the highest medieval summit. The implicit opposition between those two trends, depression and stabilization, may perhaps help us to understand a certain dualism in the general outlook of the Renaissance. Note that I said "may help to explain," not "explain." I am not postulating direct causes, but what my brilliant colleague, Mr. Ferguson, would call "permissive or partially effective causes." Some Renaissance men were pessimists: they thought of the lost heights rather than of the attained platform. Others, especially those who had managed to settle down in sufficient comfort, felt that they had definitely and finally arrived.

The pessimists may not have been the larger group, but they seem to have included some of the most significant personalities, ranging from Savonarola to Machiavelli, from Leonardo da Vinci to Michelangelo, from Dürer to Cervantes, from Thomas More perhaps to William Shakespeare. It would be useless to list more names without accounting for their inclusion, but I may be allowed, as an economic historian, to point out some of the intellectual aspects of depression. Some pessimists joined the medieval preachers in demanding an earnest return to God, or they imitated the pagan writers in exalting the golden age of primitive mankind. Others maintained that all human history, or indeed the history of the universe, is a succession of cycles in growth and decay, with no hope for permanent progress. Still others built political theories upon the assumption that men are basically gullible and corrupt, and that a statesman must adapt his strategy to human imperfection. Similar assumptions underlay many tragedies, comedies, and novels. Quite a few pessimists voiced the plight of the poor and the weak, or portrayed them in the background—but seldom in the forefront, because the forefront was reserved for the rich and the strong who purchased the work of art. A number invoked death or sleep, the brother of death. A larger number sought an escape from reality, not in Heaven but in a world of artistic, literary, philosophical, or even mathematical dreams. All of these diverse trends may of course be detected during any historical period, but they seem more pronounced during the Renaissance. It is easier to link them with economic depression than with any other economic trend.

The optimists in the Renaissance were not as different from the pessimists as one might think at first. Usually they shared with the pessimists a widespread belief in the flow and ebb of civilization, and a tendency to look for an ideal of perfection in the past and not in the future. Their standard, however, was nothing like the coarse emotionalism of the Middle Ages or the naive primitiveness of the mythical Golden Age. It was classic antiquity—another age of stability and poise in aristocratic refinement. The optimists thought that antiquity had been one of the high tides in human history, and that their own time was another high tide, intimately close to antiquity and utterly unrelated to the recent past. Now was the time to stretch one's hand for the riches which the high tide brought within reach. One could be Horatian and pluck the rose of youth and love before her beauty had faded. One could be more ambitious and make every effort to comprehend, fulfill, and enjoy the greater wealth which was now accessible to men freed from instinct and ignorance. Private individuals and political leaders were equally impatient. Their drive for self-fulfillment was humanitarian and peaceful so long as they strove to discover and develop their own self, their own moral and material resources. But it had to become aggressive individualism and political ruthlessness when success depended upon conquest of resources claimed by other individuals or nations. All of these characteristics, too, can be found in other ages, but they seem to predominate in the Renaissance. They are not surprising in an economic stagnation which still offers a good life to the elite but little hope for the outcast.

The moods of the Renaissance are so many and so various that they seem almost to defy definition. That is exactly why the Renaissance looks so modern to us—it was almost as rich and diversified as the contemporary scene. One important modern trait, however, was lacking. Most of its exponents had little faith and little interest in progress for the whole human race. Indeed this idea seems to be germane to economic expansion. The religious ideal of progress of mankind from the City of Man towards the City of God hardly survived the end of the commercial revolution and the failure of social revolts in the fourteenth century. In the later period, even the most pious men tended to exclude forever from the City of God the infidel, the heretic, and frequently all but a handful of Catholic ascetics or Protestant militant men predestined for salvation. The secular ideal of progress of mankind through the diffusion of decency and learning was seldom emphasized before the late sixteenth century, when economic stagnation began at last to be broken. In between there were nearly 200 years—the core of the Renaissance— during which any hope for progress was generally held out, not to the vulgar masses but to individual members of a small elite, not to the unredeemable "barbarians" but to the best representatives of chosen peoples.

Contrary to widespread popular belief, the society of the Renaissance was essentially aristocratic. It offered economic, intellectual, and political opportunities to only a small number. But it lacked a universally accepted standard of nobility. The commercial revolution of the High Middle Ages and the social changes connected with it already had undermined the aristocracy of blood. The great depression of the mid-fourteenth century, and the stagnation which followed shook the security and whittled down the income of the aristocracy of wealth. Blood and money, of course, were still very useful—they always are—but neither insured durable distinction by itself. Too many landowners, merchants, and bankers had lost or were threatened with losing their wealth, and high birth without wealth was of little avail in the age which has been called "the heyday of illegitimate children." Neither was there any recognized hierarchy of states and nations. The Holy Roman Empire of the Germanic people had fallen to pieces; the papacy had come close to total dissolution; France and England rose and fell many times; the Italian city-states witnessed a stunning series of coups d'état and mutations of fortune.

Perhaps this was why culture, what we still call humanistic culture, tended to become the highest symbol of nobility, the magic password which admitted a man or a nation to the elite group. Its value rose at the very moment that the value of land fell. Its returns mounted when commercial interest rates declined. Statesmen who had tried to build up their power and prestige by enlarging their estates now vied with one another to gather works of art. Businessmen who had been looking for the most profitable or the most conservative investments in trade now invested in books. The shift was more pronounced in Italy because in Italy businessmen and statesmen were the same persons. And it is in this field, I believe, that we can most profitably investigate the relation between economic and intellectual trends of the Renaissance. We ought to explore briefly the increased value of humanistic culture as an economic investment.

Quite probably the increase was relative and not absolute. It is doubtful that the Renaissance invested in humanistic culture more than any period of the Middle Ages. The precious metals which early medieval artists lavished in their works were a staggering proportion of the available stocks of gold and silver. The cathedrals and castles of the twelfth century probably absorbed a greater amount of raw materials and manpower-hours than the churches and palaces of the Renaissance. Medieval universities were far greater investments, in strictly economic terms, than the humanistic schools. But universities, cathedrals and castles were not built primarily—or, at least, not exclusively—for the sake of pure humanistic culture. Universities aimed at preparing men for professional careers, such as those of clergyman, lawyer, and physician. Castles were insurances against accidents in this life. It is not surprising that shrewd rulers and thrifty businessmen were prepared to invest part of their capital in functional works of art and in practical culture.

The investment, however, often was inversely proportional to the intensity of business spirit. We have noted that northern France, the home of most of the largest cathedrals, was one of the retarded countries in the commercial revolution. Let us now point out that cathedrals in northern Italy and Tuscany were usually smaller than those of France. Paris had the largest faculty of theology, whereas Italian universities stressed the more practical studies of law and medicine. Genoa, perhaps the most businesslike town in medieval Italy, had one of the smallest cathedrals and no university at all. Yet its inhabitants were pious and its merchants were quite cultured. Very many had gone to business schools and a good number had been graduated from a law school. But the state was run as a business proposition—and good management warned against immobilizing too many resources in humanistic culture, which was functional only to a limited extent.

The evolution from the state as a business affair to the state as a work of art, if I may still use the Burckhardtian formula, went together with the depression and the stagnation of the Renaissance. The decline of aristocracy and the recession of plutocracy left a gap through which culture, that other noblesse, could more easily shine. That culture was placed so high—higher, perhaps, than at any other period in history—is the undying glory of the Renaissance.

The transition was smooth because the seeds had been planted in the High Middle Ages. Already in the thirteenth century, culture was a creditable pastime to the nobleman and a useful asset to the merchant. It was then the fashion for kings and courtiers to write elegant lyric poems—or to have them written by the Robert Sherwoods of the time—on very subtle matters of love and courtship. So did the merchants who traded in and ruled over the Italian towns. They did still more: they elaborated a formula which vaguely anticipated the Renaissance notion that humanistic culture is the true noblesse. Real love, polite love—they said—can dwell only in a gentle heart. Though a gentle heart is not yet the well-rounded personality of the Renaissance, it resembles it in at least two ways. It is unconnected with birth or riches, and it is attainable by cultivating one's soul. Again, the Italian bourgeois of the thirteenth century were not content with building substantial houses with capacious storage rooms for their merchandise and with high towers from which to pour boiling oil on the lower towers of their neighbors. They embellished their homes as much as they could without diminishing the width of the storage rooms and the height of the towers. But a merchant of the thirteenth century would have been ill advised if he had neglected the expanding opportunities of trade for the pursuit of humanistic culture. He was too busy making money to consider lyric poetry and home decoration as a full-time occupation.

During the Renaissance many merchants were less busy—or, at least, thought they could spare more time for culture. In 1527 a Venetian merchant and ambassador was somewhat shocked at seeing that in Florence "men who govern the Republic sort and sift wool, and their sons sell cloth and engage in other work including the lowest and dirtiest." But this race of men was gradually dying out in Florence, as it had in Venice. More frequently the Italian merchant princes of the Renaissance had employees and correspondents who did the dirtier work for them.

Let us take a great merchant, indeed the head of the world's greatest financial organization in the fifteenth century, Lorenzo the Magnificent. He was at the same time the head of the Medici bank, the uncrowned king of Florence, a patron of art, and a poet in his own right. His record shows that, unlike his medieval forefathers, he was an amateur in business and a professional in literature. His mismanagement of the bank, or, rather, the mismanagement of the men he entrusted with running it, precipitated its downfall. But his patronage of the arts gave his illegitimate power a halo of respectability. His poems endeared him to his subjects—at least, to those who had not been involved in the failure of the bank—and made him famous among intellectual aristocrats throughout the world. Niccolo Machiavelli, the great historian of Florence, lauded Lorenzo for governing the state as an artist but blamed him for his poor conduct of business. Yet was this shortcoming not the inevitable counterpart of his artistic achievements? Today we no longer suffer from the ruin of the Medici bank, while we still are enchanted by the verse of Lorenzo de Medici. It is easier for us to be indulgent and to observe that business at that time was so bad that even a skillful management would not have brought many dividends. Perhaps Lorenzo may be forgiven for overlooking some opportunities to invest in trade at 5 percent interest since he invested in art at a rate which will never be exhausted.

One might even contend that investment in culture drove the Renaissance to untimely death. To obtain money for the building of Saint Peter's in Rome, the only Renaissance church that probably represented a greater investment in material and manpower than any of the Gothic cathedrals, Pope Leo X—another Medici—proclaimed a special indulgence. The sale of indulgences was the spark which ignited the Reformation. . . .

Wallace K. Ferguson

RECENT TRENDS IN THE ECONOMIC HISTORIOGRAPHY OF THE RENAISSANCE

A most distinguished historian, Professor Ferguson has long been known for his books and articles on the interpretations of the Renaissance. He taught at New York University before returning to his native land as senior professor of history at the University of Western Ontario.

. . In scarcely any other field of study dealing with the Renaissance —the history of music and of philosophy are the principal exceptions—has there been so much new material brought to light or so much significant reinterpretation as in economic history. That this should be so ought not to seem surprising, for economic history is one of the newer disciplines. So far as it touches the period of the

From Wallace K. Ferguson, "Recent Trends in the Economic Historiography of the Renaissance," in *Studies in the Renaissance* 7 (1960): 7–8, 13–14, 17–26. Reprinted by permission of the editors. The documentation of the original article has been omitted.

Renaissance, its beginnings can be dated back scarcely more than half a century. By the 1930s the pioneer work was fairly well completed. The initial hypotheses had been worked out, fought over, and in part abandoned. The main outlines of the picture had been sketched in, with a fair amount of detail, but much work still remained to be done. What has been achieved in the past two or three decades is largely the result of application of new methods, new interests, or new frames of reference. . . .

One important tendency in the past two decades has been the greatly accelerated interest in business history as a distinct discipline. This is one of the newer branches of economic history. As described by N. S. B. Gras, one of its early protagonists, business history is not the history of commerce, industry, banking, agriculture, and so forth, but that of individual units of business enterprise. Its source material is to be found, not in guild regulations, city ordinances, state legislation, or treatises on the conduct of business, but in the records of individual businessmen, partnerships, and firms—in account books, diaries, partnership agreements, notarial records, correspondence, and all the detailed evidence of the way in which a particular business actually operated. The value of this kind of study is that it sees commerce and industry, as it were, from the inside and thus frequently serves as a corrective to the generalizations of those institutionalist historians who were primarily concerned with the external structure of the various forms of economic activity. The range of focus is narrow, but the details seen thus have a realistic clarity lacking in the broader view. Above all, it concentrates attention on the practical problems of management and control of business enterprise, problems for which guild statutes and economic legislation in general offer little evidence. . . .

A second noticeable tendency in the economic historiography of the past two or three decades has been the accumulation of statistical data and the introduction of quantitative criteria in place of the earlier preoccupation with the institutional structure of commerce, industry, and finance or the still earlier qualitative criteria of those scholars whose primary concern was the capitalist spirit. In place of description or sociological analysis, the new tendency is to concentrate attention upon the discovery of secular or long-term trends and upon the measurement of the rate of change in population, prices, and the volume of production and exchange, concepts susceptible of interpretation in terms of pure economic theory. The quantitative approach is basically empirical, but it can also lead to the formation of hypotheses. In a programmatic article in 1932, entitled "The Application of the Quantitative Method to Economic History," A. P. Usher called attention to the potential usefulness of this method for the correction of institutionalist or idealist constructions of economic history. It has since become increasingly prevalent in studies of late medieval and the Renaissance economy. The combination of statistical research with economic theory has been particularly fruitful in elucidating the problems presented by the relation of money to the general economy: the fluctuating values of the monetary metals, their shifting relation to one another and to money of account, the relative rapidity of monetary circulation and the effect of governmental devaluation of coinage. E. J. Hamilton's massive study of *American Treasure and the Price Revolution in Spain* (1932), based on a vast accumulation of statistics and a quantity theory of money, was an early example and has influenced all later discussion of the economic trends of the sixteenth century. Since the early thirties English economic historians have also devoted a great deal of attention to the statistical study of trends in English foreign trade from the fourteenth to the sixteenth centuries, a study for which the preservation of the customs accounts offers unusual opportunities; but Continental scholars, too, have been increasingly preoccupied with the search for such statistical data as are available. In 1955 Armando Sapori was able to hail with satisfaction the immense progress that had been made in the collection of quantitative data on production, circulation, and prices of goods since he had urged the need for such research at the International Congress held at Zurich in 1938.

Now the value to the specialist in economic history of quantitative data, as of any other form of pertinent information, is incontestable, although it is obvious that it furnishes only one of the ingredients from which he may reconstruct the complex economic life of any period, and too exclusive reliance upon it on the part of recent historians has aroused apprehension in the minds of some thoughtful scholars. But historians of culture in general also must be interested to know whether the period they are attempting to interpret was one of rising or declining prosperity. The accumulated evidence of a great quantitative expansion of the European economy in the sixteenth century will cause no one to change his views. It has long been taken for granted. On the other hand, Fernand Braudel's study of the Mediterranean world in the age of Philip II, with its argument, supported by masses of statistical evidence, that the balance of financial and commercial preponderance did not shift from the Mediterranean to the North until well into the seventeenth century, may cause historians to reconsider some of their assumptions regarding the economic background of the decline of the Italian Renaissance in the sixteenth century, although it remains true that Italy was not the economic center of Braudel's Mediterranean world as it had been in earlier centuries.

A more serious problem for historians of the Renaissance, however, and particularly of the Renaissance in Italy, it seems to me, is that posed by a number of recent scholars whose statistical research has led them to depict the fourteenth and fifteenth centuries as, on the whole, a period of economic stagnation or decline. As Delio Cantimori pointed out in a recent article, students of the Italian Renaissance have found it disturbing to discover that the period which they think of as the Renaissance in literature, learning, and art is now depicted as one of economic decadence. English, French, and German cultural historians, accustomed to thinking of their national renaissance as beginning toward the end of the fifteenth century or in the early sixteenth, may be less concerned, as also may those who accept Huizinga's characterization of the fourteenth and fifteenth centuries as the waning of the Middle Ages. There may even be some medievalists who would welcome the idea with a feeling that an economic depression served the Renaissance right and was no more than could be expected. The thesis of economic stagnation or decline in the fourteenth and fifteenth centuries cannot, however, be so lightly dismissed by historians who, like myself, regard these centuries as marking one of the most important stages in the transition from medieval to modern civilization, not only in Italy but throughout western Europe. Whether we accept all the conclusions of the most enthusiastic proponents of this thesis or not, we must, I think, pause to reconsider the assumptions upon which our interpretation has in part been based, and to this subject I would like to devote the remainder of my paper.

A generation ago the assumption taken for granted by most

historians was that the transformation of European civilization during this period was accompanied by—if not founded upon—a steadily rising prosperity, increasing wealth, and expanding commercial and industrial activity. As stated by E. P. Cheyney in 1936 in the opening chapter of his book, *The Dawn of a New Era, 1250–1453*, "The most fundamental of the changes that marked the passage from medieval to modern times was the increase of wealth, and the principal cause of the increase of wealth was the extension of commerce." An assumption of constantly increasing wealth during this period formed part of my own conception of the Renaissance twenty years ago. It was obvious, of course, that the mortality caused by the Black Death must for a time have reduced the number of both consumers and producers, and that the devastation which accompanied the Hundred Years' War must have materially reduced the wealth of a large part of France. But I think that there was a general assumption that the development of more efficient forms of capitalist organization of commerce, industry, and finance soon made good the losses caused by the Black Death in most parts of Europe. In any case, the predominantly institutionalist approach of the majority of economic historians in the prewar period focused attention on changes in economic organization rather than upon quantitative variations or trends in the volume of production and exchange.

Now, the first serious suggestion of which I am aware that this conception was open to question appeared in Henri Pirenne's *Economic and Social History of Medieval Europe* (1937). Here he noted that the beginning of the fourteenth century marked the end of the period of medieval economic expansion, that "during the early years of the fourteenth century there is observable in all these directions [of economic activity] not perhaps a decline but a cessation of all advance. Europe lived, so to speak, on what had been acquired; the economic front was stabilized." During the next few years this revisionist thesis was echoed in scattered articles which stated it more strongly and translated stability into decline, but it did not attract general attention until after the war, when scholars were once more able to establish contact with the work of their colleagues in other countries and when the volume of scholarly research, dammed up by the war, once more flowed freely into print. It dominated the debates of the section on late medieval economy at the Ninth International Congress of Historical Sciences at Paris in 1950 and again at the Tenth Congress held in Rome in 1955, and it was given the official sanction of those august bodies in the cooperative reports subsequently published. It also formed the central theme of the second volume of *The Cambridge Economic History* (1952). The effort to revise the traditional conception of the Renaissance as a period of expanding wealth has been international in scope. Among the most prominent contributors to it are M. M. Postan in England, Renée Doehaerd in Belgium, Edouard Perroy in France, W. Abel in Germany, Armando Sapori and Carlo Cipolla in Italy, and J. U. Nef and Robert Lopez in the United States.

The first question we have to ask in relation to their thesis, it seems to me, is: has it been proven? There have been some dissenting voices, and even its protagonists are not agreed as to either the intensity or the duration of the recession. Carlo Cipolla, for example, notes a rising secular trend in Italy, beginning toward the end of the fourteenth century and continuing through the fifteenth, while Robert Lopez states flatly that the period from about 1330 to 1530, with perhaps an additional decade or two at either end, was "one of great depression followed by moderate and incomplete recovery," and that Italy "felt the impact of the economic recession most heavily." Masses of statistical evidence have been produced, but the available statistics seldom form a continuous series or are sufficiently homogeneous to serve as a basis for accurate comparison. It is difficult to determine whether the decline of some old industries, like the manufacture of fine woolen cloth in Florence and the Netherlands, was not adequately compensated by the growth of newer industries like the making of silks, light woolens, linens, and fustians; or whether the decline of some old cities was not compensated by growth in others. To what extent did the growth of rural industry in England and the Netherlands make up for the losses suffered by the old industrial cities? These and other similar questions still call for further research.

Nevertheless, the weight of the evidence does seem to justify the conclusion that, taking western Europe as a whole, there was a general cessation of economic growth in the early years of the fourteenth century, and that this was followed by a long period of contraction in the volume of production and exchange. There seems to be especially convincing evidence of a prolonged agricultural depression in England, France, and parts of Germany. Land prices fell, and not only did the clearing of land for cultivation cease, but much marginal land that had been cleared during the thirteenth century was now abandoned, either because worked out or no longer needed. The demographic curve, which had been rising for two or three hundred years, apparently began to drop in the early fourteenth century, then fell drastically with the Black Death, while normal recovery was checked for a century or more by recurrences of the plague and by the devastation caused by war. It seems reasonable to assume, too, that commerce and industry suffered quantitatively from the reduction in population and hence in both labor supply and markets. And meanwhile, the European economy had ceased to expand geographically. The eastward drive of German colonization came to a halt, while the frontiers of European trade in the Near East were beginning to shrink. The medieval frontier was closing, as A. R. Lewis argued in an article in *Speculum* in 1958, with results comparable to those which followed the closing of the American frontier at the end of the last century. The fourteenth century and the first half of the fifteenth, in short, were plagued throughout by catastrophes and crises. But did not these very crises hasten rather than retard the transition from medieval to modern civilization?

With that question in mind, let us grant for the moment the thesis of the economic revisionists, and ask what effect it may have upon our interpretations of this period. In the first place, one of the major elements in the transition from medieval to modern civilization seems to me to be a shift in the center of gravity of economic, social, and cultural life from the country to the city, and this may well have been accelerated by the relatively more severe impact of the depression upon the landholding classes—the nobles and the higher clergy—although because of falling rents and rising wages, the peasants were in most places apparently better off than they had been. A second, and related, element, the disintegration of feudalism and the rise of centralized state governments, was undoubtedly hastened by the impoverishment of the nobility and by the disruption of the manorial system, the economic basis of feudalism, which accompanied the economic and demographic crisis of the fourteenth century and the first half of the fifteenth. Despite any possible reduction in total wealth, this period saw a rapid increase in governmental income through taxation, which enabled kings and princes to extend their military and administrative authority at the expense of feudal particularism, even though it aggravated the economic crisis, as Lopez has pointed out, by imposing a crushing burden on the economy of the state. In these centuries the church, which represented the universal principle in medieval civilization, also passed through a crisis that shook it to its foundations, but this crisis seems to have been caused less by economic recession than by the intrusion of too much money into the fabric of church government. When we turn to the economic and social development within the cities, we may admit as a reasonable hypothesis that there was a reduction in total wealth corresponding to the reduction in population. But was the *per capita* wealth reduced thereby? In any case most of the exponents of the thesis of recession are agreed that shrinking markets, smaller profits, and keener competition accelerated the development of more rational and efficient techniques of business enterprise, resulting in a qualitative advance in the evolution of capitalism much greater than that which took place during the rapid quantitative expansion of the European economy in the sixteenth century. And if, as has been suggested, one result of the crisis was that the rich got richer while the poor got poorer, we must remember that it was concentrated wealth rather than widely distributed prosperity that was responsible for the patronage of art, letters, music, and all the higher forms of intellectual and aesthetic culture. Nor, in this regard, should we forget the unprecedented concentration of wealth during this period in the hands of kings and princes which accompanied the growth of central government in territorial and national states. It was the wealth of the Burgundian court as well as of the Flemish cities that furnished the material basis for the flourishing art of the Netherlands in the fifteenth century. And if, as Huizinga has so brilliantly demonstrated, an air of decadence hangs over the literature of northern France and the Netherlands in this period, this was not the result of poverty but rather of the fact that under the influence of the Burgundian royal courts literary tradition still expressed, with increasing aridity, the ideals and conventional attitudes of a noble class whose economic, social, and political roots had been cut off from the soil in which they had grown during the Middle Ages.

But it is in Italy rather than the north that the relation of economic to cultural growth poses the most serious problem for the historian, for it was here that the culture which we think of as specifically Renaissance grew in the midst of what is now portrayed as a period of economic depression. So far as patronage is concerned, I think the fruits of those years are ample proof that there was still enough to go around. In Italy, earlier than elsewhere, the concentration of wealth based on taxation furnished princes with the means of patronage. If, moreover, there was any reduction in total wealth, it was more than compensated by the growth of a tradition of culture which, more than any quantitative variation in wealth, differentiates the world of the Medici from that of the Bardi and Peruzzi. But the economic factors which helped to condition the culture of the Italian Renaissance were by no means limited to the mere existence of surplus wealth or the direct economic stimulus of patronage. The culture of the Italian Renaissance was different from that of the Middle Ages—though not, of course, completely different—because it was produced by and for a different kind of society from that characteristic of the greater part of medieval Europe. It was a society formed in large part by the early expansion of commerce and industry and the resultant growth of a wealthy urban society. One distinguishing characteristic of this society was the increasing participation in cultural activity of urban laymen, which broke the clerical monopoly of learning and the chivalric tradition in vernacular literature and which found expression in an increasingly urban and secular tone in literature, learning, art, and music. Now the growth of capitalism was, it seems to me, an important factor in stimulating this development of lay culture, first, by requiring literacy of every one engaged in business and, second, by offering opportunities for the passive investment of inherited income, which made it possible for a growing number of the upper classes in the cities to seek higher education, to qualify for the lay learned professions, and to form an appreciative public for the work of artists and writers. It seems to me, then, that the influence of capitalism upon the culture of the Renaissance depended rather more upon the evolution of its forms of business organization than upon the production of absolute wealth.

In conclusion, it seems to me that the recent tendency to concentrate attention upon the quantitative analysis of long-term trends in economic production and exchange, while undoubtedly important, tells us less that is of value in explaining and interpreting the civilization of this period than did the earlier studies of the structure of economic life, amplified, as they have been, by the more recent studies of individual business enterprises. It might be well to heed the warning of Armando Sapori not to ask of statistical data more than they can offer. Perhaps it is time now, with our increased knowledge, to return to the kind of question posed earlier in the century by Sombart, Weber, Pirenne, and others and to analyze once more the spirit which motivated Renaissance businessmen, to reconsider the relation between religion and business ethics, and to reassess the possible relation between economic individualism and the culture of the Renaissance. If we are to understand a civilization in which businessmen played an active part, it seems more important to know how they conducted their business, how they felt about it, what manner of men they were, and what were their aims and interests than to know whether the long-term trend of production and exchange was rising or falling. There may, indeed, be a point in asking whether the men of that age *thought* that things were getting better or worse, whether the psychological atmosphere was basically optimistic or pessimistic, but such subjective reactions are not susceptible of statistical analysis. Francesco di Marco Datini may have lived in an era of economic depression, but it is illuminating to know that he hopefully headed each of his ledgers with the inscription "in the name of God and of profit." Perhaps this was, after all, the spirit of capitalism.

Marie Boas

THE SCIENTIFIC RENAISSANCE: 1450–1630

Professor Marie Boas (Hall) is on the faculty of the Imperial College of Technology, University of London. She previously taught at the University of Massachusetts, Brandeis, the University of California at Los Angeles, and Indiana University. Her work on Robert Boyle (1958) was given the Pfizer Award of the History of Science Society.

> *The world sailed round, the largest of Earth's continents discovered, the compas invented, the printing-press sowing knowledge, gun-powder revolutionising the art of war, ancient manuscripts rescued and the restoration of scholarship, all witness to the triumph of our New Age.*[1]

These words of a French physician writing in 1545 might have been those of any Renaissance intellectual trying to characterize his age. Happily unaware of our modern consciousness that history is a continuous process, and that each new development has its roots in the past, men in the fifteenth century claimed complete emancipation from their medieval ancestors, proud to believe that they were founding a new stage in history which would rival that of classical antiquity in brilliance, learning and glory. As a sign and symbol of their success they could point proudly to two areas of discovery: the exploration of the intellectual world of the ancients by scholars, and the exploration of the terrestrial world by seamen. Two technical inventions aided men in their search for new worlds: the printing press and the magnetic compass. The first was a product of the fifteenth century, the second had been introduced into Europe nearly two centuries before; neither was devised by scientists, yet science somehow participated in both, and gained in importance as scholarship and practical geography each flourished in their different ways.

Nothing is more paradoxical than the relation of science and scholarship in the fifteenth century. This was the time when a man

From pp. 17–30 in *The Scientific Renaissance, 1450–1630* by Marie Boas. Copyright © 1962 by Marie Boas. Reprinted by permission of Harper & Row, Publishers, Inc. and William Collins Sons & Co. Ltd.

[1] Jean Fernel, *De Abditis Rerum Causis*, 1548; quoted by C. Sherrington, *The Endeavour of Jean Fernel* (Cambridge, 1946), p. 136.

Nel quarto lib. di Dioſcoride.   1003

POLIGONO MINORE.

FIGURE 3. Very important for the advance of science was the publication of
works by classical scientists and the accurate pictorial presentation of scientific
information. Pierandrea Mattioli, an eminent botanist, published in 1544 an Italian
commentary on Dioscorides, a Greek physician of the first century A.D. Editions
after 1554 were illustrated. A knotweed specimen is shown here. From P.
Mattioli, *Di Pedacio Dioscoride Anazarbeo della materia Medicinale* (Venice,
1568), Special Collections, Hayden Library, Arizona State University. (*Used by
permission.*)

could become famous in wide intellectual circles for his profound pursuit of the more arid reaches of philological scholarship, or for the rediscovery of a forgotten minor work of a Greek or Roman author. Humanism had already stolen from theology the foremost place in intellectual esteem. The term humanism is ambiguous; it meant in its own day both a concern with the classics of antiquity and a preoccupation with man in relation to human society rather than to God. Most humanists were primarily concerned with the recovery, restoration, editing and appraisal of Greek and Latin literature (theological literature not being entirely excluded); they regarded themselves as in rebellion against Scholasticism, the intellectual discipline of the medieval schools, which they saw as concerned with logic and theology rather than with literature and secular studies. Far from rebelling in turn against this literary and philological emphasis, which seems superficially more remote from science than the scholastic curriculum with its all-embracing interest in the works of God, the fifteenth-century scientist cheerfully submitted to the rigidity of an intellectual approach which was rooted in the worship of the remote past, and thereby strangely prepared the way for a genuinely novel form of thought about nature in the generation to follow.

Scientists were ready to adopt the methods of humanism for a variety of reasons. As men of their age, it seemed to them as to their literary contemporaries that the work of the immediate past was inferior to that of natural philosophers of Greco-Roman antiquity, and that the last few centuries were indeed a "middle age," an unfortunate break between the glorious achievements of the past and the glorious potentialities of the present. Humanists were anxious to recover obscure or lost texts, and to make fresh translations to replace those current in the Middle Ages, sure that a translation into correct (that is, classical) Latin direct from a carefully edited Greek text would mean more than a twelfth or thirteenth century version in barbarous (that is, Church) Latin, made from an Arabic translation of the Greek original, and full of strange words reflecting its devious origin. Scientists agreed that to understand an author one needed correct texts and translations; and that there were many interesting and important scientific texts little known or not at all understood in the Middle Ages. Scientists were very ready to learn Greek and the methods of classical scholarship, and

to enroll themselves in the humanists camp. So the English physicians Thomas Linacre (c. 1460–1524) and John Caius (1510–1573)
saw the restoration and retranslation of Greek medical texts as an
end in itself, a proper part of medicine, for the Greeks had been
better physicians than themselves. So, too, the German astronomers
George Peurbach (1423–1469) and Johann Regiomontanus (1436–
1476) happily lectured at the University of Vienna on Vergil and
Cicero, drawing larger audiences and more pay than they could
hope for as professors of any scientific subject; they were nevertheless able and influential professional astronomers. Scientists of
the fifteenth century saw nothing "unscientific" about an interest or
competence in essentially linguistic matters, and in editing Greek
scientific texts they saw themselves aiding both science and humanism.

Indeed, science was not, as yet, a recognized independent branch
of learning. Scientists were mostly scholars, physicians or magicians.
The practicing physician had always been in demand; with the increase in epidemic disease which had begun with the Black Death
in the fourteenth century and continued with the appearance of
syphilis and typhus in the late fifteenth, there was more need for
him than ever. A physician, especially one with a fashionable practice, was often a very wealthy man, and the professor of medicine
held the best paid chair in most universities, to the envy of his
colleagues. The success of a physician had nothing to do with his
knowledge of anatomy or physiology, for the art was still almost
entirely empirical; but the practicing physician had, if he chose,
abundant opportunity for medical research and discovery, either
literary or practical.

A slightly less respectable scientific profession—but one which
was sometimes very lucrative—was that of the astrologer. For many
reasons—as complex and diverse as the psychological shocks of
the great plagues of the fourteenth century, the shattered prestige
of the church consequent on schism and heresy, the increased
tempo of war, the wider attention paid to observational astronomy,
the popularization of knowledge through increased education and
the role of the printing press—belief in the occult flourished ex-
ceedingly in the fifteenth century and showed little sign of decrease
in the sixteenth. This was the height of the witchcraft delusion,
especially in Germany. It was a great age of magic and demonolatry:

the age of Faust. Astrology, previously almost the private domain of princes (especially in the Iberian peninsula, where every court had its official astrologer), was made available to the masses, again partly through the medium of the printing press. (It also transferred its center to Germany.) There was soon an enormous demand for ephemerides (tables of planetary positions), the essential tool of proper astrology: Regiomontanus, after he ceased lecturing on classical literature, devoted himself to their production. And every striking celestial occurrence—the conjunction of planets, the appearance of comets (especially plentiful in this period), eclipses and new stars (novae)—called forth a flood of fugitive literature scattered far and wide by the printing press, prognosticating not merely for princes but for the masses as well. Even the illiterate enjoyed the advantages of being assured by astrologers that the future held as certain doom as the past, that famine, pestilence, war and rebellion would continue to dominate the Earth; for crude but vivid woodcuts portrayed both the heavenly bodies which presaged disaster and the inevitable and all-too-familiar disaster itself. Amid the calamities of the fifteenth and sixteenth centuries, astrologers could hardly fail in their prognostications, as long as they made them dire enough.

Mystic science was, in this period, the most widely known: astrology catered for the masses by whom it was so readily understood that in the popular mind astrologer and astronomer were one. The alchemist's dream, too, was widely known. Almost unheard of in western Europe before the thirteenth century, alchemy became the preoccupation of more and more learned and semilearned men in the Renaissance; yet, rather curiously, it was often viewed with skepticism, as it had been by Chaucer's pilgrims. And now nascent experimental science was popularized as natural magic, properly the study of the seemingly inexplicable forces of nature (like magnetism, the magnification of objects by lenses, the use of air- and water-power in moving toys), more generally the wonders of nature and the tricks of mountebanks. Mathematics contributed its share to magic in the form of number mysticism, useful for prognostication.

Nonmystical aspects of science were also increasingly popularized, and turned to useful ends. Scholars were beginning to be proud to boast that they had mastered the secrets of a craft, believing that knowledge would thereby be acquired such as was not to be found in books. They repaid the debt by spreading knowledge of applied science. As in the Middle Ages, all literate men now knew something of astronomy, if only in its humbler aspects: the astronomy of timekeeping and the calendar. In the fifteenth and sixteenth centuries astronomers developed further interest in practical applications and began to make attempts, ultimately successful, to introduce astronomical methods of navigation to reluctant and conservative seamen. Mathematical practitioners, half applied scientist, half instrumentmaker, became common, and provided a new profession for the scientist. New maps and new exploration made geography an ever more popular subject. Mapmakers flourished more on the proceeds of the beautiful and colorful maps sold to the well-to-do than on the profits from the manufacture of seamen's charts, but both were produced in quantity. Algorism, reckoning with pen and paper and Arabic numerals (modern arithmetic), instead of the older practice of using an abacus and Roman numerals had been known to scholars since the introduction (in the twelfth century) of the Hindu-Arabic numerals, but it was the sixteenth century which saw the production of a spate of simple and practical books on elementary arithmetic. These, mainly in the various vernaculars, were the contribution of mathematics to merchants, artisans and sailors.

Much of the rediscovered Greek theoretical learning was also soon made available to the nonlearned, as a process of translation from Latin to the vernacular succeeded the first stage of translation from Greek to Latin, by which the learned had been made free of the new literature by the more learned. Indeed, one aspect of humanism was the popularization of ancient learning. To be sure, the humanist theory of education, designed to produce gentlemen, was an aristocratic ideal (though in fact it aimed at *creating* gentlemen, not merely at training gentlemen born). But humanism battered its way into scholastic strongholds only by adroit and clever propaganda which won sympathy from powerful forces outside the learned world of the university. To secure support from public opinion necessitated the creation of a limited but ever widening audience; and as this audience increased, it began to demand the enjoyment of humanism without its tediums. Hence the flood of translations, making science (and literature) available in a language the layman could read.

Soon, following the example of his humanist predecessors, the scientist tried to make his learning easily available to the ordinary man. To this end, the sixteenth-century scientist burned with the (somewhat premature) desire to teach the ignorant artisan how to improve his craft through better theory or more knowledge. For this purpose an increasing number of simplified manuals were written, like those of the English mathematician Robert Recorde: *The Grounde of Arts* (1542, on arithmetic), *The Pathway to Knowledge* (1551, on geometry), and *The Castle of Knowledge* (1556, on astronomy); in the process, vernacular prose was much improved. Scientists were, in this period, very ready to learn from craftsmen; having learned what the craftsmen could teach them, they naturally became convinced that they had much to teach him in turn. They were constantly disappointed to find this more difficult, when the craftsman failed to show himself eager to be taught.

The heroic stage of humanism belongs to the period before 1450: it was in 1397 that the Greek diplomat Manuel Chrysoloras (c. 1355–1415) began those lectures on Greek language and literature which had seduced clever young Florentines from their proper university studies and made them vehemently enthusiastic for Greek letters. The early fifteenth century had seen an avid international search for manuscripts of Greek and Latin authors previously forgotten, neglected or unknown. Though the major interest of the humanists was naturally in the literary classics, they took all ancient learning as their province, and scientific works were cherished equally with literary ones, always providing that they had not been studied in earlier centuries. In 1417 the Italian humanist Poggio Bracciolini was as pleased with his discovery in a "distant monastery" of a manuscript of Lucretius (little read in the Middle Ages, but to become immensely popular in the Renaissance) as he was with the manuscripts of Cicero that he found at the monastery of St. Gall. Guarino of Verona, hot in pursuit of Latin literature, was happy in finding the medical work of Celsus (in 1426) unknown for over 500 years. When Jacopo Angelo returned from Constantinople with manuscripts for baggage, only to be shipwrecked off Naples, one of the treasures he managed to pull to shore was Ptolemy's *Geography,* mysteriously unknown to the Christian West that had revered Ptolemy's work on astronomy for three centuries; he had already translated it into Latin (1406) so that it was ready for the public.

By the mid-fifteenth century this great and exciting work of collection and discovery was, of necessity, ended: the monasteries of Europe had been thoroughly pillaged, and the fall of Constantinople to the Turks in 1453 meant, as the humanists lamented, the end of the richest source of supply for Greek texts. One of the strangely persistent myths of history is that the humanist study of Greek works began with the arrival in Italy in 1453 of learned refugees from Constantinople, who are supposed to have fled the city in all haste, laden with rare manuscripts. Aside from the essential improbability of their doing any such thing, and the well-established fact that the opening years of the fifteenth century had seen intense activity in the collection of Greek manuscripts in Constantinople, there is the testimony of the humanists themselves that the fall of Constantinople represented a tragedy to them. Characteristic is the cry of the humanist Cardinal Aeneas Sylvius Piccolomini (later Pope Pius II), who wrote despairingly to Pope Nicholas in July 1453, "How many names of mighty men will perish! It is a second death to Homer and to Plato. The fount of the Muses is dried up for evermore."[2]

Cut off from the possibility of finding new manuscripts, humanists now turned from physical to intellectual discovery, from finding manuscripts to editing and translating them in ever more thorough, critical and scholarly a fashion, establishing the canons of grammar and restoring corrupt and difficult manuscripts to what was hopefully believed to be the state in which the author had left them. Here again the humanists showed a surprising impartiality, to the advantage of science. No one could be considered to have finished his apprenticeship to humanism unless, as his masterpiece, he produced a creditable Latin translation of a Greek original: the author chosen might be a medical or scientific one, especially in the sixteenth century when the supply was running short. Thus Giorgio Valla (d. 1499), a perfectly ordinary literary humanist, counted among his treasures two of the three most important manuscripts of Archimedes; he also owned manuscripts of Apollonios and of Hero of Alexandria, and made partial translations of these and other scientific texts which appeared in 1501 as part of his encyclopedic work *On Things to be Sought and Avoided (De Expetendis et*

<hr>

[2] J. E. Sandys, *A History of Classical Scholarship*, vol. 2 (London, 1908), p. 73.

Fugiendis Rebus). Guarino, discoverer of Celsus, translated Strabo's *Geography* into Latin, along with purely literary texts. Linacre was long better remembered for his share in introducing Greek studies into England than for his encouragement of medical learning through new translations of Galen and the foundation of the Royal College of Physicians (1518), but contemporaries found the mixture of activities quite natural.

It is important to realize that it was primarily the humanists who made the work of the "new" Greek science available. Although much Greek science had been widely known in Latin versions to the Middle Ages, this was chiefly either early science (fifth and fourth century B.C.) or late (second century A.D.). The works of the best period of Greek science, of the Hellenistic scientists of c. 300–150 B.C., were little known in the Middle Ages, partly because it was often highly mathematical and always complex and difficult. The humanists' role had important consequences both for what was available and how it was studied. Humanism, by nature, was intensely concerned with the establishment of the exact words of the author, with the correction of scribal errors and the restoration of doubtful passages. Consequently, humanists inevitably looked with both scorn and distrust on translations of Greek works made in the twelfth and thirteenth centuries indirectly through Arabic: these translations, whose Latin words were often separated from the Greek by four or more other languages, so tortuous had been the path of translation, were necessarily far from exact and often included what, to fifteenth-century ears, were horrible Arabicisms and neologisms, though the sense of the original was doubtless more or less preserved. (The Roman medical writer Celsus was above all at this time valued because he provided pure and proper Latin equivalents of Greek anatomical terms to replace the Latin forms of Arabicized Greek terms.) This preoccupation with exact rendering of an author's words mattered far less for scientific purposes, of course, than it did for literary ones, but no distinction was made, which explains what now seems an excessive preoccupation with "pure" texts.

The fifteenth- and sixteenth-century scientist was in complete sympathy with these ideas, imbued as he was with humanist ideals: hence his concern with "returning to" Galen or Ptolemy (*tout pur,* purged from Islamic or medieval commentary) and hence the time spent on the study of purely verbal aspects of ancient scientific texts. No doubt much of this was time wasted; on the other hand, it did force a return to original sources which was beneficial: it was certainly more useful to read Galen and Euclid direct than to read what a commentator thought an Arabic paraphrase of Galen or Euclid meant. Many ambiguities were undoubtedly cleared up. Above all, return to the original enforced a more serious considera- tion of what Aristotle, Hippocrates, Galen and Ptolemy had actually said, and this in turn involved recognition of the truth, error, fruit- fulness or uselessness of the contributions the great scientists of the past had made. This constituted a first step towards scientific advance. Greek science had by no means exhausted its inspiration in the fifteenth century; it could still, as it was to do for at least two centuries, suggest different topics of exploration to each suc- ceeding age and above all it provided authority for departing from orthodox thought. Humanism did, therefore, have much to offer science.

How is it that, nevertheless, humanists like Erasmus often seem to have attacked science? When they did so, they were attacking the science of the universities, which they regarded as part of the sterility of Scholasticism. An age determined to be new must of necessity repudiate the ideas of the immediate past; so the hu- manists turned the much-praised "subtle doctor" of the late thir- teenth century (Duns Scotus) into the nursery dunce of the sixteenth. Modern historians, admiring the ingenuity of fourteenth-century mathematics and physics, deplore this antipathy and regard the humanist worship of antiquity as having been harmful to the smooth advance of science. But however high the achievements of the fourteenth-century philosophers in certain directions, some other ingredient was needed to stimulate the development of modern science. *Il faut reculer pour mieux sauter* is often true in intellectual matters: the medieval inspiration was at a low ebb by the beginning of the fifteenth century, and the Greek inspiration had, at the mo- ment, more to offer. When the humanist attacked medieval science, he was attacking an intellectual attitude that seemed to him over- subtle, and sterile; he was emphatically not attacking science as such. He admired equally Aristotle the literary critic and Aristotle the biologist, while attacking Aristotle the cosmologer and semantic philosopher. He praised both Plato the Socratic rejecter of the material world, and Plato the cosmologer, who had insisted on the study of geometry as a preliminary to the study of higher things. Indeed, Plato's precepts were followed; for wherever humanist schools were set up, mathematics, pure and applied was always associated with the purely literary study of Latin and Greek. Infatuated as the humanist was with all that had, in his eyes, constituted the glory of the Greek past, he was eager to impart the image of the past as a whole, and to show that the Greeks had contributed to all areas of secular knowledge.[3] The humanist emphasis on Greek learning may have cast medieval learning temporarily into the shade, but it brought to light much that was fruitful and useful for a contemporary scientist to know, and which he would otherwise not have considered.

That science was not solely a scholar's concern, but was truly a part of the popular learning of the age, even if not the main point of emphasis, appears from the list of books printed before 1500, the incunabula which modern collectors have so lovingly collected and catalogued, and have made so expensive. The earliest surviving book printed in western Europe is dated 1447; by 1500 at least 30,000 individual editions had been published in all the countries of western Europe (the Iberian peninsula seeing the establishment of presses only at the very end of the century). Of these titles the bulk was, naturally, religious, from the Bible to theology; other books, equally reflecting the demand, followed, for no more then than now did printers wish to publish what they thought the public would not want to buy.

Yet perhaps 10 percent of the incunabula deal with scientific subjects, not at all a bad proportion: there is a mixture of popular science, scientific encyclopedias, Greek and Latin classics, medieval and contemporary textbooks and elementary treatises, especially on medicine, arithmetic and astronomy. There were, as yet, relatively few Greek editions of scientists—reasonably enough since the Latin translations were bound to be more popular—and few very difficult or advanced works. Thus instead of Ptolemy's *Almagest* entire (perhaps the most influential treatise on astronomy ever written, but a work of interest only to competent mathematical astronomers) one

---

[3] Thus Erasmus edited the first Greek edition of Ptolemy's *Geography* (Froben Press, 1533)—Ed.

finds the up-to-date *Epitome* of that great work by Regiomontanus. On the other hand, Ptolemy's *Geography* was printed before 1500 (in Latin, in a number of editions), reflecting the wide contemporary interest in cartography. There is nothing surprising in all this: specialist works, of interest only to a limited scientific audience were not printed as books; they remained, for the time being, in manuscript, much as specialist work today remains in learned journals; then, as now, the wider demand was for semipopular expositions. That so many scientific works appeared early in the sixteenth century shows how effective was the popularization of learning and science.

The printing press undoubtedly had a twofold influence on science: first, by making texts more readily available, it "sowed knowledge," providing a wider audience than could ever have been the case without printing, while serving as well to emphasize the authority of the written word. Secondly, it peculiarly influenced the development of the biological sciences, by making possible the dissemination of identical illustrations. Much fifteenth- and sixteenth-century work in anatomy, zoology, botany and natural history depended for its effect primarily on illustrations, which enormously aided identification (as well as standardization of technical terms); accurate illustrations could only be produced in quantity through printing. (What happened when manuscript illustrations were copied by scribes is obvious in the woeful degeneration that overtook the originally fine illustrations to Dioscorides' botanical work in the course of centuries: miniaturists could draw flower illustrations accurately, but they had no notion of scientific exactitude.) With the cooperation of contemporary artists, books of astonishing beauty, as well as technical competence and importance, poured from the presses, and again increased the popularity of science. The printing press also made easier the progress of science: it became increasingly normal to publish one's discoveries, thus assuring that new ideas were not lost, but were available to provide a basis for the work of others. Scientific advance was not dependent on the printed word: indeed, many scientists, like Copernicus (1473–1543), withheld their work from the press for many years, or like Maurolyco (1494–1577) and Eustachius (1520–1574) failed to publish important works in their lifetimes; but this attitude was increasingly rare. Publication enormously facilitated dissemination, and it is generally true that scientific work not printed had very little chance of influencing others—the work of Leonardo da Vinci being the most notable case in point. In this, as in so much else, the situation was only stabilized in the course of the sixteenth century, but the late fifteenth century prepared the way.

Hans Baron

TOWARD A MORE POSITIVE EVALUATION OF THE FIFTEENTH-CENTURY RENAISSANCE: *Part II*

The selection which follows is a continuation of an article previously introduced. In Part I (page 57) Dr. Baron examined some of the political contributions of the Renaissance to the modern state; here he presents his views on the contributions of the Quattrocento to the development of modern science.

These observations in the field of political history will help to unravel the apparent contradictions confronting us in the history of Quattrocento science. Virtually all the recent reinterpretations of phases of intellectual life in the fourteenth, fifteenth, and sixteenth centuries, to which Professor Durand refers in his memoir, have used one standard of evaluation—the question how much the authors and schools of thought studied contributed to the rise of modern natural science. But to the humanist Renaissance of the fourteenth and fifteenth centuries interest in natural science, however fundamental to the modern world, was as unfamiliar as the institutions of the modern nation-state. Natural science was the one great sector of intellectual activity that was almost wholly excluded from the humanistic program for almost a century and a half, in favor of the new study of man and history. It is in accord with this fact that Burckhardt based his evaluation of the fifteenth

From Hans Baron, "Toward a More Positive Evaluation of the Fifteenth-Century Renaissance," in the *Journal of the History of Ideas* 4 (1943): 27–49. Reprinted by permission of the editors of the *Journal of the History of Ideas*.

century on no excessive claims for any originality in the field of science. Partly for these, partly for personal reasons, he largely omitted science from his *Civilization of the Renaissance in Italy*— as did most of the subsequent accounts of the period. Only in monographic contributions to the history of the sciences has an attempt been made to establish "primacies" for the fifteenth century in positive science also—primacies outside the humanistic movement, notably of Toscanelli in Florence and of the Averroism of Padua. These studies in fifteenth-century science, long impaired by chauvinistic prejudices, as Dr. Durand has pointed out, have recently received an objective critical revision, largely through the efforts of American scholars. Closer investigation—particularly such as made by Professors Thorndike and Randall—has shown that in fact no startling innovations were made before the end of the fifteenth century, although the ban on science by humanists did not prevent studies of the medieval type from being continued throughout the Quattrocento. But when these statements are made, what does this mean for the validity of Burckhardt's picture? Apparently no errors of perspective have been detected in his analysis, but a much broader basis has been made available for reexamining the meaning of the humanist disregard of science and of the cursory treatment of this sector of intellectual life in many modern portraits of the Renaissance.

The best way to explain how temporary aloofness from science could foster the growth of humanistic thought and, indirectly, even that of later science, is to refer to the role played by early humanists in the overthrow of astrological superstition. It is well known that Petrarch's fight against the Averroists of Padua sprang to a large extent from his resistance to astrology, which permeated science in the Averroist atmosphere. So closely knit were astrological notions with the fabric of all science in the late Middle Ages that Petrarch, clinging to Cicero's scorn of superstition of every type, was almost unique in rejecting astrology as a whole. Against this fourteenth-century background one must note the following facts from the Quattrocento. When in its second half leading humanists —as well as philosophers influenced by the humanist movement— began to remove the ban on science, the result was a widespread return to astrology, a century and a half after Petrarch. Giovanni Pontano at Naples then worked out what may be called a system of

astrological psychology, while Marsilio Ficino in Florence contributed a type of astrological medicine—innovations in the field of
science that were by no means dead-born, but ushered in a new
era of astrological ascendancy which, in many respects, was to last
until the middle of the seventeenth century. Now it is true that the
same terminal decades of the Quattrocento saw the first systematic
and conclusive attack upon astrology—the famous books of *Dis-
putationum in Astrologiam* by Giovanni Pico della Mirandola. But
this criticism did not come from the most advanced scientist, but
was ventured by the very Italian thinker who kept aloof from renewed contacts with science more completely than did any of his
important contemporaries. What, then, was the source of inspiration
for this epoch-making exploit? Professor Cassirer, in his presentation of the philosophy of the Renaissance, offers the following account: "The belief in the creative power and autonomy of man, this
genuinely humanistic belief, was the factor to triumph over astrology
with Pico," not empirical-scientific motives, not "the new methods
of observation and mathematical computation. . . . The first decisive
blow was struck before these methods reached perfection. The real
motive for the liberation from astrology was not the new concept
of nature, but the new concept of the intrinsic dignity of man."
More recently Cassirer has added this perspective: "It is curious
to consider how much harder it was for Kepler, a veritable
scientific genius, to escape the bonds of the astrological way
of thinking. . . . Kepler himself could probably not have taken
the final step, had not Pico, upon whom he expressly relies,
preceded him . . . : there was needed a new attitude and a
new sense of the world." There may still be some doubt, as Cassirer
himself says, as to the extent to which lay movements outside Italy
—particularly the *Devotio Moderna*—contributed their religious spir-
itualism to the humanistic roots of Pico's critical assault, especially
through the agency of Cusanus—a problem of European interchange
to which we shall presently return. But the essential lesson to be
learned concerning the relationship between fifteenth-century science and the cultural innovations in the Quattrocento scene is clear:
the humanists were not entirely wrong in their belief that natural
science in the fourteenth- and fifteenth-century phase had little to
contribute to the new ideas championed by humanism.

But with this eclipse of natural science, however logical under fifteenth-century conditions, how could humanistic culture have been close in spirit to modern thought? To ask this question is, in Dr. Durand's eyes, to reveal its absurdity. Yet it is a precise parallel to the questions that we have tried to answer in the field of political history. There, in fact, we observed a structure of Quattrocento life that did in many respects foreshadow the modern pattern, despite the circumstance that certain fundamentals of the modern state (nationwide unity and representative government) were lacking in the Italian Renaissance. These facts should warn us to withhold judgment with regard to "tradition" and "innovation" in intellectual life, until both possible perspectives—that of similarities in "structure" as well as that of "continuity"—have been discerned.

A milestone in our knowledge of the rise of science, no doubt, is the discovery that positive scientific work, gradually expanding beyond the ancient legacy, was started in the late medieval schools; that in this way a tradition was built up which was still an essential element in Galileo's day; and that fifteenth-century Italy contributed but little to this coherent growth. Yet with our knowledge of the effects of humanistic thought on astrology, we must conclude that this discovery does not settle the problem in all its aspects. It certainly does not exclude the possibility that, outside the continuity of academic science, the Quattrocento may have produced such philosophic views and intellectual habits as on the one hand could foreshadow characteristics of the later "scientific mind" and on the other in due time react on science itself. This means that the question still remains, to what extent did the general transformation of the cultural atmosphere in the Quattrocento either anticipate or even *indirectly* influence the change from "medieval" to "modern" science in the sixteenth century?

Couched in these general terms, the problem seems to threaten to lead us into that blind alley of search for an "intangible spirit," against which Dr. Durand warns us in his paper. But the vagueness disappears as soon as the inquiry is reduced to the concrete questions, how far the scientific revolution of the sixteenth century was a consequence solely of the intrinsic growth of thought, a product of the cooperative efforts of schools and academic associations; and how far, in the critical stage, even science was dependent on contemporary changes in moral values, religious and philosophical convictions, and on the relations of thought and practical experience in the life of those engaged in scientific pursuits. This problem, already attacked by recent students, is open to proof or disproof by historical evidence. Should we find essential contributions made by factors reacting on science from outside, then fifteenth-century Italy, despite its barrenness in science in the proper sense, may still appear as instrumental in producing the indispensable frame for the sixteenth-century revolution of science.

The first example to be examined in this light concerns the possible role of the "Quattrocento spirit" only in part, since the developments of lay society and thought outside Italy had a large share in its intellectual formation. But as the case of Cusanus, which I have in mind, contains the most challenging implications for every approach to fifteenth-century science, it has become a focal point for Renaissance debate and has been used as such by Dr. Durand. However, as the intellectual forces by which Cusanus's mind was molded were largely of non-Italian origin—an earlier counterpart to the mixture of northern and Italian elements in Pico della Mirandola—it should be emphasized that our characterization of the Renaissance as a "prototype" of the modern world is not meant to imply that every aspect of modern thought must first have appeared in fifteenth-century Italy. Many well-known phases of Quattrocento life undoubtedly had parallels in the contemporary culture of other European countries, and not a few characteristics of the modern mind—particularly all those connected with the rise of a new lay piety—found even more favorable conditions outside of Italy. Quattrocento culture gives the well-known illusion of a "radical break with the Middle Ages," because the peculiar structure of Italian society and its kinship with ancient Roman civilization intensified cultural change and caused so rapid a pace of evolution that fifteenth-century Italy experienced many social and intellectual developments which did not appear in the rest of Europe until centuries later. Yet, even so, the Italian Renaissance was merely part of a greater phenomenon, which, in different ways, and with varying speed, was appearing all over Europe. There was constant interrelation between the "Italian Renaissance" and the Renaissance as a movement continental in scope. The first great personality in whom all the elements of Renaissance "innovation," both inside and outside Italy, combined was Nicholas of Cusa.

Cusanus's role in the overthrow of medieval cosmology—before cosmology had become a part of Renaissance interests in Italy—has given rise to the most conflicting interpretations. Professor Durand has recalled the fact that certain German scholars made the mistake of reading "anticipations of Copernicus into the mystico-scientific speculations of Nicholas of Cusa," while they attributed heliocentric ideas to this mystic of the fifteenth century—an error that has been bitterly assailed by Thorndike. One must insist, however, that these corrections have settled the matter only so far as the time and circumstances of the emergence of modern astronomical concepts are concerned. The general historical problem in the background, the real cause of those misinterpretations, is left unsolved. The intricacy of this problem is revealed by the fact that, although Cusanus did not have at his disposal, nor did he anticipate, the relevant astronomical data, he did develop the notion that the earth was not low and vile, far below the divine heavens of the stars, but was itself a "noble star," along with the others. He rejoiced over this vindication of the earth in words that were well known to and almost literally repeated by the founders of the heliocentric theory in the sixteenth century—while even in the seventeenth century acceptance of the Copernican system was still obstructed by the argument that the earth, in consequence of her "vileness," must be in the center of the universe, this being the worst possible place and farthest removed from the incorruptible bodies of the stars. All these facts and similar aspects of the Cusanus case have been emphatically pointed out by two philosophers who can hardly be suspected of having any chauvinistic axes to grind—Professor Cassirer (in the introductory chapter of his *Individuum und Kosmos in der Renaissance*) and Professor Lovejoy (in the chapter "The Principle of Plenitude and the New Cosmology," in his *Great Chain of Being*).

From this the only plausible conclusion seems to be that in the case of cosmology the isolated study of the history of science leads one astray; that the perspective that emerged from mysticism—or, better, from a combination of mysticism, Platonism, and stimuli from the Italian Renaissance—for the evaluation of life and a metaphysical interpretation of the world, anticipated observations in astronomical science leading to similar conceptions of the universe.

But if in this case the growth of science was closely intertwined with strands of thought which had their origin outside the scientific sphere, can we believe that a profound mutation of culture and society, such as that which took place in Italy, would not have finally reacted on science in a similar way, on an even grander scale, and with more conclusive results? It is, of course, impossible to attempt any exhaustive inquiry into this problem within the compass of this critique. Moreover, the selection of evidence depends largely upon the notions of "science" that are taken as a standard—notions that are disputed and must be adapted to the changing needs of Renaissance research by experts in the history of science. Still, certain general conclusions suggest themselves immediately when for the Quattrocento such problems are raised as have been recently discussed by students of the period of Galileo.

There is no better subject to begin with than cosmology, as the discussion of Cusanus has revealed. It is not necessary to emphasize the bonds of kinship which had existed between the Weltanschauung of the Middle Ages and a type of cosmology which held that the heaven of the stars was composed of ether, an element purer than anything on this sinful earth; where man lifted up his eyes to the changeless movements of the stars—signs of divine perfection and eternal laws, for which he knew no parallel on earth. Not for scientific reasons alone, therefore, did the idea of the universe as a hierarchy composed of pure and less pure spheres hold the allegiance of medieval man. This cosmic system was consistent with this habit of thinking in terms of a gradational hierarchy and a static divine order in all spheres of life. When Galileo struck the final blow against this old cosmology, proving that the stars are made of stuff no different from earthly things, and that they follow the same natural laws that rule the human sphere, he rebelled against the medieval past not only as a scientist, but also as a son of an epoch in which man rejoiced in the idea that earth and stars and every particle of the universe are equal in perfection, none degraded for eternity. To regard this new frame of mind as sufficient cause for Galileo's attempt to prove the operation of the same laws in the stellar sphere and on earth, would be to overstress a single factor. But the distortion is equal when the profound change in the human evaluation of life, which was a necessary concomitant of the transition from a gradational and static to a decentralized and dynamic universe, is regarded as negligible. When Galileo jubilantly noted the definite proof that this our earth is physically one with moon and stars, "non autem sordium mundanarumque fecum sentinam esse," he knew that he was repeating the triumphant words of Cusanus, uttered long before the claim was supported by scientific discoveries. He also knew that he was transforming and expressing in exact mathematical language the lofty idea of a decentralized, infinite Nature, evolved from philosophical speculation—first through the vitalism and panpsychism dominating biology, medicine, and chemistry early in the sixteenth century, and finally by Giordano Bruno's pantheistic conviction that one and the same divine power unfolds itself restlessly in every particle of the world.

Today, because of the prevailing tendency to accept the coming of the mathematical method as the decisive factor distinguishing "new" from "old," Giordano Bruno, who once seemed to represent the climax of Renaissance philosophy, has receded into the background. Yet Bruno, standing at the crossroads, provides the best evidence that genuine elements of the Renaissance went into the crucible of modern scientific thought. Although he failed to perceive the full meaning of the mathematical method and the mathematical concept of the infinite, he had a firm grip on the cosmological idea of the infinity of the universe, and in it found a sufficient basis for revolt against the Aristotelian-scholastic concepts of finite space and a finite world. From Bruno's work one can perceive the almost logical train of the phases of Renaissance thought: experience of the boundlessness of human passion and of the search for knowledge —the basis common to Renaissance ethics and psychology since Petrarch—found a corollary in the idea of the infinitude of the physical universe; while the infinitude of physical energies in turn needed as its vehicle, as it were, the infinitude of space—the idea that was to burst asunder the concept of a static finite world. "Here too"—quoting from Cassirer's description of this fundamental concatenation of Renaissance thought—"it is a dynamic motive which overcomes the static structure of Aristotelian-scholastic cosmology, . . . not [yet] as a new science of dynamics, but as a new dynamic feeling underlying the cosmological outlook."

In other words, the story of the birth of modern science cannot be fully told before inquiry is made into the causes of the rising tendency to see life in a "dynamic" vision; before it is explained how the belief in the universe as an immovable, God-given order was overcome by the idea of a decentralized, infinite universe, a world in evolution, and so paved the way for the later readiness to reduce all physical phenomena to a successive flux, and for the evolutionary views characteristic of modern thought.

To reconstruct this story means to find a place for the fifteenth-century Renaissance in the rise of science. The static world of medieval man had inspired conviction as long as the idea of hierarchic order had reigned supreme in every field, in human history as well as nature. The famous doctrine of four universal empires succeeding one another as a divinely created frame of history, with the Roman Empire as the last, placed above historical flux and destined to endure to the end of history, was the exact equivalent in historical outlook of the gradation of the crystal spheres in the Ptolemaic system. Again, when the idea of a *Sacrum Imperium,* more "perfect" than the other states, was destroyed by the notion of a decentralized history with empires and smaller states all on one level of natural growth and decay, the revolution in historical outlook thus revealed was a precise counterpart to the emergence of a dynamic, decentralized view of nature. The intellectual and psychological effects of rebellion in either sphere were bound to be akin and to react on one another.

But the two processes, although related in their meaning for intellectual life, did not occur at the same time. At the end of the Middle Ages, as in all other periods of history, intellectual energy was first concentrated on certain sectors of life until, with revolutionary results achieved, interest shifted to other fields. By the end of the humanistic Renaissance of the Quattrocento, a dynamic, decentralized view had emerged in history and political science, with its first great expression in the works of Machiavelli and Guicciardini. In the sixteenth century the same vision began to transform cosmology and, indeed, all notions of nature. Machiavelli's *Discorsi sopra la prima deca di Tito Livio* (finished, in substance, in 1513) and Galileo's *Dialogo sopra i due massimi sistemi del mondo* (finished in 1632) were complementary phases of one historical process. Both deal with the same problem of the dynamic vision of a decentralized reality; both represent the triumph of the vernacular, and thus of closer contacts with the lay world, in their respective fields. Finally, to the question why the "discovery of man and history" should have occurred first in the Renaissance, while the "discovery of nature" followed, the answer seems to be that the experience and sentiments of the citizen of the Italian Commune first produced new conceptions of culture, politics, and history. When the historical outlook and the ideas of human nature had been remade, the change in perspective, in a second phase, would react on natural science.

If these considerations are sound, fifteenth-century Italy contributed one of the most decisive "innovations" to the development of modern science. This contribution, it is true, had little immediate effect on science, but in the broader intellectual life it caused the rise of those very problems and attitudes of mind that were to provide the indispensable frame of thought for the transition from "medieval" to "modern" science, a hundred years later. Now one may wonder whether inquiry into the nature of such general cultural relations must be included in the discussion of the evolution of natural science and should not be left rather to the care of students in other fields, particularly in the history of philosophy. However, the need for specialization in practical research is one thing, while the need to give to individual results their proper place in a synoptic vision of all the vital forces of a period is another. If it is true that mental attitudes and problems are apt to spread across the separate departments of culture, and that this dissemination of new concepts often requires the span of generations, two inferences seem inevitable: first, that no estimate of the forces of "tradition" and "innovation" in any period is reliable if based on research in a single field; and second, that neither science, nor political thought, nor any single cultural activity can be understood in its specific evolution, unless allowance is made for cases in which essentials of progressive growth—for instance, the awareness of natural laws, or the power to make causal observation and research—are born and first elaborated in sectors of intellectual life remote from the particular field of our learned specialization.

In historical sciences older and riper than the comparatively recent Renaissance scholarship, integration of the results of study in neighboring fields has undoubtedly progressed much farther than in present Renaissance research. A familiar example is, in the history of early Greece, the unraveling of the subtle threads connecting Ionic nature philosophy and the political thought of the Sophists. It may be useful to bring home the point by quoting the following account from Professor Sabine's recent *History of Political Theory:*

> At the start the fundamental [Greek] idea of harmony or proportionality was applied indifferently as a physical and as an ethical principle and was conceived indifferently as a property of nature or as a reasonable property of human nature. The first development of the principle, however, took place in natural philosophy, and this development reacted in turn upon its later use in ethical and political thought. . . . The objects that made up the physical world were to be explained on the hypothesis that they were variations or modifications of an underlying substance which in essence remained the same. The contrast here is between fleeting and ever-changing particulars and an unchangeable "nature" whose properties and laws are eternal. . . . But at about the middle of the fifth century . . . [there was] a swing in the direction of humanistic studies, such as grammar, music, the arts of speech and writing, and ultimately psychology, ethics, and politics. . . . The Greeks had [now] become familiar . . . with the variety and the flux of human custom. What more natural, then, than that they should find in custom and convention the analogue of fleeting appearances and should seek again for a "nature" or a permanent principle by which the appearances could be reduced to regularity? The "substance" of the physical philosophers consequently reappeared as a "law of nature," eternal amid the endless qualifications and modifications of human circumstance.

There is no reason why, in the fifteenth and sixteenth centuries of our era, the inverse sequence of, first, humanism and politico-historical science and, secondly, natural science should not be interpreted in similar terms. When viewed in this light, the balance between "promise" and "prejudice" in the Quattrocento will take on a different aspect.

So far we have attempted to show that a change in the structure of intellectual life did have a part in the growth of positive science in the sixteenth century, and that there had been precedents in fifteenth-century Italy for the new frame of mind essential in Galileo's period. With these facts as a background, there is more concrete meaning in the claim that the importance of the Quattrocento lay in a new type of thinking, in a fresh approach to intellectual problems, and not in the extent of the innovations that were immediately effected in the specific sciences and arts.

We may now add a second illustration—one hardly less decisive, taken from the *sociological* aspects of modern science. This factor Dr. Durand touches upon when he mentions "the happy union of the hand, the eye, and the mind, which reached its perfection in Leonardo da Vinci," i.e., the observational and experimental work of Quattrocento artists and engineers outside of humanism and academic science—a trend unfortunately excluded from Dr. Durand's picture because (in his own words) the assessment of its "theoretical contributions to the whole of Quattrocento science must wait for further monographic research." But are we really justified, on this ground, in omitting an appraisal of these artist groups from an attempted "balance sheet" of the fifteenth-century Renaissance? If their "fruitful work," as Dr. Durand says, was "undeniably a chief glory of Quattrocento Italy," it is difficult to see how one could reach any fair balance between its elements of tradition and innovation, while eliminating one of the most interesting potential factors of "innovation." Fortunately for our purposes, the point about these groups most strongly emphasized by recent students is not so much their possible contribution of clearly defined theories, as the psychological and intellectual consequences of the appearance of foci of practical, unacademic investigation in the field of science. But before applying the sociological perspective of the fifteenth-century set-up, we must provide a framework by summarizing the results already gained with this approach for the history of science in the period of Galileo.

The import of Galileo's scientific work springs, roughly speaking, from two major achievements: his bringing to a triumphant conclusion the cosmological revolution that had been growing throughout the Renaissance; and his reduction, final and irrevocable, of science to measurement, quantity, and motion—to mathematics working on data supplied by observation, checked by experiment. To the problems of the origin of this mathematical method much study has been given in recent years. To a degree, stress of mathematics as the core of true knowledge, had long been an element of Platonist epistemology and metaphysics. In the wake of Platonism, it had come to the fore with Cusanus, and again with Kepler, a fact highly emphasized by Cassirer in his various works. Yet, though positive science—in its Averroist and its Ockhamite branches—developed at the late medieval universities, and induction, observation, and even the precedents of Galileo's combination of analytic-resolutive and constructive-compositive methods gradually appeared, mathematics did not, until the middle of the sixteenth century, obtain its modern place in scientific research. In the School of Padua—as shown by Professor Randall and reemphasized by Professor Durand —it was largely from the Latin revisions of Archimedes by Tartaglia in 1543 and by Commandino in 1558, that mathematical interests and methods slowly began to penetrate physical science.

These conclusions, important and definite though they are, seem to require some comment. The appearance of a convenient revised edition of the familiar work of an ancient mathematician, however eagerly welcomed and utilized by leading Paduan scholars, would not in itself explain the triumph of the mathematical method. The publication and its effects are remarkable rather as a straw in the wind, because they signalize a trend of interest which was developing in the second half of the sixteenth century. The origin of Tartaglia's interest in mathematics had little to do with the science of Padua or with any of the older schools. Tartaglia was a self-taught man, who had made all his discoveries in mathematics and mechanics in intercourse with practical engineers, gunners, merchants, and architects in northern Italy. A few decades later there were similar conditions affecting the development of Galileo. In his youth, unable to find an opportunity for mathematical training in the University of Pisa, Galileo acquired the mathematical interest characteristic of his later work by making contacts with the same type of practical mathematics. His studies were pursued under a teacher who belonged to the Accademia del Disegno in Florence, a kind of technical institute for the preparation of artists, architects, and engineers.

Thus the conclusion is suggested that it was contact with experimenting, practically minded technicians and masters outside the schools that infused the decisive element, a fresh compound of experiment and mathematics, into late medieval science. It is this point that serves as a leitmotif in the monograph on *Galilei und seine Zeit* published by Professor Olschki in 1927—a work which first called full attention to the connection of Tartaglia and Galileo with the mathematical pursuits of artists, architects, and engineers outside the academic circles. More recently, studies by Dr. Edgar Zilsel, still in progress, have traced the early contacts of the academic world with the new class of workshop engineers and foremen in the countries outside Italy—particularly from the middle of the sixteenth century onward, when scholars first undertook observational studies in the mines and foundries of the new capitalistic industries. There may be some danger of exaggeration in Zilsel's claim that the "decisive event in the genesis of science" about 1600 lay in the uniting of the two previously separated groups—the educated, theoretically minded "upper stratum," and the practical workmen in the shops and mines, the "lower stratum," which "added causal spirit, experimentation, measurement, quantitative rules of operation, disregard of school authority, and objective co-operation." Yet there is one outstanding fact which may be definitively inferred from Olschki's and Zilsel's findings: it is now better understood why natural science in the modern sense depended on the rise of a new society, no less than did humanistic education and the new political and historical sciences. The point in common is that the emergence of a new phase was everywhere bound up with the appearance of lay circles living a life of work and action from which evolved new practical skills and subsequently new theories, ideas, and evaluations of life. What the rise of an urban society, composed of practical men participating as readers and writers in a type of literature no longer produced for one rank only, meant for humanist education; what the reappearance of active political citizenship in the Italian city-states meant for political studies: this the emergence of groups educated and engaged in technological pursuits meant for the beginnings of the new natural science.

Viewed in this light the Quattrocento reveals itself once more as a prototype of the modern pattern—as a precursor, even if on a somewhat variant basis. It is true that the high tide for the new technical classes, as Zilsel emphasizes, did not come until the full rise of capitalism in the mining, metal and related industries in the sixteenth century, while fifteenth-century Italy clung to the "ancient distinction between liberal and mechanical arts," with the one exception of painters and sculptors, who were "gradually detached from handicraft and slowly rose to social esteem." But it was in fact this exception which in the Quattrocento brought about the first contacts of any practical profession with scientific theory, awakening scientific interest in a general cultured public outside humanism and the academic schools. In the conditions of Renaissance Italy the workshop of the artist, in fostering experimental work and stimulating observation and causal thinking, performed precisely the intellectual function that was in later centuries discharged by the industrial workshop and the scientific laboratory.

There were in the art of the Renaissance several elements capable of promoting this effect. To begin with, a type of art that placed proportion first, made truth to nature an indispensable standard, and included in the work of the artist-architect town planning and the technique of fortifications, was bound to promote mathematical and experimental methods far beyond the reach of the medieval Schoolmen. Moreover, it was in the heart of the new urban society that the new technical skills were practiced. While passing from the detached, collectivist orbit of the masons' guild engaged in the construction and adornment of a medieval church, to the workshop of the "artist-engineer" in a busy Florentine street, art had in fact traveled a distance equivalent to that covered in the intellectual transition from the clerical atmosphere of medieval monasteries and universities to the symbiosis of thought and action in the society of the Renaissance. Thanks to the pioneering work of Professors Olschki and Julius von Schlosser we are able to form a very clear idea of those early counting, measuring, experimenting masters, accustomed to pursue self-taught studies in optics, perspective, anatomy, and the engineering work connected with the great architectural projects of the Renaissance. From Florentine groups which included Ghiberti, Brunelleschi, L. B. Alberti, and Filarete, there extended a coherent tradition of skills and interests down to circles subsequently formed at the courts of Urbino and Milan, with the climax in the great figure of Leonardo. Continued throughout the sixteenth century, this trend became an essential influence (as was said above) on Galileo in his youth.

For Florence our documents permit us to observe the existence of constant and intimate contacts between the most diversified groups of citizens, including the humanist literati, and masters of this type working on technical as well as artistic projects. The universal curiosity aroused by the public competition of Florentine artists for the adornment of the doors of the Baptistry in 1401 is mentioned in every history of the Renaissance, and the emotional appeal to the Florentine public of the pioneering problems involved in the construction of the cathedral dome strikingly foreshadowed the general interest in great technical feats in later centuries. Professor Krey, in a recent pamphlet, has given a convincing account of the importance and intensity of this exchange between the craftsman and the cultured citizen, the artist and the humanist. That early humanists did not include scientific studies in their program should therefore not cause us to forget this subtle education of Renaissance society in scientific interests and ways of thought. There was a growing effect on intellectual life and even on humanism in the second half of the Quattrocento. If it did not produce originality in the field of natural science, it still reacted on the literary production of the mature Renaissance, providing writers with a scientific background which aided them in finding realistic ways of thought in many fields of literature and learning. In the Florence of Lorenzo de' Medici the neoplatonists as well as humanists of the type of Poliziano were all in intercourse with Toscanelli's circle, and the effects are palpable in their work. As to Machiavelli, his dependence on medical and biological ideas was demonstrated by O. Tammasini in his huge monograph thirty years ago. Had scientific pursuits as yet not played a part, side by side with classical and political interests, in the Florentine groups which influenced the growth of Machiavelli's thought, he would hardly have possessed the intellectual tools he needed for his naturalistic analysis of political disintegration and growth.

All these factors throw light upon the existence of subtle interrelations between the "realism" of the Renaissance and the subsequent rise of the scientific spirit. But it is necessary to turn to the lonely, gigantic figure of Leonardo da Vinci to realize fully the promise for the future inherent in the scientific by-ways of the Quattrocento. Whatever may be the final verdict upon the thesis offered by Duhem—i.e., that Leonardo as a scientist largely exploited the work of Scholastic predecessors—it is evident even today that by the artist of the Renaissance something substantial was added to the legacy of the Schoolmen—a new achievement springing from the milieu of the artist-engineers of the Quattrocento. This addition was not only an advance in practical experimental skills; it included the very element which was to become the mark of modern science —the ascendancy of the mathematical method. Leonardo, long before mathematics became the royal road of academic science, contended unambiguously that "no human investigation can be called true science without passing through mathematical tests." He was convinced that any step beyond this solid foundation would lead to the illusion of understanding the substance of things, a knowledge of which "the human mind is incapable." And in place of the old hierarchy of sciences, with metaphysics and theology supreme, he first envisaged a gradation of studies in terms of the certitude they derived from the degree in which they were penetrated by mathematics.

This sudden and unique anticipation of the method of modern science is, of course, more than an isolated fact. It points to a substantial affinity between Leonardo's vision of nature and the modern scientific outlook. Indeed, viewed from any angle of the great transition from a static-centralized to a dynamic-evolutionary view of life, Leonardo's ideas and discoveries herald the things to come. With him Cusanus's exultation over the earth as one with the other stars—the "glory of our universe," as Leonardo said with Cusanus—led to the first dynamic interpretation, not only of the cosmos, but of nature as a whole. To Leonardo, in the geological history of the earth, the Deluge had ceased to be the all-determining event—a counterpart to the eclipse of the *Sacrum Imperium* in historical thought—giving way to a vision of incessant flux and change. For the first time the geological scene of human life appeared as the work of oceans, rivers, winds, a world in which plants, animals, and men grow in a natural way—until this planet in some distant future shall have become cold and dry, by the workings of the same natural forces, in the same natural cycle of growth and decay. It is the keenness of his perception of the dynamic rotation of nature from destruction to reproduction that led Leonardo to many of his startling discoveries—such as his understanding of the change of species in flora and fauna in the course of geological history, and of the incessant processes of consumption and reproduction in all living substance. For an historical perspective of the Renaissance the most important point is not the fact that these discoveries along with many of Leonardo's technological inventions foreshadowed some of the later attainments of science in an astounding way, but that in their entirety they revealed the same dynamic vision contemporaneously at work in the remaking of political and historical science by Machiavelli—the vision of reality that was to transmute cosmology and, subsequently, all positive sciences, from the second half of the sixteenth century onward. One may attempt to indicate Galileo's place in intellectual history with the three key words of experimental observation, mathematical method, and the dynamic view of a decentralized nature. All these basic avenues of the later science Quattrocento thought had entered a century before, and in no half-hearted fashion.

With this delineation of the historical role of the "artist-engineer" we are in a position to appraise, in a fresh and concrete way, the meaning of the claim that a new type of man and thought appeared with the Quattrocento. The older interpretations of the Renaissance, based on fifteenth-century humanism and the political conditions of the Quattrocento, have been repeated and confirmed in the investigation of a new sector of Quattrocento life. Wherever, we may say, creative individuals belonged to social groups which had direct contacts with the new life of work and action—whether we think of the official-secretary, or the merchant-statesman, or the artist-engineer—there the transformed relationship of life and thought rapidly gave to experience, interests, and accepted values the shape that differentiates the modern from the medieval mind.

In the perspective of present-day research, the upshot then seems to be that Burckhardt's analysis of the Renaissance as a new phase of psychological and intellectual development still holds its own. The definition and formulation of the results attainable through his approach have been, no doubt, modified and remodified in the course of eighty years of subsequent investigation. What in Burckhardt's day appeared as one perspective, is now refracted in divergent strains of thought. Most of the students who still follow Burckhardt as a guide feel that his dictum of "the discovery of the world and of man" in the Italian Renaissance, i.e., his characterization of the period as that of the triumph of "realism" and "individualism," is in the light of the concrete problems of present scholarship incomplete, and needs specification. One group of recent students has emphasized the place of the Renaissance in what we have described as the transition from a static-gradational and centralized idea of life and the world to a dynamic-evolutionary and decentralized concept of man, history, and nature. Others, under the impact of increasing evidence that there was much of realism in medieval thought and art, feel it imperative to redefine the "realism" of the Renaissance—a redefinition which shifts the emphasis to the fifteenth-century discovery of objective laws in nature, history, and human psychology, with the laws of mathematics in a place of special significance for the rise of science. In the last analysis these varied views are not alternative, but complementary to each other. They represent the different avenues along which recent scholarship has been developing the Burckhardtian thesis that at the basis of the fifteenth-century Renaissance there was a fundamental change in man's outlook on life and the world—the coming of the "firstborn among the sons of modern Europe."

If, on the other hand, we are today more aware than Burckhardt of the immense importance of the continuity binding the ideas and institutions of the modern world to the medieval past, this insight neither needs nor has the power to undo the lesson learned from a century of studies of the Italian Renaissance. The task before us is increasingly to integrate the two great vistas opened up by medieval and Renaissance research, neither of which gains by their mutual disparagement.

Paul Oskar Kristeller

THE PLACE OF CLASSICAL HUMANISM IN RENAISSANCE THOUGHT

Paul Oskar Kristeller, professor of philosophy at Columbia University, was born and educated in Germany. His research and publications reveal a wide and profound knowledge of Renaissance thought and its classical background. Much of his attention has been centered on the person of Marsilio Ficino as the outstanding Platonist in the intellectual and philosophical history of the Italian Renaissance. Professor Kristeller is also widely known as a special lecturer and visiting professor both here and abroad.

The "problem of the Renaissance," as it has been widely discussed in the last few decades, is largely a pseudoproblem. A complex historical period with a great variety of cross-currents, in which each European country and each field of interest underwent its own particular development, can hardly be interpreted in terms of a brief

From P. O. Kristeller, "The Place of Classical Humanism in Renaissance Thought," in the *Journal of the History of Ideas* 4 (1943): 59–63. Reprinted by permission of the editors of the *Journal of the History of Ideas.*

definition which would at the same time distinguish it from all other periods of history. Such definitions are apt to be too narrow or too broad. The discussion has been further complicated by the tendency of many scholars to take the Renaissance as an imaginary battle-ground on which to fight out contemporary political, social and ideological conflicts, or as a test case for the solution of such metahistorical questions as the possibility and the causes of his-torical change. On the other hand, there seems no doubt about the distinctive physiognomy of the Renaissance, and the claim that the very existence of "the Renaissance" has to be proved by a satisfac-tory definition of it, must be rejected. With the same right, we might as well conclude that there was no "eighteenth century," since we are unable to describe its distinctive characteristics in a brief definition. The best procedure would be rather to start with a tenta-tive conception of the Renaissance, and to take this idea as a guiding principle when investigating the actual facts and sources of the period under consideration.

The question which Professor Durand sets out to answer is much more specific: what is the contribution of fifteenth-century Italy to the progress of natural science? I think the question is worth asking, and we must be grateful for the judicious way in which he has presented and evaluated the facts discovered through recent studies in the history of science. He rightly emphasizes the continuity of the university tradition, and at the same time recognizes the impor-tance of the new translations from the Greek, as in the case of Ptolemy's *Geography*. Many other scientific translations, commenta-ries, and treatises of the fifteenth century are still awaiting a more detailed investigation, and many other branches of science and learning will have to be examined. But most probably Professor Durand's conclusion will be confirmed, that fifteenth-century Italy brought no basic change in the methods and results of natural science, although it contributed numerous observations and theories in the various fields.

I disagree, however, with the conclusions for the general inter-pretation of the Renaissance Professor Durand seems to draw from this result. I fully agree with Professor Baron's excellent definition of the relation between the history of science and intellectual history in general, and his emphasis on the powerful influence which impor-tant changes in other fields eventually exercised on the development of natural science. The question of tradition and innovation in Renaissance science cannot be definitely settled without taking into consideration the nonprofessional writers on science, the non-Italian scientists, many of whom were more or less indebted to the Italians, and possibly even the scientists of the sixteenth century who largely reaped what the fifteenth century had sown. Moreover, science has not always occupied that dominating place among the other fields of culture which it has held during the last few centuries of occidental history. We cannot accept the claim that historical changes are unimportant unless they are changes in the field of science or immediately affect science. In the case of the Renaissance, the cultural change did not primarily concern science. Since Burckhardt's conception of the Renaissance is not based on any claim for a basic change in natural science, I do not see how it can be disproved by showing that actually no such basic change in science took place. On the other hand, I agree with Professor Baron that a change did take place in fields other than science, and that this change did influence the development of science, though indirectly and in a later period.

But when I try to answer the question, what kind of change was characteristic of the Renaissance, and especially of fifteenth-century Italy, I find myself less in agreement with Professor Baron than with Professor Durand. I do believe that classical humanism was, if not the only, certainly the most characteristic and pervasive intellectual current of that period. With its merits and with its limitations, humanism pervaded more or less all achievements and expressions of the fifteenth century. When its influence declined in the sixteenth century, its work had been already done. The influence of humanism on science as well as on philosophy was indirect, but powerful. The actual performance of the humanists in these fields was rather poor. But they popularized the entire body of ancient Greek learning and literature and thus made available new source materials of which the professional scientists and philosophers could not fail to take advantage. This was important, because at that time occidental science and thought had not yet reached or surpassed the results of classical antiquity, and hence had still something to learn from the ancients. Moreover, medieval science had developed in definite patterns, and the introduction of new sources and "authorities" eventually prepared the way for new methods and theories. Those who claim that ancient science was completely known to the Middle Ages are as mistaken as those who deny that it was known at all. At least some of the classical Latin authors became more widely known in the Renaissance, Lucretius, for example. Numerous Greek manuscripts were brought over from the East, and more men were able to read them in the original. Moreover, practically all the Greek texts were translated into Latin by the humanists, many for the first time. The question of how many were translated for the first time and whether the new translations were better or more influential than the extant earlier translations, cannot be settled by dispute, but only by a careful bibliography of the Latin translations from the Greek, which should include the manuscript materials. In the field of philosophy, humanism introduced most of the works of Plato, Plotinus, Epictetus, Diogenes Laertius, Plutarch, Lucian, as well as many works of the commentators on Aristotle and of the Greek Fathers, not to speak of the Greek poets, historians, and orators. In science the contribution may be less impressive, but it has still to be investigated. Archimedes and Hero came at least to be more widely known, and many of the minor mathematicians were translated for the first time. The Latin translations were followed by extensive commentaries, and by translations into the various vernacular languages which reached an ever wider public.

The humanists were certainly not the only representatives of science and learning in the fifteenth century. On the one hand, there were the followers of the medieval traditions who carried on the work of their predecessors, especially at the various universities. On the other hand, there were the artists and engineers who through their practical work came face to face with mathematical and scientific problems and sometimes made important contributions, as has been recently emphasized. But in the fifteenth century both of these latter groups were influenced by humanism, as was the general public. If the humanists failed to make substantial contributions to the various fields of traditional learning, they did introduce source materials and problems which could be applied to those fields. By the end of the fifteenth century, humanism had not indeed replaced the traditional learning, but the representatives of traditional learning had absorbed the achievements of humanism. This accounts for the changes and progresses which took place in the sixteenth century—just as the achievements of the artists and engineers were taken over by the professional scientists after the middle of that century. On the other hand, even the artists and engineers were subject to the influence of humanism, as Professor Baron rightly emphasizes. The personal relations between the humanists and the artists need further investigation, especially as they appear from numerous letters and poems of the humanists which have not yet been utilized for this purpose. The number of artists and engineers who made active contributions to science was still comparatively small in the fifteenth century as compared with the sixteenth. But the case of Leon Battista Alberti shows that this scientific activity of the artists cannot be separated from, or opposed to, contemporary humanism.

I cannot agree with those who identify these artists with the general public of the unlearned or who make a sharp contrast between the "Academic" humanists who wrote in Latin, and the "popular" writers who used the vernacular language. Those artists who also wrote scientific treatises certainly had some learning beyond that of the general public, and drew something from the professional learning of their time, whether it was in the medieval or in the humanistic tradition. The humanists themselves, no less than these artists, impressed the popular imagination of their time, as many anecdotes show. Since this was a matter of fashion, no real understanding on the part of the public was required. If today many admire the achievements of modern science without understanding its methods, we may well grant that in the early Renaissance many admired the humanists without understanding their Latin. Moreover, the question of language is less important for our problem than might be supposed. In the fifteenth century there is abundant evidence for the mutual influence between vernacular and neo-Latin literature, and when the vernacular definitely won out in the sixteenth century, it had already absorbed the characteristic achievements of humanism, in style, terminology, literary form, and subject matter. Otherwise, it could not have replaced Latin.

To conclude, I should like to add to the statements of Professors Durand and Baron that by popularizing in the fifteenth century the works of classical antiquity, the humanists made an important, though indirect contribution to the development of science and philosophy, and that this contribution bore fruit not only in the work of the humanists themselves, but also in that of the professional

FIGURE 4. The woodcut portrait of Andreas Vesalius of Brussels from the first edition of his *De humani corporus fabrica* (Basel, 1543). From *The Illustrations from the Works of Andreas Vesalius of Brussels,* annotated and translated by J. B. deC. M. Saunders and C. D. O'Malley (Cleveland, 1950), reprinted by Dover Publications, Inc. (New York, 1973). (*Used by permission.*)

scientists and artists of their time and of the following century. All these statements, however, are tentative rather than final, and subject to further revision. The only thing that really counts in Renaissance studies is the actual investigation of the extensive source materials which have not yet been included in any extant synthesis. This investigation must proceed with the cooperation of all scholars interested in the period, regardless of their point of view. In this study we should try to eliminate so far as possible our personal preference for or against this or that nation, language, class, current, or field, and to arrive at a fair evaluation of the contribution each of them has made to the whole of occidental civilization. Such an evaluation will not depend wholly on the influence, direct or distant, which each phenomenon has exercised on later developments, but will also acknowledge the inherent, "absolute" significance of many ideas and achievements which for some reason or other failed to have any visible influence. It is this significance, rather than any incidental sequence of changes or influences, which in my opinion should be the ultimate purpose of the history of ideas, if not of all history.

Lynn Thorndike

RENAISSANCE OR PRENAISSANCE?

Lynn Thorndike was widely known as a distinguished teacher at Columbia University before his death in 1965. His many books and articles reveal a vast knowledge of the Middle Ages, particularly of medieval science. He was a founding fellow of the Mediaeval Academy of America and of L'Académie Internationale d'Histoire des Sciences. He served as president of the History of Science Society (1929) and as president of the American Historical Association (1955).

Professor Dana B. Durand has accused me of harboring a personal antipathy to the Renaissance. Whether my motive is personal or rational, objective or subjective, conscious or subconscious, it must be confessed that my aversion to the term in question is even more sweeping than Durand perhaps thinks and extends to such catchwords as the Carolingian Renaissance and the twelfth-century Renaissance, as well as to the more often mentioned Italian Renaissance of the fifteenth century or somewhere thereabouts. Religion may have its resurrections and revivals, but I have even less faith than Nicodemus in rebirths or restorations of whole periods of human history. I take my stand with the blind writer of Christian hymns, Fanny Crosby, who sang,

> *But the bird with the broken pinion never soared so high again;*

with William Muldoon who said of former heavyweight champions,

> *They never come back;*

with Omar Khayyam who mused,

> *The moving finger writes and having writ*
> *Moves on; nor all your piety nor wit*
> *May lure it back to cancel half a line*
> *Nor all your tears wipe out one word of it;*

and with a verse from the light opera *Tom Jones,*

From Lynn Thorndike, "Renaissance or Prenaissance?" in the *Journal of the History of Ideas* 4 (1943): 65–74. Reprinted by permission of the editors of the *Journal of the History of Ideas*. The documentation of the original article has been omitted.

> *Time is not a necromancer;*
> *Time's a thief and nothing more.*

Legacies from the past? Yes. Inheritances from previous periods? Yes. Survivals? Yes. Resemblances to our forebears? Yes. Reformations? Perhaps. Reactions? Unfortunately. But no rebirths and no restorations!

Books and works of art are about all that remains to us of the past. The latter are all too soon sadly altered, and their restoration, whether by some German professor or by a Thorwaldsen or Viollet-le-Duc, only makes them less like what they originally were. Books remain less changed by the lapse of time, but even their text may become corrupt, or the meaning of the very words they use alter in the interim. The humanists of the so-called Italian Renaissance had only a bookish knowledge of antiquity; they failed almost as dismally as have Mussolini and his Fascists to make the reality of ancient Rome live again. If, even in our own day, all the resources of the art of history aided by archaeology can give us only a faint and imperfect idea of the past, how can we expect actual renaissances of it or recognize them as such, if they were to occur? At the age of sixty I am perhaps more like myself at the age of twenty than I am like anyone else. But I couldn't possibly put myself back into the frame of mind that I had then. I have a dim recollection of it; my present state of mind is an outgrowth of it; that is all. A girl of eighteen, dressed up in the clothes which her grandmother wore when a girl of eighteen, may look more like her grandmother as she was then than her grandmother herself does now. But she will not feel or act as her grandmother felt and acted half a century or more ago. Much more tenuous is the connection between distant historical periods, and much less likely is it that historians can successfully venture upon glittering generalities about them. Who can evoke from the past more than a wraith, a phantasy, a specter, which murmurs, like the ghost in *Hamlet,* "Historian, remember me!"

It is true that history offers examples of human customs which somewhat resemble the conception of a renaissance. For instance, at Tonalamatl in ancient Mexico the recurrence of the year date 2. acatl every fifty-two years was considered a critical occasion, it being feared that the sun might fail to rise next day and that the evil spirits might destroy the world and mankind. Accordingly, a festival of ceremonial fire-making was held. All the old fires were carefully extinguished and at midnight on the mountain top the high priest by rubbing sticks together kindled a new fire on the breast of a prisoner who was forthwith sacrificed. The new fire was then distributed to the temples of the surrounding cities and thence to the adjacent peoples. Old garments were thrown away and household dishes and utensils were broken or freshly painted over in token of the new lease of life given to mankind. But this rekindling and renewal was immediate, continuous, and perfunctory. Only a part of one night intervened between the two periods, not centuries of dark ages. There was no intellectual or spiritual rebirth.

We might also adduce the influence upon our notions of revolutions and periods in history of the astrological theory of conjunctions and revolutions of the planets.

But let us turn to the development of the concept of an Italian Renaissance and begin with the translation into Latin of Ptolemy's *Geography* in the first decade of the fifteenth century. Durand is inclined to censure the previous medieval translators for neglecting this work. If they did—for a previous translation may have escaped our notice—it is to be remembered that after all the text in question consists largely of lists of ancient place-names, many of which cannot be identified and located with any assurance and are of purely historical and linguistic interest. Moreover, Ptolemy had made the Mediterranean Sea too short by one-third, whereas one of the medieval *portolani* is more accurate than any other map of the Mediterranean until the eighteenth century. Concerning the Far East, too, and islands in the Atlantic the thirteenth and fourteenth centuries were much better informed than Ptolemy. The translation and subsequent vogue of his *Geography* were therefore in some ways regrettable. Be that as it may, in the dedication of his translation to Pope Alexander V, Jacobus Angelus, who was a booster of his native town of Florence, says:

> *This very age of ours, especially in our city of Florence, has sparkled with how many wits, who to their great glory have resuscitated liberal studies which had grown almost torpid.*

In the fifth volume of *A History of Magic and Experimental Science* I have given various examples of this notion of a resuscitation of liberal studies becoming stereotyped and being extended to most inappropriate fields, such as astronomy by Moravus and Santritter, chiromancy and physiognomy by Cocles, anatomy by Vesalius, and magic in the case of Antiochus Tibertus. Abstemius depicted Pope Paul III as restoring astrology after it had lain in darkness, disrepute, barbarism and sordid squalor for many centuries past; Pena praised Charles, cardinal of Lorraine, for having resuscitated the prostrate mathematical sciences. Just as the humanists who found manuscripts of the Latin classics in monasteries represented themselves as discovering the work in question and rescuing it from neglect and decay, saying nothing of the fact that the monks had copied it in Carolingian times and preserved it ever since, but leaving their own manuscripts when they died to some monastery as the safest place in which to keep them, so publishers who printed a text for the first time, even if it was a typical product of medieval scholasticism, represented themselves as snatching it from Gothic filth and dust and mildew and cobwebs and bringing it to the light of fairest impressions with the text carefully restored to its pristine purity and freed from barbarisms, when in reality they were very likely using a single inferior manuscript and neglecting a dozen older and superior versions.

When was the word, Renaissance, first used? Nicolaus Prucknerus, or Prugner, approached such usage when, in the preface to his reedition of the ancient Roman astrologer, Julius Firmicus Maternus, addressed from Strasbourg on January 28, 1551, to young King Edward VI of England, he spoke of religion reviving in that realm (*una cum renascente religione istius regni*). But evidently he was speaking of the Protestant Reformation. Two years later, however, the French naturalist, Pierre Belon, in the dedicatory epistle of his *Les observations . . . de plusieurs singularitez* to François Cardinal Tournon, assured him that, as a result of his patronage of learning and education of promising young scholars, it had followed that the minds of men, which were formerly as it were asleep and sunk in a profound slumber of long-standing ignorance, had begun to awake, to come forth from the shadows where they had so long dwelt, and to develop in all sorts of good disciplines a happy and desirable Renaissance, like plants that, after the rigors of winter, regain their strength with the sun and sweetness of springtime.

Peter Ramus, in an oration delivered in 1546, made the following vivid contrast between his own and the preceding century. Suppose, he said, a master of a century ago should return to life now, what progress he would discover, how astounded he would be! He would be as surprised as one who, risen from depths of earth, should see for the first time sun, moon and stars shining bright. For then he heard no one speak except in a barbarous and inept manner, while now he would hear countless persons of every age speaking and writing Latin correctly and ornately. Then no one could read Greek, now men not only read it but understand it thoroughly. He used to hear as grammarians, poets and orators, Alexander of Villa-Dei, Facetus, the *Graecismus;* in philosophy, Scotists and followers of Petrus Hispanus; in medicine, the Arabs; in theology, I know not what upstarts. Now he would hear Terence, Caesar, Virgil, Cicero, Aristotle, Plato, Galen, Hippocrates, Moses and the prophets, the Apostles and other true and genuine messengers of the Gospel, and indeed voices in all languages.

Except for the closing allusions to vernacular translations of the Bible, this passage well expresses the original restricted significance of the Renaissance as a purification of Latin diction and grammar, a revival of Greek, and a return from medieval compilers, commentators and originators to the old classical texts. This was all that the revival of learning meant to the Italian humanists of the Quattrocento and to their fellows beyond the Alps, and for them it was enough. The mere thought of it aroused in Ramus a grand and glorious feeling of enthusiasm tempered with complacency. He neither sensed any change in the political and economic set-up nor was aware of any alteration in social and moral values.

As the study and reading of Latin and Greek waned, however—and this was partly because the humanists and classicists had substituted a dead for a living language—fewer and fewer persons could sincerely share in this thrill or impart it to others. Such fervor as the concept of the Renaissance still invoked was largely in the realm of the fine arts, where the term had been applied to the post-Gothic period. It was at this juncture that Michelet called the Renaissance "the discovery of the world and of man," and was followed in this lead by the very influential book of Burckhardt, in which, on what seem too often to be dogmatic or imaginary grounds without sufficient presentation of facts as evidence, the Renaissance was no longer regarded as primarily a rebirth of classical learning and culture but rather as a prebirth or precursor of present society and of modern civilization—"a period," to quote the *Boston Transcript* (February 27, 1926) concerning Elizabethan England, "that witnessed the birth pangs of most that is worth while in modern civilization and government."

This made a well-calculated appeal to the average reader who is little interested to be told that Erasmus was a great Greek scholar or that Leonardo da Vinci copied from Albert of Saxony, but whose ego is titillated to be told that Leonardo was an individual like himself or that Erasmus's chief claim to fame is that he was the first modern man—the first one like you and me. All this was quite soothing and flattering and did much to compensate for one's inability to read Horace or to quote Euripides. It even had its appeal for professors of modern European history and for teachers of the modern languages. It appears to be the concept of the Renaissance which such recent advocates thereof or apologists therefor as Wallace K. Ferguson and Hans Baron are concerned to defend, retreating to new standing ground by plausible hypothesis and ingenious conjecture, when some of Burckhardt's old bulwarks are proved to be untenable by new masses of facts concerning either or both the Middle Ages and the Quattrocento. But would it not make things clearer, if they ceased to employ the old name, since the old concept has been abandoned, and, instead of talking of the Renaissance, spoke of the period or movement or whatever it is they have in mind as the Prenaissance?

With regard to the work of Burckhardt I may perhaps be permitted a few further comments. Of its six parts, the third on the Revival of Antiquity seems to me scholarly and just, recognizing the defects as well as the merits of the Italian humanists and containing many bits of illuminating detail. But most of the political, social, moral and religious phenomena which he pictures as Renaissance seem almost equally characteristic of Italy at any time from the twelfth to the eighteenth century inclusive. The fourth part on the discovery of the world and man uses only popular, not scientific literature, nor may this be dismissed as merely a sin of omission, since elsewhere in the volume are such atrocious misstatements as that few works of Aristotle had been translated into Latin by the fourteenth century. By including such personalities as Frederick II and such authors and literary composition as Dante and the *Carmina burana* within the Renaissance, Burckhardt freed the movement from the embarrassment of chronological limits and made any differentiation between it and medieval culture well-nigh impossible. At bottom this was a wholesome tendency, equivalent to recognition that there is no dividing line between "medieval" and "renaissance" culture, just as most historical museums have a single section labeled "Middle Ages and Renaissance." In general, Burckhardt devoted so much of his pages and energy to the attempt to trace intangibles, such as personality, imagination, passion, spirit, the popular mind, the feeling for this and that, such and such a sentiment, that his book hardly touches the domain of intellectual history and seems to possess a will-o'-the-wisp sort of character.

The attraction which this kind of writing has for many has been well expressed by Professor Schevill in reviewing another book:

> *If the modern scientific method, a well coordinated plan, and the view-point regarding the character of the social process which obtains among present-day scholars are the indispensable requirements of a good history, it would have to be conceded that Mrs. Taylor's book stands self-condemned. But if there is salvation outside the ruling formulas, if a work may still be history, and good history, when, instead of building up a solid edifice of fact, it occupies itself with the spirit behind the facts in the hope of communicating the color and perfume of a segment of human experience, this book can be confidently recommended not only to the notoriously unscientific lovers of the Renaissance but to those grave and reverend signors, the professional historians themselves.*

The trouble is that this kind of writing is almost invariably based upon an insufficient acquaintance with the facts and misinterpretation of them. Of the same genus is another bête-noire of mine, those writers who proclaim that this or that person was far in advance of his time, like Roger Bacon or Leonardo da Vinci. But should you ask them to name a few contemporaries of the person in question who were typical of that time, they would hardly be able to do so.

Was the individual freed and personality enhanced by the Renaissance or Prenaissance? Burckhardt affirmed that with it "man became a spiritual *individual* and recognized himself as such," whereas "in the Middle Ages both sides of human consciousness— that which was turned within as that which was turned without— lay dreaming or half-awake beneath a common veil." It might be remarked that individualism may be a mark of decline rather than progress. The self-centered sage of the Stoics and Epicureans rang the knell of the Greek city-state. Basil, on the verge of the barbarian invasions, complained that men "for the greater part prefer individual and private life to the union of common life." Carl Neumann held that "true modern individualism has its roots in the strength of the barbarians, in the realism of the barbarians, and in the Christian Middle Ages." Cunningham believed that the Roman Empire "left little scope for individual aims and tended to check the energy of capitalists and laborers alike," whereas Christianity taught the supreme dignity of man and encouraged the individual and personal responsibility. Moreover, in the thirteenth century there were "fewer barriers to social intercourse than now." According to Schäfer, "So far as public life in the broadest sense, in church and state, city and country, law and society, is concerned, the Middle Ages are the time of most distinctive individuality and independent personality in volition and action." We may no longer think of the Gothic architects as anonymous, and de Mely discovered hundreds of signatures of miniaturists hidden in the initials and illuminations of medieval manuscripts. No period in the history of philosophy has discussed individuality and its problems more often or more subtly than did the medieval Schoolmen. Vittorino da Feltre and other humanist educators may have suited their teaching to the individual pupil; at the medieval university the individual scholar suited himself. The humanists were imitative in their writing, not original. Vitruvius was the Bible of Renaissance architects who came to follow authority far more than their creative Gothic predecessors. For the Middle Ages loved variety; the Renaissance, uniformity.

Not only has it been demonstrated that the thirteenth and fourteenth centuries were more active and penetrating in natural science than was the Quattrocento, but the notion that "appreciation of natural beauty" was "introduced into modern Europe by the Italian Renaissance" must also be abandoned. Burckhardt admitted that medieval literature displayed sympathy with nature, but nevertheless regarded Petrarch's ascent of Mount Ventoux (which is only 6260 feet high) in 1336 as epoch-making. Petrarch represented an old herdsman who had tried in vain to climb it fifty years before as beseeching him to turn back on the ground that he had received only torn clothes and broken bones for his pains and that no one had attempted the ascent since. As a matter of fact, Jean Buridan, the Parisian Schoolman, had visited it between 1316 and 1334, had given details as to its altitude, and had waxed enthusiastic as to the Cevennes. So that all Petrarch's account proves is his capacity for story-telling and sentimental ability to make a mountain out of a molehill. Miss Stockmayer, in a book on feeling for nature in Germany in the tenth and eleventh centuries, has noted various ascents and descriptions of mountains from that period. In the closing years of his life Archbishop Anno of Cologne climbed his beloved mountain oftener than usual.

As for the feeling for nature in medieval art, let me repeat what I have written elsewhere anent the interest displayed by the students of Albertus Magnus in particular herbs and trees.

This healthy interest in nature and commendable curiosity concerning real things was not confined to Albert's students nor to "rustic intelligences." One has only to examine the sculpture of the great thirteenth-century cathedrals to see that the craftsmen of the towns were close observers of the world of nature, and that every artist was a naturalist too. In the foliage that twines about the capitals of the columns in the French Gothic cathedrals it is easy to recognize, says M. Mâle, a large number of plants: "the plantain, arum, renunculus, fern, clover, coladine, hepatica, columbine, cress, parsley, strawberry-plant, ivy, snapdragon, the flower of the broom, and the leaf of the oak, a typically French collection of flowers loved from childhood." *Mutatis mutandis,* the same statement could be made concerning the carved vegetation that runs riot in Lincoln cathedral.

> *The thirteenth-century sculptors sang their* chant de mai. *All the spring delights of the Middle Ages live again in their work—the exhilaration of Palm Sunday, the garlands of flowers, the bouquets fastened on the doors, the strewing of fresh herbs in the chapels, the magical flowers of the feast of Saint John—all the fleeting charm of those old-time springs and summers. The Middle Ages, so often said to have little love for nature, in point of fact gazed at every blade of grass with reverence.*

It is not merely love of nature but scientific interest and accuracy that we see revealed in the sculptures of the cathedrals and in the notebooks of the thirteenth-century architect, Villard de Honnecourt, with its sketches of insect as well as animal life, of a lobster, two parakeets on a perch, the spirals of a snail's shell, a fly, a dragonfly, and a grasshopper, as well as a bear and a lion from life, and more familiar animals such as the cat and the swan. The sculptors of gargoyles and chimeras were not content to reproduce existing animals but showed their command of animal anatomy by creating strange compound and hybrid monsters—one might almost say, evolving new species—which nevertheless have all the verisimilitude of copies from living forms. It was these breeders in stone, these Burbanks of the pencil, these Darwins with the chisel, who knew nature and had studied botany and zoology in a way superior to the scholar who simply pored over the works of Aristotle and Pliny. No wonder that Albert's students were curious about particular things.

Finally, can we accept the altered concept of a Prenaissance as the vestibule to modern times and seedbed of the modern spirit? Chronologically, perhaps. But, aside from the circumstance that modern times and spirit seem at present to be swiftly shifting, are not our political, economic, charitable, educational and ecclesiastical institutions quite as much an outgrowth from medieval life? Without attempting here to argue this larger question, I would merely recall that medieval men coined the word, modern, and regularly spoke of themselves or the last generations of themselves as such. "Maurus, Matthew, Solomon, Peter, Urso are modern physicians through whom reigns the medicine of Salerno." About 1050 Berengar of Tours was accused of "introducing ancient heresies in modern times"; about 1108 Hugh de Fleury wrote his *Historia moderna.* "On all sides they clamor," wrote John of Salisbury in the twelfth century, "what do we care for the sayings or deeds of the ancients? . . . The golden sayings of the ancients pleased their times; now only new ones please our times." When in the next century Robertus Anglicus composed his treatise on the quadrant, it was called *Tractatus quadrantis secundum modernos.* But then improvements were made in the quadrant and Robert's work became *Tractatus quadrantis veteris.* Even scholastic philosophy had its *via moderna* as well as *via antiqua.*

The concept of the Italian Renaissance or Prenaissance has in my opinion done a great deal of harm in the past and may continue to do harm in the future. It is too suggestive of a sensational, miraculous, extraordinary, magical, human and intellectual development, like unto the phoenix rising from its ashes after 500 years. It is contrary to the fact that human nature tends to remain much the same in all times. It has led to a chorus of rhapsodists as to freedom, breadth, soaring ideas, horizons, perspectives, out of fetters and swaddling clothes, and so on. It long discouraged the study of centuries of human development that preceded it, and blinded the French philosophes and revolutionists to the value of medieval political and economic institutions. It has kept men in general from recognizing that our life and thought is based more nearly and actually on the Middle Ages than on distant Greece and Rome, from whom our heritage is more indirect, bookish and sentimental, less institutional, social, religious, even less economic and experimental.

But what is the use of questioning the Renaissance? No one has ever proved its existence; no one has really tried to. So often as one phase of it or conception of it is disproved, or is shown to be equally characteristic of the preceding period, its defenders take up a new position and are just as happy, just as enthusiastic, just as complacent as ever.

> *You may break, you may shatter the vase, if you will,*
> *But the scent of the roses will hang round it still.*

Still lingers the sweet perfume of the Renaissance; still hovers about us the blithe spirit of the Prenaissance.

Rudolf Wittkower

INDIVIDUALISM IN ART AND ARTISTS: A RENAISSANCE PROBLEM

Rudolf Wittkower was born and educated in Berlin. He taught at Cologne University and the University of London before becoming the Avalon Foundation Professor of Art and Architecture at Columbia University in 1956. The recipient of many honors, he was the author of a number of books on the art and architecture of early modern Europe. Professor Wittkower died in 1971.

Let me start this talk by reminding you of a present-day phenomenon which many of us accept without much questioning. A joke on paper by Picasso, a doodle by Paul Klee are snatched up in the salesrooms for thousands of dollars. If explanations are given, we hear—usually with a shrug of the shoulder—of a passing fashion, of an infatuation of the public, of the flight of money into works of art, and so forth.

All this may be true, but it is also true that the joke on paper and the doodle hold our attention; they hold our attention because we know their authors are Picasso and Klee. Without the pedigree or the signature these works would sometimes hardly be worth the paper they are drawn on.

It is the name that works the magic. Behind the name looms the man, the great artist, about whom we know so much, of whose genius we are convinced, and in whose integrity we believe. Clearly, for an appreciation of these works, a knowledge of the artist's personality is more important than the visual evidence. Even though the work may lack individual quality one cannot argue that the public deceives itself, since it evidently places the artist above the work (of course, often without being aware of it).

The very opposite also happened in history. Seneca reflected on people who venerate the images of the gods but decry the sculptors who make them. A generation later Plutarch exclaimed: "We enjoy the work and despise the maker."

From Rudolf Wittkower, "Individualism in Art and Artists: A Renaissance Problem" in the *Journal of the History of Ideas* 22 (1961): 291–302. Reprinted by permission of the editors of the *Journal of the History of Ideas.* The documentation of the original article has been omitted.

These somewhat hackneyed observations are of importance for my subject because it appears that the problems of individualism of artists and individualism in art are not necessarily reciprocally related. I therefore want to separate these two aspects and discuss first at some length when, where, and why the image of the individualist artist arose and then mention, much more briefly, some phenomena which we may associate with special problems of individualism in art.

The criteria to assess these two sides of the inquiry are of an essentially different order, for the one problem is primarily a sociological and psychological, the other primarily a visual one. On the one hand, we have to ask what traits of personality did artists develop, and what traits did the public attribute to artists viewed as apart from, and superior to, the rest of mankind (implicitly valuing the artist higher than his work); and on the other hand, whether at some periods in the history of art one can detect individualistic features not occurring at other periods in the works of artists.

In order to find out what artists thought about themselves and how the public viewed them, we have to rely on literary sources. Such sources begin to flow only from the fifteenth century on, and first exclusively in Italy. But a previous lack of this sort of literature does not necessarily mean that artists had no individuality. Conversely, even where we have a literary tradition at our disposal, we cannot be sure that, what might look like individual and distinctive traits, are not, in fact, legends or literary *topoi*. Before the war Ernst Kris and Otto Kurz published an illuminating collection of such legends which had currency in the Far East and in the West and may easily be misread as personal characteristics by the uninitiated.

When Pliny tells us that the sculptor Callimachus was nicknamed the "niggler" because of his overzealous application to detail, or Apollodorus the "madman" because he often broke up a finished statue being unable to reach the ideal he had aimed at, we may or may not be dealing with factual biographical material. Nor can we be certain that the single-minded devotion to work of the painter Protogenes took on the form transmitted to us. We are told that, while engaged on his main work, "he lived on lupins steeped in water that he might satisfy at once his hunger and thirst without blunting his faculties by over-indulgence."

Nevertheless, these and similar stories prove that the ancient world, in any case at a late period, associated certain behavioral traits with artists. In the eyes of an elite at least, artists were looked upon, to use a colloquial term, as "queer fish."

It was not until the fourteenth century that the theme of the extravagant behavior of artists enters literature once again. In the *Decamerone* and the Tuscan *novelle* of the period they appear mainly as the perpetrators of entertaining and burlesque practical jokes. For Boccaccio a painter was a man full of fun, high-spirited, quite shrewd, of somewhat lax morals, and not burdened by too much learning. And in one of Francesco Sacchetti's *novelle,* written in the late fourteenth century, one finds a painter's wife exclaiming: "You painters are all whimsical, you build castles in the air, you are permanently drunk and are not even ashamed of yourselves!" This remarkable statement sounds like a prophetic definition of the bohemian, but it should not tempt us to arrive at weighty conclusions.

It is an entirely different matter if 200 years later—to be precise, in 1561—Cardanus, in his *De utilitate,* listing the characteristics of a great many professional men, described painters as "fickle, of unsettled mind, melancholic, and changeable in their manners." His assessment surely reflected current opinions. In fact, the material describing the oddities and idiosyncrasies of artists from the Renaissance on is vast and circumstantial and helps to give substance to Cardanus's dictum.

In support of this claim I want to submit some observations which may throw light on personality problems arising among artists at the time of the Renaissance. It would seem that with the breaking of the guild monopoly in the course of the fifteenth century the artist's attitude to his work changed. Instead of being subjected to the regulated routine of a collective workshop, he was now often on his own and developed habits compatible with his freedom. Periods of most intense and concentrated work alternate with unpredictable lapses into inactivity.

A contemporary who saw Leonardo working on the *Last Supper* describes how he stayed on the scaffolding from dawn to dusk without putting down his brush, forgetting to eat and drink, painting all the time. Then for two, three, or four days he would not touch his work and yet be staying there, sometimes an hour, sometimes two hours a day wrapped in contemplation. Similarly, Pontormo would set out to work and go away in the evening "without having done anything all day but standing lost in thought," as Vasari informs us. I need not give more examples.

Solitude and secrecy became the hallmark of many artists. Michelangelo allowed no one—not even the pope—to be near him while he worked. Tintoretto would rarely admit friends, let alone other artists, to his studio. The sculptor Rustici explained that one should never show one's work to anybody before it was finished. Why this insistence on creating in solitude? The answer is not far to seek. Leaving aside professional and artistic jealousies, it was the need for undisturbed concentration that made solitude necessary. . . .

More than once Michelangelo allows us an insight into the problems that moved him to the core. The essence is contained in the three lines of a sonnet that remained a fragment:

Non ha l'habito intero	Entire understanding none can have
Prima alcun, c'ha l'estremo	Before he's experienced the immensity
Dell'arte et della vita	Of art and life

That experience can only be gained in isolation. And isolation spells agony.

His suffering is the red thread running through many of his letters. Already as a young man of twenty-two he wrote to his father: "Do not wonder if I have sometimes written irritable letters, for I often suffer great distress of mind and temper." And fifteen years later: "I live in a sordid way, regarding neither life nor honors—that is, the world—and suffer the greatest hardships and innumerable anxieties and dreads." As a man of fifty he reports to Sebastiano del Piombo about a dinner party: "This gave me exceeding great pleasure, since it drew me forth a little from my melancholy, or shall we call it my mad mood." Again, at the age of seventy-four he writes to a friend: "You will say that I am old and mad [*che io sia vecchio e pazo*]; but I answer that there is no better way of keeping sane and free from anxiety than being mad." At about the same period he put the paradox differently in a famous sonnet:

La mia allegrez' è la maninconia	Melancholy is my joy
E'l mio riposo son questi disagi	And discomfort is my rest.

The last quotations seem to leave no doubt that the agonized reveling in self-reflection was a satisfying experience to an artist like Michelangelo. But it would be wrong to believe, as is often done, that Michelangelo was an exception. In actual fact, he has the traits of personality, enhanced and to excess, which we find in a number of Renaissance artists.

Michelangelo's choice of the words "madness" and "melancholy" leads us on and I shall discuss them in turn. Madness not in the clinical but in a broader sense as emotional instability or behavioral nonconformity is attributed in Renaissance and post-Renaissance sources to scores of artists. Often they are called "bizarre" and "fantastic."

An early occurrence of this terminology in a historical context is to be found in Girolamo Borselli's late fifteenth-century chronicle of Bologna where the sculptor Niccolò dell'Arca is described as "*fantasticus [erat] et barbarus moribus.*" Here *fantasticus* is perhaps best translated as "eccentric." Later sources, Vasari in particular, abound with reports of the eccentric behavior of artists.

The cases of Piero di Cosimo and Pontormo stand out among many others, but are too well known to need a lengthy discussion. Both had misanthropic habits of the oddest kind. The essential correctness of Vasari's report is borne out by a diary which Pontormo kept from 1554–1556—a moving testimony of a lonely, introspective man, wrapped up in his thoughts and beset by morbid worries for his physical well-being. . . .

As to Michelangelo's claim of being melancholic, suffice it to say at the moment that in this respect too he was not an exception. On the contrary, the sources from the sixteenth century on abound with reports about melancholy among artists.

This brief survey has familiarized us with some of the important distinctions in the personality of Renaissance artists. Their approach to work is characterized by frantic activity alternating with creative pauses; their psychological make-up by agonized introspection; their temperamental endowment by a tendency to melancholy; and their social behavior by a craving for solitude and by eccentricities of an endless variety. While we seem thus to be able to talk of a highly individualized professional type, we must not forget that our general picture is derived from such marked individualists as Leonardo, Michelangelo, Pontormo, Parmigianino, Barocci, and a number of minor stars.

In addition, the question arises to what extent were these artists themselves and those who observed them and wrote about them dependent on new or traditional patterns of thought? To what extent were modes of behavior, the individualized way of life, as well as the traits selected by writers, determined by philosophical fashions and literary conventions?

Where Michelangelo talks of his madness and melancholy, his reactions and his thoughts cannot be divorced from Platonic and Aristotelian concepts which were given wide currency in the age of the Renaissance. It is true that Michelangelo by using the word *pazzia* to characterize his state of mind refers to his nonconformist obsessions rather than to the Platonic "madness." Yet such almost narcissistic emphasis on *pazzia* would be unthinkable without a familiarity with Plato's concept of μανία by which the poets and seers are possessed. It is well known that Renaissance artists appropriated this condition of inspired frenzy to themselves, for it gave their art the aura Plato had conceded to poetry.

Moreover, Aristotle had shown that only men of melancholic temperament were capable of "manic" creativity. Michelangelo's *pazzia* and *maninconia* were thus closely allied conditions which Ficino in *De vita triplici* had authoritatively postulated for the man of genius. Melancholy became the password for artistic talent from the Renaissance on, but as Robert Burton said in the *Anatomy of Melancholy* of 1621: "The Tower of Babel never yielded such confusion of tongues as the Chaos of Melancholy doth of Symptoms," while the clear-headed mystic St. Teresa simply decreed: melancholy "is more common in our day than it used to be; the reason is that all self-will and license are now called melancholy." A perhaps too liberal interpretation of these words might conclude that melancholy stands here for individualism.

Although in the sixteenth century the term "melancholy" acquired many shades of meaning, Timothy Bright's detailed analysis, in his *On Melancholy* of 1586, probably came close to the generally accepted usage. He described a melancholic as "suspicious, painful in studies, and circumspect; given to fearful and terrible dreams; in affection sad and full of fear . . . envious and jealous . . . out of measure passionate. . . . Of pace slow, silent, negligent, refusing the light and frequency of men, delighted more in solitariness and obscurity." This *homo melancholicus* shows many of the distinguishing marks of the race of individualistic artists.

Looking back on this position, one feels bound to infer that the artists developed traits of personality which would tally with current ideas on creative talent and that consciously or subconsciously writers adjusted their reports accordingly.

Is then the breakthrough to individualism in Renaissance artists a myth—one of the many myths depending on Burckhardt's thesis of the liberation of the individual in the age of the Renaissance?

Let us approach this tricky problem from another angle. We know a great many names of medieval artists, architects, and craftsmen from documents and inscriptions. In documents they may be praised as ingenious, learned, skilled, excellent, wise, admirable, zealous, illustrious, and so forth. More important, in the inscriptions the masters themselves proudly proclaim their own and their works' excellence. Thus about 1063 Rainaldus, the architect of Pisa Cathedral, boasted that he had executed a remarkable and magnificent structure; a generation later, Lanfrancus of Modena calls himself *clarus, doctus,* and *aptus.* However one may interpret such inscriptions, it is clear that these masters saw their work in a class distinct from other crafts, as a unique accomplishment. It was precisely this quality of uniqueness that warranted the mention of their names. Can we doubt that this attitude reflects a strong sense of individual achievement?

But how can we combine such an interpretation with the social organization and social standing of artists in the Middle Ages? It would seem that the guilds, which, admittedly, became all-powerful not until the twelfth century, exercised an equalizing influence, for artists were de jure and de facto craftsmen with a well-regulated training and a well-regulated daily routine. Specialists have come to contradictory conclusions: Coulton believes that the guild system had a leveling effect on originality, while Doren, the historian of the Florentine guilds, does not admit any interference of the system with the free development and manifestation of individualism. It is certainly true that the city breeds individualism, but it is just against the background of the guild-controlled craftsman that the personality problems of Renaissance artists appear as of a revolutionary nature and emphatically real.

We may have to agree that the individual was not liberated because he had not been fettered or, more correctly, that he exchanged new fetters for the old ones. With this proviso Burckhardt's thesis remains valid. If anywhere, it remains valid in the field of the visual arts, which Burckhardt excluded from his *Civilization of the Renaissance.*

It is an undeniable achievement of Renaissance artists that they raised art from the level of a mechanical to that of an intellectual occupation. By allying art to science, they drove a wedge between the arts and the crafts and, at the same time, rose in their own eyes and those of the world to the level of an elite. For the first time the artists were also capable of seeing their art as an act of self-expression. And although the modern concept of genius belongs to a later period, statements abound that artists are *born.* For the first time in Western history the initiated public bowed before the artist and acknowledged his special place in society. During his lifetime Michelangelo was called "divine" and ranked above the princes of the blood. Never before had such honors been accorded to an artist.

It was also then that for the first time the artist's personality was placed above his art. In his *Dialogues* Francisco de Hollanda, the Portuguese painter who was in Rome between 1538 and 1540, makes Vittoria Colonna say that those who knew Michelangelo had greater esteem for his person than for his work. Whether this is rhetorical gallantry or not, the fact that such an idea could be verbalized, illustrates the direction of the volte face and shows that the position on which I commented at the beginning had been reached so soon.

Let me sum up: the artists, freed from the protective bond of the guilds, faced the struggle with their environment alone. Early in the sixteenth century they emerged in Italy as an idiosyncratical professional caste with immensely strong leading individuals, who yet developed along the grooves prepared for them. The modern type of artist had come into existence.

The reality of this new type is put into relief by the violence of the reaction against it. As early as the middle of the sixteenth century the individualist artist with his foibles and eccentricities was no longer "fashionable." It was not felt that artists should unobtrusively merge with the social and intellectual elite. Vasari himself, to whom any form of extravagance was anathema, reports in the most glowing terms that Raphael had superseded the qualities common among artists, i.e. their detachment from reality and their eccentricity admixed with madness and uncouthness (*"un certo che di pazzia e di salvatichezza"*). At almost the same moment, the end of the 1540s, Francisco de Hollanda ascribes the following statement to Michelangelo, surely in order to give it the weight of highest authority: "People spread a thousand pernicious lies about famous painters. They are strange, solitary, and unbearable, it is said, while in fact they are not different from other human beings. Only silly people believe that they are *fantasticos e fantesiosos*—eccentric and capricious."

The strongest and most illuminating stricture comes from the pen of Giovan Battista Armenini, who was trained as a painter in Rome between 1550 and 1556. In his *Dei veri precetti della pittura* (1587) he writes: "An awful habit has developed among common folk and even among the educated to whom it seems natural that a painter of highest distinction must show signs of some ugly and nefarious vice allied with a capricious and eccentric temperament springing from his abstruse mind. And the worst is that many ignorant artists believe to be very exceptional by affecting melancholy and eccentricity." By quoting examples of great and learned masters, ancient and modern, Armenini intends to drive home his point "that artists must keep away from the vices of madness, uncouthness, and extravagance, nor should they aim at originality by acting disorderly and using nauseating language."

Nevertheless, the bohemian, or rather protobohemian, type of artist had come to stay, but it was now overshadowed by its counterpart, Leon Battista Alberti's far-sighted vision-come-true: the gentleman artist, whose easy deportment and impeccable manners marked him as a man of the world. This type, unthinkable without the rising social and educational institution of the academies which had their heydey between the seventeenth and the nineteenth centuries, traced its ancestry to Vasari's literary portrait of Raphael. During long periods the conforming academic type retained the upper hand. It was only with the arrival of the true bohemian, the child of the Romantic era, that the tables were turned and the nonconforming type was once again in the ascendancy.

The Renaissance artist's fight for liberation from the encumbrance of the guilds was reenacted in the Romantic artist's fight for liberation from the ties of the academy. The specter of the artist as a member of a privileged group, as a kind of being elevated above the rest of mankind, alienated from the world and creating in splendid isolation, arose once again: the image of the bohemian took shape, fostered as much by the behavior of the artists as by the reaction of the society on the fringe of which they lived. Thus we see at the turn of the nineteenth century problems of personality in the making which, under kindred circumstances, had beset the artists of the Italian Renaissance. Paradoxically, the untrammeled individualism of twentieth century avant-garde artists, their personality and social problems were ultimately derived from the Italian Renaissance, the period in history on which they heaped the fullness of their scorn.

The moment has come to turn from the men to their work. I shall briefly mention here three different topics which seem to me of a particular relevance: first, the question of individual styles; secondly, that of rapid changes of style within the work of one artist; and thirdly, that of the *non finito.*

Regarding individual styles, I want to stress only one single aspect. We can no longer doubt that many masters of the Middle Ages—great as well as mediocre ones—often had highly individual manners of their own. How else could we ascribe with assurance certain statues of the west porch of Chartres to the great revolutionary master and others to his pupils and followers? Attributing works of art, the notorious pastime of art historians, implies an absolute trust in the individuality of style without barriers of time and place.

But the conception of an individual style, the awareness of it, the wish to develop it in a definite direction—this, I believe, could not exist until Renaissance artists began to see themselves as historical beings in a new sense, to which the writing of autobiographies, starting with Ghiberti's, bears witness. It was only then that artists were able to survey the panorama of history and make a considered choice of their allegiance. No medieval artist could have said or written what the architect Filarete wrote about 1460: "I ask everybody to abandon the modern tradition [by modern, he of course referred to the Gothic style]; do not accept council from masters who work in this manner. . . . I praise those who follow the ancients and I bless the soul of Brunelleschi who revived in Florence the ancient manner of building."

The freedom of choice was accompanied by a freedom to change. So far as we can judge, Renaissance artists were the first to change their manner considerably from one phase to another and not rarely from year to year. Without literary evidence and a highly developed technique of analysis it would often be impossible to state that a great master's works from different periods are actually by the same hand. This is true of many artists from Raphael on and particularly so of modern artists. . . .

The change from a comparative stability to a comparative mobility of style is also reflected in a new approach to the training of artists. In accordance with medieval workshop traditions, Cennini, in his late medieval manual, written in Florence after 1400, advises the reader that the student should follow one master in order to acquire a good manner. At the end of the century Leonardo reversed this position by counseling that the aspiring artist should study not only one but many masters, apart from nature. By and large this remained the accepted pattern of art education for almost four centuries. In art historical jargon the method is described by the wooly term "eclecticism" which by the very freedom of choice it implies, should stand, in fact, for individualism of style, as it does in Picasso's case.

It is true, however, that for long periods in the history of art the freedom of choice became illusory because it was made subservient to a dictatorship of taste and fenced in by an art theory which, following literary theory, accepted *imitatio* as a central notion. A leveling in the individualism of style resulted, for instance, during the second half of the sixteenth century in Italy, the second half of the seventeenth in France, and the first half of the eighteenth in England. This led a man like Clive Bell, in a spirited and not yet forgotten book of 1913, to the not entirely paradoxical conclusion that Giotto was at once the climax and anticlimax of medieval individualism; "for Giotto [he claimed] heads a movement towards imitation. . . . Before the late noon of the Renaissance, art was almost extinct." . . .

The *non finito* affords perhaps an even deeper insight into the process of individualization than problems of style. There are, of course, unfinished medieval works, but where we can check, it appears that they remained incomplete for external reasons. With Leonardo and Michelangelo the *non finito* enters a new phase, for it is now the result of internal rather than external causes.

Never before had a tension existed between the conception and the execution of a work. But now self-criticism, dissatisfaction with the imperfect realization of the inner image, the gulf between mind and matter, between the purity of the Platonic idea and the baseness of its material realization—often the subject of Michelangelo's sonnets—prevented these masters from finishing some of their works.

Later, with Rodin and so many others, the *non finito* may be due to a deliberate decision to bring the creative process to an end at any moment of the artist's choice, so that the torso, the roughly hewn work, the half-finished picture, the sketchy execution *are* the finished product. The intentional *non finito* requires a new form of self-analysis and introspection, for the artist has to develop a sophisticated control of the act of creation. Moreover, if only half is said and so much hidden and hinted at, the umbilical cord between the work and its maker is never truly severed. In other words, the personality of the artist asserts itself in the work and through the work more demandingly than at any other period of the history of art.

Without trying to tie together the loose ends of this paper, I may yet claim that we are back at the beginning; for now we find the artist, by the visual evidence of his work, requesting the public to pay due regard to his genius, to follow him even where he seems indistinct, sure in his conviction that all he does is important. The readiness of the public to comply with this unspoken request has its roots in the Renaissance which first raised the artist's personality upon a lofty pedestal.

FIGURE 5. Title page from the large folio of Masses, *Liber quindecim Missarum* (Rome, 1516), by Andrea de Antiquis. The printer is shown presenting his work, printed from wood blocks, to Pope Leo X. From G. S. Fraenkel's *Decorative Music Title Pages* (New York, 1968). (*Used by permission of Dover Publications, Inc.*)

LIBER QVINDECIM
MISSARVM ELECTA
RVM QVAE PER EXCEL
LENTISSIMOS MVSICOS
COMPOSITAE FVERVNT

Edward E. Lowinsky

MUSIC IN THE CULTURE OF
THE RENAISSANCE

*Edward Lowinsky, an eminent musicologist, was born in Stuttgart, Germany,
in 1908. He came to the United States in 1940 and taught in a number of
institutions, including the University of California, Berkeley, before becoming the Ferdinand Schevill Distinguished Service Professor in Music at the
University of Chicago. He is the author of a number of articles and books
on Renaissance music and, since 1964, general editor of* Monuments of
Renaissance Music.

We return . . . to our initial question: can the study of music make
a relevant contribution to the problem so hotly debated among historians of culture, whether or not there was a "Renaissance" and
if so, what precisely it means. In spite of the considerable reluctance
on the part of eminent musical scholars to use the term "Renaissance" in music, I believe that a justification for so doing may be
established on the foundation of the following ten theses:

1. In the fifteenth century a reorganization of musical institutions
was begun which created the material foundation for an unsur-
passed flowering of music. The initial impulse came from the
prosperous and music-loving Netherlands and developed such force
that it reached into all corners of western, and even parts of eastern, Europe before it was spent. The constant migration of Netherlands musicians to Italy and the interaction between Italian harmony
and northern counterpoint were essential factors in the direction
of musical development during the Renaissance, to which the
English made an early but decisive contribution through their insistence on the consonant character of thirds and sixths in spite
of mathematical evidence adduced by Puritanic Pythagoreans.

2. The outstanding characteristic of the musical innovations of
the Renaissance was a movement of emancipation carried on along
the whole front of creative activity: emancipation from the *formes
fixes,* from the dominion of rhythmic modes, and later from the

From Edward E. Lowinsky, "Music in the Culture of the Renaissance" in the
Journal of the History of Ideas 15 (1954): 550–553. Reprinted by permission of the
editors of the *Journal of the History of Ideas.*

shackle of isorhythmic construction, emancipation, above all, from the *cantus firmus* and *cantus prius factus* principle, and emancipation, also, from the hold of Pythagorean tuning.

3. Emancipation is impossible without criticism. Zarlino's criticism of the Gregorian chant and its ensuing reform were as typical for the humanistic attitude as they would have been unthinkable on the part of medieval composers. But this criticism was only a symptomatic manifestation of the rejection of the whole code of medieval musical aesthetics and the procedures of composition. Even where medieval techniques remained in force side by side with the new—as e.g., with regard to *cantus firmus* composition—their nature was essentially changed.

4. The emancipation from the Gregorian chant went hand in hand with the gradual emancipation from the old system of modes. The introduction of new modes, Aeolian, Ionian and their plagal companions (Aeolian is the predecessor of our minor, Ionian that of our major scale), the development of harmony, the intensive development of *musica ficta,* the introduction of chromaticism and of harmonic modulation, brought about a crisis in the modal system which was to lead gradually to modern tonality.

5. The most radical innovation in the process of composition in the Renaissance is the transition from a successive to a simultaneous conception of parts: in the case of simultaneous harmonic conception it is the newly acquired capacity to "think in harmonies," in the case of simultaneous polyphonic conception it is the projection of each part in connection with every other part. The result is a completely unified musical organism.

6. Unprecedented was the enlargement of the tonal world: the tone space was extended in both directions, instruments were being built in lower and higher registers than ever before. The territory of remote tones in the circle of fifths, inaccessible before because of the monopoly held by Pythagorean tuning laws, was newly discovered; chromaticism was introduced, the use of quartertones was considered and tried experimentally; harmonic modulation was discovered.

7. None of this was used for its own sake. The wealth of new musical means was born from the overwhelming desire to express and paint in tones the outer world of nature and the inner reality of man. The expansion of the text repertory of the Renaissance

composer corresponded to the enlargement of tonal means. "Homo sum nil humani mihi alienum puto" was a sentiment that the Renaissance composer could utter with full justification. Thus the real heart of Renaissance music is the new relation to the word and to language. To sing the text in each part so that it can be understood and felt, so that the subject matter becomes, as it were, "visible through tones," this is the deepest motivation of the stylistic revolution in Renaissance music. Though this can still be demonstrated in much greater detail, it may be said that this is the contribution of humanism to music. It was not necessary, as has been claimed, for the Renaissance musician to know actual Greek music. It was sufficient for him to read Plato to discover that the intimate relationship with poetry was at the root of Greek musical thought and practice. But the preoccupation with chromatic and with quartertone composition, too, had its source in the Greek chromatic and enharmonic genders, while the idea of adapting different modes, rhythms, and genders to different texts was at the bottom of the Greek theory of musical ethos. This humanistic spirit, equally with the progressive "harmonization" of music, was responsible for the vocalization of polyphony and for the emergence of the new choral art.

8. The great freedom with regard to the performance of music for voices, or instruments, or a combination of both, facilitated also, for better or for worse, the development of the vocal and instrumental virtuoso. Polyphonic pieces could be sung by one voice accompanied by lute, harpsichord, or organ; they could also be played entirely by instruments. The vehicle of virtuoso exhibitionism was the art of improvising embellishments and coloraturas, an art assiduously cultivated by singers and players. The endless warnings against excess and improper application, coupled with all the instructions on how to improvise embellishments, show what sins against style and taste were committed out of the desire for individual distinction. It is safe to make two statements in this connection: *the virtuoso is a Renaissance phenomenon; the virtuoso precedes virtuoso music.*

9. Though instrumental music learned to walk hand in hand with its older sister, vocal music, it was in the Renaissance that instrumental music became independent and developed a number of autonomous forms from which could develop prelude, toccata,

fugue and ostinato forms. The emancipation of instrumental music was furthered by the vast expansion of the instrumentarium, by the tremendous changes undergone by every type of instrument, and by the keen sense for timbre and color developed during the Renaissance and leading to the art of orchestration in the Baroque.

10. Whether it be improvements of old or invention of new instruments, whether it is a matter of resurrecting ancient music or of probing into unexplored tonal regions, whether it concerns new tuning systems, new modal theories, new calculations of intervals, new melodic, harmonic, rhythmic, or formal designs—every musical enterprise of the Renaissance is characterized by an endless curiosity, a firm—if at times concealed—refusal to abide by authority for authority's sake, an intrepid pioneering spirit and an inexhaustible joy in theoretical speculation, personal and literary controversy and debate, and practical experimentation. . . .

Douglas Bush

THE RENAISSANCE AND ENGLISH HUMANISM: MODERN THEORIES OF THE RENAISSANCE

Douglas Bush is professor of English literature at Harvard University. The selection which follows is part of his first lecture given in 1939 under the provisions of the Alexander Lectureship in English of the University of Toronto. Ferguson considers his first lecture "an excellent general account, certainly the best in our language, of the history of the Renaissance concept."

A more recent religious interpretation of the Renaissance is that of Giuseppe Toffanin. For him individualism, in Burckhardt's sense of the word, is a late medieval phenomenon and a short-lived one. Toffanin sees classical humanism rising, not as a contributory cause of irreligious individualism, but as an anti-individualistic wall of

From Douglas Bush, *The Renaissance and English Humanism* (Toronto, 1939), pp. 24–38. Reprinted by permission of the University of Toronto Press.

learned orthodoxy. The spirit of the age of transition from medievalism to modernity is a faith in the progressive and final religious
and cultural unity of the world under the auspices of classical
humanism. Humanism has a bond of union with Scholasticism,
for both originated in an antidemocratic and antiheretical impulse. Like Scholasticism, humanism arrested for a time the
eruption of the various rationalistic and naturalistic forces which
we call modern. In concentrating on the Italian humanistic
tradition, which many writers of late have tended to neglect or
disparage, Toffanin may perhaps be charged, like other theorists,
with a too narrow exclusiveness, yet to me at least the tradition
of Christian humanism seems a broad and central road. Toffanin's
view of a strong Italian orthodoxy is, I think, fundamentally sound,
and one large result is the emergence of the true harmony, rather
than the conventional differences, between Italian and northern
humanism. But this subject must be postponed for the present.

We may turn now to those theories which reject the notion of
Italy as the matrix of the Renaissance. The only other country which
can be set up as a rival is France—that is, pending an official
proclamation from Germany of purely Teutonic origins. The significance of medieval French culture was already a commonplace in
the time of Pater's volume, and some modern scholars have urged
that the Renaissance was not Italian and of the fifteenth century,
but French and of the twelfth. All the manifestations of ripe culture
found in Italy, from conversation to cathedrals, are found in France
at an earlier date—civilized towns and polished courts; cultivated
society in which women play an important role; an abundant and
sophisticated literature; achievements in the fine and useful arts;
and so on. In many things, such as the romances of chivalry and
the lyrical poetry of love, France is the teacher of Italy. Even the
classical primacy of the Italians may be questioned. Old French
literature shows wide and intelligent knowledge and adaptation of
the Latin classics. The classical revival under Charlemagne, which
caused Bishop Modoin to exclaim that golden Rome was reborn for
the world, was carried on in such centers as Chartres and flowered
in the great renaissance of the twelfth century. This early renaissance was of major importance on the classical side and it was
still more important in the development of philosophy, science, and
mathematics. And all this fertile activity is going on in France before

Italy is well awake. As even a summary partly indicates, this thesis can be carried to extreme lengths, as it has been by Johan Nordström, and we find a French scholar declaring, for instance, that until the sixteenth century English literature was hardly more than an offshoot of French! But even chauvinistic claims may have an ultimately salutary effect. We cannot ignore the international character of medieval culture and isolate the French or the Italian Renaissance as a purely self-contained phenomenon.

The various strands of our large problem are too closely interwoven to be kept separate and the question of Italian origins has already partly anticipated the question of chronology. We must have some rough chronological limits in mind when we use the word "Renaissance." Even if we use it to indicate an individual outlook and attitude we imply that there was some period when that outlook and attitude were characteristic and dominant, or as characteristic and dominant as a particular Weltanschauung ever is in any age. Burckhardt saw the Renaissance as beginning in Italy in the fourteenth century and reaching its climax around 1500. It was a simple matter for him, since Renaissance day banished medieval night, and the few gleams of individualism that he discerned in the Middle Ages, such as the Goliardic songs, were obviously the first rays of dawn. Michelet had already taken a wider view. He had in fact observed so many medieval expressions of individualism that he was compelled to ask why the Renaissance arrived 300 years later than it should have. The answer seemed to be that the medieval mind, entrenched behind its walls of religious conservatism and superstition, stubbornly resisted the forces making for a return to nature. Of later nineteenth-century historians, some saw the Middle Ages as a broad plain, without much on it but churches and monasteries, sloping up slightly from the early barbarian period and then rising suddenly to a mountain range. For others the plain was studded with hills, but they were the foothills of the Renaissance. When we stop to think of it, the term "Middle Ages," though both the phrase and the idea have a long pedigree, is unhistorical. It implies that a period of a thousand years, a fairly large segment in the recorded life of man, was not itself, an integral and consecutive part of the great panorama, but a sort of interlude between the two periods which really mattered. André Maurois somewhere caricatures the unhistorical attitude by having a knight address his followers in this fashion: "In truth, then, we men of the Middle Ages must not forget that tomorrow we set off for the Hundred Years' War."

One reason for the general readiness to play fast and loose with the Middle Ages has been the general ignorance which has prevailed until a relatively recent time. William Morris was a medieval enthusiast, with great knowledge in some directions, yet his conception of the medieval world was quite unrealistic. Of late years we have had the religious, social, and alcoholic romanticism of Chesterton and Belloc, the twin exponents of "the Mass and Maypole" school of history. And many secularly minded people still believe that the Middle Ages were romantic, though a medieval knight, sitting down at a modern breakfast table beside a toaster and a percolator, would think he had been transported out of his own prosaic world into the land of Prester John. But the more serious fault of serious historians has been the drawing of picturesque contrasts between the religiosity of the Middle Ages and the paganism of the Renaissance. Symonds, for example, can indulge in a paragraph like this, in which you will observe, incidentally, the usual echoes of Michelet:

> *During the Middle Ages man had lived enveloped in a cowl. He had not even seen the beauty of the world, or had seen it only to cross himself, and turn aside and tell his beads and pray; . . . humanity had passed, a careful pilgrim, intent on the terrors of sin, death, and judgment, along the highways of the world, and had scarcely known that they were sight-worthy or that life is a blessing. Beauty is a snare, pleasure a sin, the world a fleeting show, man fallen and lost, death the only certainty, judgment inevitable, hell everlasting, heaven hard to win; ignorance is acceptable to God as a proof of faith and submission; abstinence and mortification are the only safe rules of life: these were the fixed ideas of the ascetic mediaeval Church. The Renaissance shattered and destroyed them, rending the thick veil which they had drawn between the mind of man and the outer world, and flashing the light of reality upon the darkened places of his own nature. For the mystic teaching of the Church was substituted culture in the classical humanities; a new ideal was established, whereby man strove to make himself the monarch of the globe on which it is his privilege as well as his destiny to live. The Renaissance was the liberation of the reason from a dungeon, the double discovery of the outer and the inner world.*

At least we should acknowledge that Jean de Meung and Chaucer wore their cowls with a difference, even if they did not enjoy life like Savonarola and Calvin.

To return to the specific problem of chronology, modern critics may be roughly divided into two camps. One view extends the Renaissance backward to include the Middle Ages, the other extends the Middle Ages forward to include the Renaissance. It may serve as a useful warning of my own set of prejudices if I say that I incline to the latter. These two groups often appear in unnecessarily rigid opposition, when logic as well as history would recommend a compromise, but they have one basic attitude in common: they do insist on an historical continuity which makes the Middle Ages and the Renaissance much more alike than they used to be thought. The great watershed of the Renaissance has been, if not leveled down, at any rate made a less conspicuous eminence than it was. If we take the metaphysical view of man and the universe to be the most fundamental criterion, some scholars would say that the later Middle Ages and the seventeenth century witnessed more essential and far-reaching changes than the intervening period. The wholesale introduction of Aristotle in the twelfth century enabled St. Thomas Aquinas to build his great structure of rational theology; it also started the stream of scientific rationalism which was to undermine that structure; and these two movements, especially the latter, may be said to have given the modern mind its direction. At the same time, to be indecisively and exasperatingly judicial, undue insistence on continuity and undue depreciation of the Renaissance may result in missing the woods for the trees, in blurring really significant alterations in the contours of the spiritual landscape. There has been a danger in modern scholarship, a danger which is perhaps being illustrated in these discourses, but our concern at the moment is with the older attitude which brought on the reaction just described.

Depreciation of the Middle Ages has had a number of more or less traditional reasons behind it. One has been noticed, the lack of real knowledge and understanding of medieval culture. Another reason is that historians have been over-ready to take at its face value the scorn which many Renaissance humanists and neoclassicists felt for things medieval, such as degenerate Scholasticism and Gothic art. A future historian would be injudicious if he allowed his estimate of the Victorian age to be guided by twentieth-century rebels against effete Victorianism. Thirdly, there has come down from the sixteenth and seventeenth centuries a considerable Protestant prejudice against the Catholic Middle Ages. Finally, and perhaps chiefly, the Michelet-Burckhardt conception of the Renaissance, which has been so congenial to the modern mind, while it was, to be sure, based on historical research, was also largely predetermined by the philosophic outlook of its authors. It was, in short, a conception engendered by modern secular liberalism, by the nineteenth-century faith in rationalistic enlightenment and progress. From that point of view the Middle Ages appeared as not much more than a long cultural lag, a period in which man was enslaved by a system based on religious superstition and unnatural restraint. Hence anything in the way of revolt was a step toward the Renaissance and, ultimately, toward the triumphant freedom of the nineteenth century.

As I have remarked already, Burckhardt's conception of the Renaissance is still the popular one, and there are still scholars who celebrate the secularizing of the human mind, its emancipation from the shackles of superstition. But nowadays such verdicts command less immediate assent than they once did. As we look around our world and consider where the emancipated mind has landed us, we may think that liberal historians might be a little less complacent about progress. And, in spite of our long subservience to secular liberalism, the climate of opinion in some quarters has changed a good deal. Voices can be heard declaring that the Renaissance, so far as it involved a secular revolt, was more of a calamity than a triumph. Our concern, however, is with less nostalgic and more historical ideas. On the one hand we might defend the Middle Ages by saying that they were full of rebels against religious, ethical, social, and political authority. But such a defense, though obvious and true, is not the one I would choose to offer. The Middle Ages can rest sufficient claims to greatness on their leaders of orthodoxy, however important the rebels may have been. On the other hand, until quite recent times historians, partly through prejudice and partly through ignorance, have much exaggerated the suddenness and completeness of the Renaissance emancipation from medievalism. Since these lectures will be largely occupied with some Good Things which the Renaissance inherited from the Middle Ages, we can afford to admit that many Bad Things also survived. The so-called enlightenment did not banish astrology and witchcraft; indeed such sciences flourished with fresh vigor. And countless other irrational and uncritical beliefs and habits of mind persisted not merely among the multitude but among the educated, including such heralds of modernity as Bodin and Bacon and Descartes.

It is self-evident that the Renaissance, even in its narrower meaning of a classical revival, was a heterogeneous movement which contained many mutually antagonistic impulses. Without forgetting the various pitfalls of generalization we have encountered, and without denying the importance, the necessity, of the rebellious side of the Renaissance, I wish in these discussions to emphasize the more neglected and, I think, more truly representative elements of orthodox conservatism. That means, of course, emphasis on the continued strength of medieval attitudes and ways of thought, in union with a richer and fuller appreciation of the classics than medieval men ordinarily possessed. To put the matter briefly and somewhat too bluntly, in the Renaissance the ancient pagan tradition (which does not mean neopaganism), with all its added power, did not overthrow the medieval Christian tradition; it was rather, in the same way if not quite to the same degree as in the Middle Ages, absorbed by the Christian tradition. And that, after all, is only what we would, or should, expect.

If we are more accustomed to think of the Renaissance in terms of emancipation and rebellion and are more familiar with the rebels than with the conservatives, it is partly because all the world loves a rebel and partly, as I have said, because the historians have stressed what appealed to them. We look at the voluptuous Venuses of the Italian painters and exclaim, "How typical of the Renaissance lust of the eye and pride of life!" But why are they more typical than the multitudinous Madonnas of the same period? For one person who has heard of Vittorino da Feltre, the Christian humanist whose teaching flowered in the culture of Urbino, a score have heard of that really insignificant scoundrel, Pietro Aretino. It is a cliché of English literary history that Marlowe is the very incarnation of the pagan Renaissance. But is Marlowe's half-boyish revolt against traditional faith and morality more, or less, typical and important than Hooker's majestic exposition of the workings of divine reason in divine and human law?

Before we leave general definitions of the Renaissance for classical humanism, I should like to dwell a bit longer on the theory of individualism. There is not much time for it, but one may ask a few questions. In the first place, was the medieval church so crushing a weight upon the individual? One might reply that Chaucer's pilgrims do not seem to feel crushed. On a more philosophic if not necessarily a more convincing level one might appeal to the thoroughgoing moral individualism of Aquinas. It is dubious history as well as dubious praise to claim for the Renaissance the distinction of having established immoral individualism. If that were true, the medieval church would have had an easier task than it had.

But, it may be said, was not Protestantism itself the expression of Renaissance individualism par excellence? While on the one hand Protestantism made every man his own priest, on the other it substituted the absolute authority of the church. And if in practice the medieval church was often repressive, it was less so than Protestantism, as soon as the latter achieved organization and power. Besides, we must remember that the Reformation was only the climax of a widespread medieval movement; Luther's chief guides, apart from the Bible, were Augustine and medieval pietists.

In the field of political thought there is the bogeyman of Europe, the exponent of unscrupulous Italian individualism. Machiavelli was a conscientious official and ardent patriot who was daring enough to find lessons for his troubled time and country in the pages of Livy. His ideal was not the despotism of the ruthless strong man, it was the ancient Roman republic; but he believed that despotism might be a necessary prelude to a republic, since only the strong man could create order out of chaos. Machiavelli's view of the state, as his avowed modern disciple has realized, has much in common with fascism. Further, his supposedly revolutionary doctrine of expediency was in the main a formulation of the principles on which medieval statecraft had operated. As Professor J. W. Allen remarks, in connection with Machiavelli, the further you go into the political thought of the sixteenth century, the more medieval you will find it.

In the field of personal ethics there is that philosophic individualist, Montaigne, who devotes his life to the study of himself as he is, without excuses and without unduly exacting aspirations, and who seems to be, in his quiet ironic way, a solvent of all traditional external restraints. Yet, although Montaigne draws his rationalism from the classics and from himself, he respects religion as a plane of experience above his own. And he is a good if not overactive Catholic, partly by instinct and inheritance, but much more because he believes in the necessity and efficacy of the church as a bulwark of solidarity. Moreover, if Montaigne secularizes personal ethics, he is no modern advocate of "self-expression." He had a large share in creating the ideal of the *honnete homme,* and the very definition of the civilized man is that he obeys standards of good taste, a norm of rational behavior free from individual eccentricities. Thus, however much Montaigne might be invoked by *libertins,* he is to be found on the side of order, authority, reason. His essays may be called, in the words of Lanson (who makes due qualifications), the great reservoir from which is to flow the classic spirit. . . .

Altogether, our theory of the Renaissance must be, like the Copernican hypothesis, the simplest theory which explains the phenomena. That of rebellious individualism is much too simple and exclusive.

Charles Homer Haskins

THE RENAISSANCE OF THE TWELFTH CENTURY

Charles Homer Haskins (1870–1937) is remembered by many as a profound scholar, a great teacher, and a respected author and editor. Educated at Johns Hopkins University, he was a member of its faculty until 1902 when he became professor of history at Harvard University, where he served for many years as dean of the Graduate School of Arts and Sciences. His scholarship and publications in the field of medieval history were recognized when he was elected to the presidency of the Mediaeval Academy of America in 1926. He also served as editor of The American Historical Series.

Preface

The title of this book will appear to many to contain a flagrant contradiction. A renaissance in the twelfth century! Do not the Middle Ages, that epoch of ignorance, stagnation, and gloom, stand in the sharpest contrast to the light and progress and freedom of the Italian Renaissance which followed? How could there be a renaissance in the Middle Ages, when men had no eye for the joy and beauty and knowledge of this passing world, their gaze ever fixed on the terrors of the world to come? Is not this whole period summed up in Symonds's picture of St. Bernard, blind to the beauties of Lake Leman as he bends "a thought-burdened forehead over the neck of his mule," typical of an age when "humanity had passed, a careful pilgrim, intent on the terrors of sin, death, and judgment, along the highways of the world, and had scarcely known that they were sightworthy, or that life is a blessing"?

The answer is that the continuity of history rejects such sharp and violent contrasts between successive periods, and that modern research shows us the Middle Ages less dark and less static, the Renaissance less bright and less sudden, than was once supposed. The Middle Ages exhibit life and color and change, much eager search after knowledge and beauty, much creative accomplishment in art, in literature, in institutions. The Italian Renaissance was preceded by similar, if less wide-reaching movements; indeed it came out of the Middle Ages so gradually that historians are not agreed when it began, and some would go so far as to abolish the name, and perhaps even the fact, of a renaissance in the Quattro-cento.

To the most important of these earlier revivals the present volume is devoted, the Renaissance of the Twelfth Century which is often called the medieval Renaissance. This century, the very century of St. Bernard and his mule, was in many respects an age of fresh and vigorous life. The epoch of the Crusades, of the rise of towns, and of the earliest bureaucratic states of the West, it saw the culmination of Romanesque art and the beginnings of Gothic; the emergence of the vernacular literatures; the revival of the Latin classics and of Latin poetry and Roman law; the recovery of Greek science, with its Arabic additions, and of much of Greek philosophy; and the origin of the first European universities. The twelfth century left its sig-nature on higher education, on the scholastic philosophy, on Euro-pean systems of law, on architecture and sculpture, on the liturgical drama, on Latin and vernacular poetry. The theme is too broad for a single volume, or a single author. Accordingly, since the art and the vernacular literature of the epoch are better known, we shall confine ourselves to the Latin side of this renaissance, the revival of learning in the broadest sense—the Latin classics and their in-fluence, the new jurisprudence and the more varied historiography, the new knowledge of the Greeks and Arabs and its effects upon Western science and philosophy, and the new institutions of learn-ing, all seen against the background of the century's centers and materials of culture. The absence of any other work on this general theme must be the author's excuse for attempting a sketch where much must necessarily rest upon secondhand information. . . .

The Historical Background

The European Middle Ages form a complex and varied as well as a very considerable period of human history. Within their thousand years of time they include a large variety of peoples, institutions, and types of culture, illustrating many processes of historical development and containing the origins of many phases of modern civilization. Contrasts of East and West, of the North and the Mediterranean, of old and new, sacred and profane, ideal and actual, give life and color and movement to this period, while its close relations alike to antiquity and to the modern world assure it a place in the continuous history of human development. Both continuity and change are characteristic of the Middle Ages, as indeed of all great epochs of history.

This conception runs counter to ideas widely prevalent not only among the unlearned but among many who ought to know better. To these the Middle Ages are synonymous with all that is uniform, static, and unprogressive; "medieval" is applied to anything outgrown, until, as Bernard Shaw reminds us, even the fashion plates of the preceding generation are pronounced "medieval." The barbarism of Goths and Vandals is thus spread out over the following centuries, even to that "Gothic" architecture which is one of the crowning achievements of the constructive genius of the race; the ignorance and superstition of this age are contrasted with the enlightenment of the Renaissance, in strange disregard of the alchemy and demonology which flourished throughout this succeeding period; and the phrase "Dark Ages" is extended to cover all that came between, let us say, 476 and 1453. Even those who realize that the Middle Ages are not "dark" often think of them as uniform, at least during the central period from c. 800 to c. 1300, distinguished by the great medieval institutions of feudalism, ecclesiasticism, and Scholasticism, and preceded and followed by epochs of more rapid transformation. Such a view ignores the unequal development of different parts of Europe, the great economic changes within this epoch, the influx of the new learning of the East, the shifting currents in the stream of medieval life and thought. On the intellectual side, in particular, it neglects the medieval revival of the Latin classics and of jurisprudence, the extension of knowledge by the absorption of ancient learning and by observation, and the creative work of these centuries in poetry and in art. In many ways the differences between the Europe of 800 and that of 1300 are greater than the resemblances. Similar contrasts, though on a smaller scale, can be made between the culture of the eighth and the ninth centuries, between conditions c. 1100 and those c. 1200, between the preceding age and the new intellectual currents of the thirteenth and fourteenth centuries.

For convenience's sake it has become common to designate certain of these movements as the Carolingian Renaissance, the Ottonian Renaissance, the Renaissance of the Twelfth Century, after the fashion of the phrase once reserved exclusively for the Italian Renaissance of the fifteenth century. Some, it is true, would give up the word renaissance altogether, as conveying false impressions of a sudden change and an original and distinct culture in the fifteenth century, and, in general, as implying that there ever can be a real revival of something past; Mr. Henry Osborn Taylor prides himself on writing two volumes on *Thought and Expression in the Sixteenth Century* without once using this forbidden term. Nevertheless, it may be doubted whether such a term is more open to misinterpretation than others, like the Quattrocento or the sixteenth century, and it is so convenient and so well established that, like Austria, if it had not existed we should have to invent it. There was an Italian Renaissance, whatever we choose to call it, and nothing is gained by the process which ascribes the Homeric poems to another poet of the same name. But—thus much we must grant— the great Renaissance was not so unique or so decisive as has been supposed. The contrast of culture was not nearly so sharp as it seemed to the humanists and their modern followers, while within the Middle Ages there were intellectual revivals whose influence was not lost to succeeding times, and which partook of the same character as the better known movement of the fifteenth century. To one of these this volume is devoted, the Renaissance of the Twelfth Century, which is also known as the Medieval Renaissance.

The renaissance of the twelfth century might conceivably be taken so broadly as to cover all the changes through which Europe passed in the hundred years or more from the late eleventh century to the taking of Constantinople by the Latins in 1204 and the contemporary events which usher in the thirteenth century, just as we speak of the Age of the Renaissance in later Italy; but such a view becomes too wide and vague for any purpose save the general history of the period. More profitably we may limit the phrase to the history of culture in this age—the complete development of Romanesque art and the rise of Gothic; the full bloom of vernacular poetry, both lyric and epic; and the new learning and new literature in Latin. The century begins with the flourishing age of the cathedral schools and closes with the earliest universities already well established at

Salerno, Bologna, Paris, Montpellier, and Oxford. It starts with only
the bare outlines of the seven liberal arts and ends in possession
of the Roman and canon law, the new Aristotle, the new Euclid and
Ptolemy, and the Greek and Arabic physicians, thus making possible
a new philosophy and a new science. It sees a revival of the Latin
classics, of Latin prose, and of Latin verse, both in the ancient style
of Hildebert and the new rhymes of the Goliardi, and the formation
of the liturgical drama. New activity in historical writing reflects the
variety and amplitude of a richer age—biography, memoir, court
annals, the vernacular history, and the city chronicle. A library of
c. 1100 would have little beyond the Bible and the Latin Fathers,
with their Carolingian commentators, the service books of the
church and various lives of saints, the textbooks of Boethius and
some others, bits of local history, and perhaps certain of the Latin
classics, too often covered with dust. About 1200, or a few years
later, we should expect to find, not only more and better copies
of these older works, but also the Corpus Juris Civilis and the
classics partially rescued from neglect; the canonical collections
of Gratian and the recent popes, the theology of Anselm and Peter
Lombard and the other early Scholastics; the writings of St. Bernard
and other monastic leaders (a good quarter of the 217 volumes of the
Latin *Patrologia* belong to this period); a mass of new history, poetry,
and correspondence; the philosophy, mathematics, and astronomy
unknown to the earlier medieval tradition and recovered from the
Greeks and Arabs in the course of the twelfth century. We should
now have the great feudal epics of France and the best of the
Provençal lyrics, as well as the earliest works in Middle High German. Romanesque art would have reached and passed its prime,
and the new Gothic style would be firmly established at Paris,
Chartres, and lesser centers in the Ile de France.

A survey of the whole Western culture of the twelfth century would
take us far afield, and in many directions the preliminary studies are
still lacking. The limits of the present volume, and of its author's
knowledge, compel us to leave aside the architecture and sculpture
of the age, as well as its vernacular literature, and concentrate our
attention upon the Latin writings of the period and what of its life
and thought they reveal. Art and literature are never wholly distinct,
and Latin and vernacular cannot, of course, be sharply separated,
for they run on lines which are often parallel and often cross or

converge, and we are learning that it is quite impossible to maintain the watertight compartments which were once thought to separate the writings of the learned and unlearned. The interpenetration
of these two literatures must constantly be kept in mind. Nevertheless, the two are capable of separate discussion, and, since far
more attention has been given to the vernacular, justification is not
hard to find for a treatment of the more specifically Latin Renaissance.

Chronological limits are not easy to set. Centuries are at best but
arbitrary conveniences which must not be permitted to clog or distort our historical thinking: history cannot remain history if sawed
off into even lengths of hundreds of years. The most that can be said
is that the later eleventh century shows many signs of new life,
political, economic, religious, intellectual, for which, like the revival
of Roman law and the new interest in the classics, specific dates
can rarely be assigned, and that, if we were to choose the First
Crusade in 1096 as a convenient turning point, it must be with a
full realization that this particular event has in itself no decisive importance in intellectual history, and that the real change began some
fifty years earlier. At the latter end the period is even less sharply
defined. Once requickened, intellectual life did not slacken or
abruptly change its character. The fourteenth century grows out of
the thirteenth as the thirteenth grows out of the twelfth, so that there
is no real break between the medieval renaissance and the Quattrocento. Dante, an undergraduate once declared, "stands with one foot
in the Middle Ages while with the other he salutes the rising star of
the Renaissance"! If the signature of the thirteenth century is easy
to recognize in the literature, art, and thought of c. 1250, as contrasted with the more fluid and formative epoch which precedes, no
sharp line of demarcation separates the two. We can only say that,
about the turn of the century, the fall of the Greek Empire, the reception of the new Aristotle, the triumph of logic over letters, and the
decline of the creative period in Latin and French poetry, mark a
transition which we cannot overlook, while two generations later the
new science and philosophy have been reduced to order by Albertus
Magnus and Thomas Aquinas. By 1200 the medieval renaissance is
well advanced, by 1250 its work is largely done. In a phrase like
"the renaissance of the twelfth century," the word "century" must
be used very loosely so as to cover not only the twelfth century

proper but the years which immediately precede and follow, yet with sufficient emphasis on the central period to indicate the outstanding characteristics of its civilization. For the movement as a whole we must really go back fifty years or more and forward almost as far.

Furthermore, the various phases of the movement do not exactly synchronize, just as in the later Renaissance there is not complete parallelism between the revival of classical learning, the outburst of Italian art, and the discoveries of Columbus and Copernicus. Certainly the revival of the Latin classics begins in the eleventh century, if indeed it may not be regarded as a continuous advance since Carolingian times, while the force of the new humanism is largely spent before the twelfth century is over. The new science, on the other hand, does not start before the second quarter of the twelfth century, and once begun it goes on into the thirteenth century in unbroken continuity, at least until the absorption of Greek and Arabic learning is completed. The philosophical revival which starts in the twelfth century has its culmination in the thirteenth. Here, as throughout all history, no single date possesses equal importance in all lines of development.

Unlike the Carolingian Renaissance, the revival of the twelfth century was not the product of a court or a dynasty; and unlike the Italian Renaissance, it owed its beginning to no single country. If Italy had its part, as regards Roman and canon law and the translations from the Greek, it was not the decisive part, save in the field of law. France, on the whole, was more important, with its monks and philosophers, its cathedral schools culminating in the new University of Paris, its Goliardi and vernacular poets, its central place in the new Gothic art. England and Germany are noteworthy, though in the spread of culture from France and Italy rather than in its origination; indeed, the period in Germany is in some respects one of decline as we approach the thirteenth century, while England moves forward in the closest relation with France, as regards both Latin and vernacular culture. Spain's part was to serve as the chief link with the learning of the Mohammedan world; the very names of the translators who worked there illustrate the European character of the new search for learning: John of Seville, Hugh of Santalla, Plato of Tivoli, Gerard of Cremona, Hermann of Carinthia, Rudolf of Bruges, Robert of Chester, and the rest. Christian Spain was merely a transmitter to the North.

FIGURE 6. An outstanding achievement of early Spanish humanism and of printing skill was the publication (delayed until 1522) of the famous Complutensian Polyglot Bible in six volumes. In the specimen page given here (*Jeremiah*, 14–15), the Greek Septuagint on the left has an interlinear Latin translation, the authoritative Vulgate is in the middle column, and the original Hebrew is on the right. From *Biblia* (Alcalá, 1514–1517), Special Collections, Hayden Library, Arizona State University. (*Used by permission.*)

Such names, for the most part only names to us, suggest that the twelfth century lacks the wealth and variety of striking personalities in which the Italian Renaissance abounds. It has no such mass of memoirs and correspondence, its outstanding individuals are relatively few. Nor can it claim the artistic interest of portraiture. Its art is rich and distinctive both in sculpture and architecture, but it is an art of types, not of individuals. It has left us no portraits of scholars or men of letters, very few even of rulers or prelates. It has not even given us likenesses of its horses, such as adorn the palace of the Gonzaga dukes at Mantua.

Johan Huizinga
THE WANING OF THE MIDDLE AGES

Johan Huizinga (1872–1945), the Dutch historian, served as professor of history at the universities of Gröningen and Leyden. A capacity for projecting himself imaginatively into historical ages and personalities makes his writings reveal deep impressions of the spirit and inner life of the subject he was describing. His contributions to cultural history were great and his artistic style and impressionistic manner remind one of Burckhardt.

According to the celebrated Swiss historian, the quest of personal glory was the characteristic attribute of the men of the Renaissance. The Middle Ages proper, according to him, knew honor and glory only in collective forms, as the honor due to groups and orders of society, the honor of rank, of class, or of profession. It was in Italy, he thinks, under the influence of antique models, that the craving for individual glory originated. Here, as elsewhere, Burckhardt has exaggerated the distance separating Italy from the western countries and the Renaissance from the Middle Ages.

The thirst for honor and glory proper to the men of the Renaissance is essentially the same as the chivalrous ambition of earlier times, and of French origin. Only it has shaken off the feudal garb.

From J. Huizinga, *The Waning of the Middle Ages* (London, 1948), pp. 58–60, 297–308. Reprinted by permission of Edward Arnold and Co. The English translations of the French passages have been taken from the footnotes of the book.

The passionate desire to find himself praised by contemporaries or by posterity was the source of virtue with the courtly knight of the twelfth century and the rude captain of the fourteenth, no less than with the beaux esprits of the Quattrocento. When Beaumanoir and Bamborough fix the conditions of the famous combat of the Thirty, the English captain, according to Froissart, expresses himself in these terms: "And let us right there try ourselves and do so much that people will speak of it in future times in halls, in palaces, in public places and elsewhere throughout the world." The saying may not be authentic, but it teaches what Froissart thought.

The quest of glory and of honor goes hand in hand with a hero worship which also might seem to announce the Renaissance. The somewhat factitious revival of the splendor of chivalry that we find everywhere in European courts after 1300 is already connected with the Renaissance by a real link. It is a naive prelude to it. In reviving chivalry the poets and princes imagined that they were returning to antiquity. In the minds of the fourteenth century, a vision of antiquity had hardly yet disengaged itself from the fairyland sphere of the Round Table. Classical heroes were still tinged with the general color of romance. On the one hand, the figure of Alexander had long ago entered the sphere of chivalry; on the other chivalry was supposed to be of Roman origin. "And he maintained the discipline of chivalry well, as did the Romans formerly," thus a Burgundian chronicler praised Henry V of England. The blazons of Caesar, of Hercules, and of Troilus, are placed in a fantasy of King René, side by side with those of Arthur and of Lancelot. Certain coincidences of terminology played a part in tracing back the origin of chivalry to Roman antiquity. How could people have known that the word *miles* with Roman authors did not mean a *miles* in the sense of medieval Latin, that is to say, a knight, or that a Roman *eques* differed from a feudal knight? Consequently, Romulus, because he raised a band of a thousand mounted warriors, was taken to be the founder of chivalry.

The life of a knight is an imitation; that of princes is so too, sometimes. No one was so consciously inspired by models of the past, or manifested such desire to rival them, as Charles the Bold. In his youth he made his attendants read out to him the exploits of Gawain and of Lancelot. Later he preferred the ancients. Before retiring to rest, he listens for an hour or two to the "lofty histories of

Rome." He especially admires Caesar, Hannibal and Alexander, "whom he wished to follow and imitate." All his contemporaries attach great importance to this eagerness to imitate the heroes of antiquity, and agree in regarding it as the mainspring of his conduct. "He desired great glory"—says Commines—"which more than anything else led him to undertake his wars; and longed to resemble those ancient princes who have been so much talked of after their death." The anecdote is well known of the jester who, after the defeat of Granson, called out to him: "My lord, we are well Hannibaled this time!" . . .

Thus the aspiration to the splendor of antique life, which is the characteristic of the Renaissance, has its roots in the chivalrous ideal. Between the ponderous spirit of the Burgundian and the classical instinct of an Italian of the same period there is only a difference of nuance. The forms which Charles the Bold affected are still flamboyant Gothic, and he still read his classics in translations.

The Advent of the New Form

The transition from the spirit of the declining Middle Ages to humanism was far less simple than we are inclined to imagine it. Accustomed to oppose humanism to the Middle Ages, we would gladly believe that it was necessary to give up the one in order to embrace the other. We find it difficult to fancy the mind cultivating the ancient forms of medieval thought and expression while aspiring at the same time to antique wisdom and beauty. Yet this is just what we have to picture to ourselves. Classicism did not come as a sudden revelation, it grew up among the luxuriant vegetation of medieval thought. Humanism was a form before it was an inspiration. On the other hand, the characteristic modes of thought of the Middle Ages did not die out till long after the Renaissance.

In Italy the problem of humanism presents itself in a most simple form, because there men's minds had ever been predisposed to the reception of antique culture. The Italian spirit had never lost touch with classic harmony and simplicity. It could expand freely and naturally in the restored forms of classic expression. The Quattrocento with its serenity makes the impression of a renewed culture, which has shaken off the fetters of medieval thought, until Savonarola reminds us that below the surface the Middle Ages still subsist.

The history of French civilization of the fifteenth century, on the contrary, does not permit us to forget the Middle Ages. France had been the motherland of all that was strongest and most beautiful in the products of the medieval spirit. All medieval forms—feudalism, the ideas of chivalry and courtesy, Scholasticism, Gothic architecture—were rooted here much more firmly than ever they had been in Italy. In the fifteenth century they were dominating still. Instead of the full rich style, the blitheness and the harmony characteristic of Italy and the Renaissance, here it is bizarre pomp, cumbrous forms of expression, a wornout fancy and an atmosphere of melancholy gravity which prevail. It is not the Middle Ages, it is the new coming culture, which might easily be forgotten.

In literature classical forms could appear without the spirit having changed. An interest in the refinement of Latin style was enough, it seems, to give birth to humanism. The proof of this is furnished by a group of French scholars about the year 1400. It was composed of ecclesiastics and magistrates, Jean de Monstreuil, canon of Lille and secretary to the king, Nicolas de Clemanges, the famous denouncer of abuses in the church, Pierre and Gontier Col, the Milanese Ambrose de Miliis, also royal secretaries. The elegant and grave epistles they exchange are inferior in no respect—neither in the vagueness of thought, nor in the consequential air, not in the tortured sentences, nor even in learned trifling—to the epistolary genre of later humanists. Jean de Monstreuil spins long dissertations on the subject of Latin spelling. He defends Cicero and Vergil against the criticism of his friend Ambrose de Miliis, who had accused the former of contradictions and preferred Ovid to the latter. On another occasion he writes to Clemanges: "If you do not come to my aid, dear master and brother, I shall have lost my reputation and be as one sentenced to death. I have just noticed that in my last letter to my lord and father, the bishop of Cambray, I wrote *proximior* instead of the comparative *propior;* so rash and careless is the pen. Kindly correct this, otherwise our detractors will write libels about it." . . .

It suffices to recall that we met Jean de Monstreuil and the brothers Col among the zealots of the *Roman de la Rose* and among the members of the Court of Love of 1401, to be convinced that this primitive French humanism was but a secondary element of their culture, the fruit of scholarly erudition, analogous to the so-called renaissance of classic Latinity of earlier ages, notably the ninth and the twelfth century. The circle of Jean de Monstreuil had no immediate successors, and this early French humanism seems to disappear with the men who cultivated it. Still, in its origins it was to some extent connected with the great international movement of literary renovation. Petrarch was, in the eyes of Jean de Monstreuil and his friends, the illustrious initiator, and Coluccio Salutati, the Florentine chancellor who introduced classicism into official style, was not unknown to them either. Their zeal for classic refinement had evidently been roused not a little by Petrarch's taunt that there were no orators nor poets outside Italy. In France Petrarch's work had, so to say, been accepted in a medieval spirit and incorporated into medieval thought. He himself had personally known the leading spirits of the second half of the fourteenth century; the poet Philippe de Vitri, Nicholas Oresme, philosopher and politician, who had been a preceptor to the dauphin, probably also Philippe de Mézières. These men, in spite of the ideas which make Oresme one of the forerunners of modern science, were not humanists. As to Petrarch himself, we are always inclined to exaggerate the modern element in his mind and work, because we are accustomed to see him exclusively as the first of renovators. It is easy to imagine him emancipated from the ideas of his century. Nothing is further from the truth. He is most emphatically a man of his time. The themes of which he treated were those of the Middle Ages: *De contemptu mundi, De otio religiosorum, De vita solitaria.* It is only the form and the tone of his work which differ and are more highly finished. His glorification of antique virtue in his *De viris illustribus* and his *Rerum memorandarum libri* corresponds more or less with the chivalrous cult of the Nine Worthies. There is nothing surprising in his being found in touch with the founder of the Brethren of the Common Life, or cited as an authority on a dogmatic point by the fanatic Jean de Varennes. Denis the Carthusian borrowed laments from him about the loss of the Holy Sepulcher, a typically medieval subject. What contemporaries outside Italy saw in Petrarch was not at all the poet of the sonnets or the *Trionfi*, but a moral philosopher, a Christian Cicero.

In a more limited field Boccaccio exercised an influence resembling that of Petrarch. His fame too was that of a moral philosopher, and by no means rested on the *Decamerone*. He was honored as the "doctor of patience in adversity," as the author of *De casibus virorum illustrium* and of *De claris mulieribus*. Because of these queer writings treating of the inconstancy of human fate "messire Jehan Bococe" had made himself a sort of impresario of Fortune. As such he appears to Chastellain, who gave the name of *Le Temple de Bocace* to the bizarre treatise in which he endeavored to console Queen Margaret, after her flight from England, by relating to her a series of the tragic destinies of his time. In recognizing in Boccaccio the strongly medieval spirit which was their own, these Burgundian spirits of a century later were not at all off the mark.

What distinguishes nascent humanism in France from that of Italy, is a difference of erudition, skill and taste, rather than of tone or aspiration. To transplant antique form and sentiment into national literature the French had to overcome far more obstacles than the people born under the Tuscan sky or in the shadow of the Coliseum. France too, had her learned clerks, writing in Latin, who were capable at an early date of rising to the height of the epistolary style. But a blending of classicism and medievalism in the vernacular, such as was achieved by Boccaccio, was for a long time impossible in France. The old forms were too strong, and the general culture still lacked the proficiency in mythology and ancient history which was current in Italy. Machaut, although a clerk, pitifully disfigures the names of the seven sages. Chastellain confounds Peleus with Pelias, La Marche Proteus with Pirithous. The author of the *Pastoralet* speaks of the "good king Scipio of Africa." But at the same time his subject inspires him with a description of the god Silvanus and a prayer to Pan, in which the poetical imagination of the Renaissance seems on the point of breaking forth. The chroniclers were already trying their hand at military speeches in Livy's manner, and adorning their narrative of important events by mentioning portents, in close imitation of Livy. Their attempts at classicism did not always succeed. Jean Germain's description of the Arras congress of 1435 is a veritable caricature of antique prose. The vision of Antiquity was still very bizarre. . . .

In so far as the French humanists of the fifteenth century wrote in Latin, the medieval subsoil of their culture is little in evidence. The more completely the classical style is imitated, the more the true spirit is concealed. The letters and the discourses of Robert Gaguin are not distinguishable from the works of other humanists.

But Gaguin is, at the same time, a French poet of altogether medieval inspiration and of altogether national style. Whereas those who did not, and perhaps could not, write in Latin, spoiled their French by Latinized forms, he, the accomplished Latinist, when writing in French, disdained rhetorical effects. His *Débat du Laboureur, du Prestre et du Gendarme,* medieval in its subject, is also medieval in style. It is simple and vigorous, like Villon's poetry and Deschamps's best work. . . .

Classicism then was not the controlling factor in the advent of the new spirit in literature. Neither was paganism. The frequent use of pagan expressions or trophies has often been considered the chief characteristic of the Renaissance. This practice, however, is far older. As early as the twelfth century mythological terms were employed to express concepts of the Christian faith, and this was not considered at all irreverent or impious. Deschamps speaking of "Jupiter come from paradise," Villon calling the Holy Virgin "high goddess," the humanists referring to God in terms like *"princeps superum"* and to Mary as *"genetrix tonantis,"* are by no means pagans. Pastorals required some admixture of innocent paganism, by which no reader was duped. The author of the *Pastoralet* who calls the Celestine church at Paris "the temple in the high woods, where people pray to the gods," declares, to dispel all ambiguity, "If, to lend my Muse some strangeness, I speak of the pagan gods, the shepherds and myself are Christians all the same." In the same way Molinet excuses himself for having introduced Mars and Minerva, by quoting "Reason and Understanding," who said to him: "You should do it, not to instil faith in gods and goddesses, but because Our Lord alone inspires people as it pleases Him and frequently by various inspirations." . . .

To find paganism, there was no need for the spirit of the waning Middle Ages to revert to classic literature. The pagan spirit displayed itself, as amply as possible, in the *Roman de la Rose.* Not in the guise of some mythological phrases; it was not there that the danger lay, but in the whole erotic conception and inspiration of this most popular work of all. From the early Middle Ages onward Venus and Cupid had found a refuge in this domain. But the great pagan who called them to vigorous life and enthroned them was Jean de Meun. By blending with Christian conceptions of eternal bliss the boldest praise of voluptuousness, he had taught numerous generations a very ambiguous attitude towards Faith. He had dared to distort Genesis for his impious purposes by making Nature complain of men because they neglect her commandment of procreation, in the words:

> *So help me God who was crucified,*
> *I much repent that I made man.*

It is astonishing that the church, which so rigorously repressed the slightest deviations from dogma of a speculative character, suffered the teaching of this breviary of the aristocracy (for the *Roman de la Rose* was nothing less) to be disseminated with impunity.

But the essence of the great renewal lies even less in paganism than in pure Latinity. Classic expression and imagery, and even sentiments borrowed from heathen antiquity, might be a potent stimulus or an indispensable support in the process of cultural renovation, they never were its moving power. The soul of Western Christendom itself was outgrowing medieval forms and modes of thought that had become shackles. The Middle Ages had always lived in the shadow of antiquity, always handled its treasures, or what they had of them, interpreting it according to truly medieval principles: scholastic theology and chivalry, asceticism and courtesy. Now, by an inward ripening, the mind, after having been so long conversant with the forms of antiquity, began to grasp its spirit. The incomparable simpleness and purity of the ancient culture, its exactitude of conception and of expression, its easy and natural thought and strong interest in men and in life,—all this began to dawn upon men's minds. Europe, after having lived in the shadow of antiquity, lived in its sunshine once more.

This process of assimilation of the classic spirit, however, was intricate and full of incongruities. The new form and the new spirit do not yet coincide. The classical form may serve to express the old conceptions: more than one humanist chooses the sapphic strophe for a pious poem of purely medieval inspiration. Traditional forms, on the other hand, may contain the spirit of the coming age. Nothing is more erroneous than to identify classicism and modern culture.

The fifteenth century in France and the Netherlands is still medieval at heart. The diapason of life had not yet changed. Scholastic thought, with symbolism and strong formalism, the thoroughly dualistic conception of life and the world still dominated. The two poles of the mind continued to be chivalry and hierarchy. Profound pessimism spread a general gloom over life. The Gothic principle prevailed in art. But all these forms and modes were on the wane. A high and strong culture is declining, but at the same time and in the same sphere new things are being born. The tide is turning, the tone of life is about to change.

Wallace K. Ferguson
THE REINTERPRETATIONS OF THE RENAISSANCE

Wallace K. Ferguson is widely known for his The Renaissance in Historical Thought: Five Centuries of Interpretation *(1948), a work which is basic to an understanding of the various interpretations of the problem of the Renaissance.*

Historians of every generation since Petrarch have contributed to the interpretation or reinterpretation of the Renaissance; but it is only in the past half century that it has become an acutely controversial problem in historiography. Bit by bit, generations of humanists, Protestant historians, rationalists, and romantics built up the conception of the revival of art, letters, and learning, until in the mid-nineteenth century Jacob Burckhardt fused the traditional views, with some very significant additions of his own, into a synthetic picture of the Renaissance as a distinct period in the cultural history of western Europe. The historians who followed in Burckhardt's footsteps must have been very happy men. They knew what the Renaissance was. This period of idyllic certainty, however, was

From Wallace K. Ferguson, "The Reinterpretations of the Renaissance," in *Facets of the Renaissance,* ed. W. H. Werkmeister (Los Angeles, 1959; reprint, 1971), pp. 1–17. Reprinted by permission of the University of Southern California Press. The documentation of the original article has been omitted.

not left long undisturbed. Criticism of the master's conception began even before the end of the nineteenth century, though it was generally ignored. Since that time revisionists in increasing numbers and working from a variety of directions have collaborated in the task of bringing chaos out of order. And so far as can be discerned at the moment, the end is not yet.

No Renaissance historian today can be unaware of the conflict of interpretations. Most of the historians in this country, whose specialty lies in other fields, however, have tended, at least until very recently, to take the various interpretations of the Renaissance more or less for granted, and have been unconsciously rather than consciously influenced by them. Busy with their own specific tasks, they have not taken the time to study the varying trends of Renaissance historiography nor, perhaps, to consider very definitely their own stand in relation to them. In this country we have been rather wary of definite historical interpretations and philosophies of history. And perhaps rightly so. But however much we may shy away from the *Begriff*-stricken Teutonic tendency toward the abstract conception and the *ismus,* we cannot write or teach history without giving it some interpretation, and it may be as well that that interpretation should be a conscious one and that we should be aware of its relation to the historical writing of the past and present. The following brief sketch of the main currents in the history of Renaissance historiography, concluding somewhat rashly with the approach to the interpretation of the Renaissance which I myself have found most satisfactory, is directed primarily to scholars who are not specialists in Renaissance history and is proffered in the hope that it may provoke some thought and discussion, even if it does not, God save the mark, help to clarify the issue.

Looking back over the long evolution of the idea of the Renaissance and its more recent vicissitudes, I am impressed by the fact that the relation of the Renaissance to the Middle Ages is the crucial point. Its relation to modern civilization is a subsidiary problem, dependent on the historian's notion of the extent to which Renaissance culture differed from that of the Middle Ages and the directions in which the deviation occurred. For centuries the conceptions of the Renaissance were shaped by men who disliked what they knew of medieval culture, and the more recent revisions of the traditional interpretation have come, for the most part, from men

who for one reason or another felt drawn to some aspect of medieval civilization. In either case Renaissance historiography has
fairly bristled with value judgments.

The Italian humanists, who laid the first foundations for the modern periodization of history, as well as for the conception of a
rebirth of art and letters after the Middle Ages, were certainly guilty
enough in this respect. Their admiration for classical culture led
them to draw a clear line of demarcation between antiquity and
the period of barbaric darkness that followed the decline of the
Roman Empire. Petrarch thought ancient history ended when the
emperors became Christian. Flavio Biondo set the date somewhat
later and more definitely at the year 410. The humanists thus set
up one of the boundaries of the Middle Ages; but their view of the
thousand years that were later given that name varied, depending
on the aspect of history which occupied them at the moment. As the
political historians of the Italian states, they treated the whole
period from the first appearance of the communes as one of steady
growth down to their own day. But as classical scholars, the products
of an urban and secular society, they found much less to value in
the culture of the period between the decline of ancient civilization
and the recent revival of art and classical learning in Italy. Almost
without exception they ignored the whole body of medieval feudal
and ecclesiastical literature and leaped straight from the decline
of ancient culture to the age of Giotto and Dante or, more commonly, Petrarch. Between those two ages art and letters were dead,
neglected, buried, sleeping, prostrate in the dust—these phrases
occur over and over again—until they were revived or restored to
the light by the great Italian masters of the fourteenth and fifteenth
centuries. For this revival the humanists as a rule suggested no
cause except the unexplained phenomenon of individual genius;
though Leonardo Bruni, the Florentine historian, found a causal
relation in the recovery of freedom by the Italian cities. The Italian
humanists, in their capacity as historians, contributed only these
ingredients to the full conception of the Renaissance: that art and
letters were dead for a period of centuries; that the revival coincided
with the restoration of classical literature; and that it was the work
of the genius of the Italian masters. But these ideas were to live
for centuries among men whose tastes were formed by the classical
traditions of education.

Where the Italian humanists had been generally content to pass over medieval culture as though it were nonexistent, the Erasmian humanists of the North added a positive factor to the conception of medieval darkness by a vitriolic attack upon Scholasticism. Erasmus was convinced that both religion and learning had declined sadly since the time of the last classical writers and the Fathers of the Church, and that a reform could come only through a return to the sources in their ancient purity. The medieval system of education, he thought, was largely responsible for the *de*formation of both Christianity and good letters and in his own day it was still the principal barrier to reform.

After the Reformation, the Protestant historians seized eagerly upon the conception of medieval culture thus developed by the humanists and used it as a propagandist weapon against the Roman church. For two centuries and more, Protestant interpretations of medieval history were oriented by the necessity of proving that the light of the Gospel had been progressively obscured by the malign influence of the popes and their scholastic agents, with the result that Western Christendom had remained for a thousand years sunk in barbaric ignorance, superstition, and spiritual sloth. Philipp Melanchthon described medieval learning as a barbaric mixture of two evils: ignorant yet garrulous philosophy and the cult of idols. And Bishop John Bale, popularly known as "bilious" Bale because of his talent for invective, in one of his milder moments concluded that the mere description of this sordid, obscure, and ignoble kind of writing was enough to move generous and well-born minds to nausea.

For the Protestant historians the Reformation was the beginning of a new age in the history of the church, but they also hailed the revival of learning as marking the dawn of the new day. Viewed from this angle the renaissance of letters became a movement inspired by Divine Providence to prepare the way for the acceptance of the Gospel. The genius of the Italian masters dropped into the background as the theologians sought some more evident sign of God's handiwork. John Foxe, the author of the *Book of Martyrs,* found the origins of the movement in that "admirable work of God's Wisdom," the invention of printing, through which by God's grace "good wits" were stirred up "aptly to conceive the light of knowledge and judgment, by which light darkness began to be espied and ignorance to be detected, truth from error, religion from superstition to be discerned." Théodore de Bèze, on the other hand, ascribed the revival to the fall of Constantinople and the flight of the Greek refugees to Italy.

This latter idea took firm root in the following centuries among northern historians who were but slightly interested in the earlier history of the Italian revival and to whom the cataclysmic cause appealed with all the charm of a theory that made further thought unnecessary. Thanks to Vasari, whose *Lives of the Great Painters, Sculptors and Architects* had made the *rinascità dell'arte* in the age of Giotto and his contemporaries a standard conception, the early history of the revival of art was never forgotten; but through the seventeenth and eighteenth centuries the revival of learning was generally regarded as beginning in the age of the Medici. Meanwhile, the periodization of history implicit in the humanist pattern of cultural history and in the Protestant scheme of church history was reinforced by a growing appreciation of the significance of the explorations and discoveries and of the rise of the national states around 1500. Before the end of the seventeenth century it had hardened into the formal divisions of ancient, medieval, and modern history which still dominate our historical thought. In this scheme of periodization, the Renaissance, in its limited identification with the revival of learning and art became merely one of the phenomena that marked the beginning of the modern age.

It was thus that the eighteenth century historians treated it, but they gave the revival of learning a new interpretation and a new significance. For them it was the first stage in the modern progress of reason. David Hume regarded it as one of the symptoms of what he called "the dawn of civility and science." Like the Protestant historians, if for different reasons, the historians of the Enlightenment condemned both the religion and the learning of the Middle Ages as ignorant, superstitious, and barbarous. Like the humanists, too, they judged the literature and art of the past by classical standards, though their classicism was more rigid than that of the humanists and they added to the condemnation of medieval culture a more positive revulsion against its irrationality, eccentricity, and general formlessness. For the eighteenth century, then, the revival of art and learning under classical influences meant both the restoration of good taste and the liberation of human reason. Edward Gibbon summed up this classical-rationalist interpretation of the literary revival with the ponderous authority that only he could achieve:

> Before the revival of classic literature, the barbarians in Europe were immersed in ignorance; and their vulgar tongues were marked with the rudeness and poverty of their manners. The students of the more perfect idioms of Rome and Greece were introduced to a new world of light and science; to the society of the free and polished nations of antiquity; and to a familiar intercourse with the immortal men who spoke the sublime language of eloquence and reason. . . . As soon as it had been deeply saturated with the celestial dews, the soil was quickened into vegetation and life; the modern idioms were refined; the classics of Athens and Rome inspired a pure taste and a generous emulation; and in Italy, as afterwards in France and England, the pleasing reign of poetry and fiction was succeeded by the light of speculative and experimental philosophy.

But if Gibbon placed the greater emphasis on the influence of the classics, Voltaire laid greater stress on intellectual progress, and on the spontaneous development of Italian genius. He described the history of western Europe as "l'histoire de l'extinction, de la renaissance, et du progrès de l'esprit humain." And of all the European peoples the Italians were the first to emerge from the *grossièreté* of the Middle Ages. In the fourteenth and fifteenth centuries, "barbarism, superstition, and ignorance covered the face of the earth, except in Italy." The Italians had a monopoly on genius. They were the most intelligent people in the world, and only in their rich cities could men live with comfort and enjoy the good things of life. Voltaire gave full value to the independent rebirth of the vernacular literature and the fine arts in the fourteenth century, but described the age of the Medici, which followed the fall of Constantinople and the revival of learning, as one of the four ages in human history that might be counted happy by a man of thought and taste. Voltaire's picture of Renaissance society, however, was not without its dark side. He was the first to stress the moral confusion, the irreligious attitude, and the criminal tendencies which were to become the distinguishing characteristics of the Italian Renaissance in nineteenth century historiography. Apparently assuming that such would be the natural result of the growth of learning and reason, Voltaire concluded that the leading classes in Italy had rejected Christianity. But true philosophy and natural religion, the products of the Age of Reason, had not yet been discovered. Hence the moral chaos of the Renaissance. "No century," he declared, "was so prolific in assassinations, poisonings, treasons, and monstrous debauches."

The tradition of medieval darkness and of the rebirth of art, letters, and reason lasted into the nineteenth century. It was reechoed by Roscoe, Hallam, and Michelet. True, it was no longer undisputed. The Romantic movement introduced a rehabilitation of the Middle Ages. In reaction against rationalist values, the Romantic historians idealized the chivalry, the religious aspirations, the poetry, and art forms of feudal and monastic society. Yet this reversal of values did nothing to minimize the contrast between medieval and Renaissance culture. If anything, the Romantic historians heightened the contrast, added color to the rational wickedness of the Renaissance, and regarded the age of the Medici and the Borgias with a kind of fascinated horror.

Thus far the conception of the Renaissance per se had been limited to the revival of learning or the *renaissance des lettres et des beaux arts.* Nearly all the ingredients of what became the traditional conception of the Renaissance were already present, but they had not yet been fused together into a comprehensive synthesis, extended to include the whole civilization of the period. The Hegelian philosophy of history, with its emphasis on the creative action of the Idea, on the *Volksgeist* and the *Zeitgeist,* pointed the way toward a periodic conception of the Renaissance as a "moment in the life of the spirit," and Michelet had used the term "Renaissance" in a periodic sense. But it was not till the publication of Jacob Burckhardt's *Civilization of the Renaissance in Italy* that the Renaissance was finally established as a separate period in *Kulturgeschichte.*

Burckhardt's Renaissance marked the culmination of the long tradition of medieval darkness and the rebirth of culture. In it the classical and rationalist strains of interpretation were particularly strong, but the whole synthesis would have been impossible before the nineteenth century, and some of its most characteristic features were a direct reflection of Burckhardt's own personality. Burckhardt combined historical insight and a rare capacity for synthesis with the mental and emotional bias of the aesthete and the intellectual aristocrat. Hence his peculiar emphasis on the conscious artistry of Renaissance institutions and on the liberation of individual personality from the corporate bondage of the Middle Ages. His interpretation appealed strongly to the aestheticism and liberalism as well as to the Hegelian idealism of the later nineteenth century. It carried conviction by the consummate artistry with which every aspect of Renaissance life was fitted into its place in an integrated whole, and the perfection of the synthesis helped to conceal the fact that it was a static picture.

But there is little need to dwell upon the Burckhardtian conception of the Renaissance. It is familiar enough. For half a century Renaissance historians did little more than repeat and amplify it, extending it to the northern countries and appropriating to the Renaissance every indication of new life that they discovered in the Middle Ages. Even when historians began to depart from it in one direction or another, it remained the norm by which the deviations were measured.

The revisions of Burckhardt's formula, which have become increasingly numerous in the past four or five decades, proceeded from a variety of sources; from the religious Romanticism of the late nineteenth century, which carried over into the Thomist revival of more recent Catholicism; from the growing nationalism, which in Germany was identified with a Pan-Germanic racial doctrine and in France with a belligerent assertion of French national culture; from a great increase in both the quantity and intensity of medieval studies, which coincided with a general decline in classical education, particularly in this country; and, closely associated with this, the extension of historical research to economic and social fields. Perhaps I might add, too, the natural tendency of historians, most of whom are professors, to think otherwise.

From these and other sources has come an increasing criticism of the following characteristics of the Burckhardtian Renaissance: the causative and determining influence of the revival of classical antiquity; the exclusively Italian origins of Renaissance thought; the unique individualism of Renaissance society; and, finally, the whole conception of the Renaissance as a separate period with a coherent and unchanging character, sharply contrasted with the Middle Ages.

The first notable departure from the classical-rational aspects of Burckhardt's interpretation appeared in the religious Romanticism of Henry Thode's *Franz von Assisi und die Anfänge der Kunst der Renaissance in Italien,* first published in 1885. It was Thode's thesis that the individualism of the Renaissance, its subjective energy, and its reconciliation of religion with nature were the results not of the revival of antiquity, but of the religious mysticism and subjectivism of the Middle Ages. The figure of the saint of Assisi occupied the center of his picture. He was represented as both the culmination of one great trend in medieval religion and the inspiration of the Italian culture of the following two centuries, out of which, in turn, grew both humanism and the Reformation. Thode's book made little stir among the historians until his conception of St. Francis was reinforced by Paul Sabatier's unforgettable biography. Since then, however, there has been a growing appreciation of the Christian content in Renaissance thought at the expense of the classical and rational. Émile Gebhardt and Konrad Burdach were directly influenced by Thode, and one might also mention among those who have stressed the continuity of Christian tradition in Italian humanism H. O. Taylor, Alfred von Martin, Ernst Walser, Giuseppe Toffanin, and more recently, Douglas Bush. It was not so necessary to demonstrate the Christian quality of northern humanism, though Augustin Renaudet and others have done so at great length. The relation between humanism and late medieval mysticism in the North has been pointed out by Paul Mestwerdt and Albert Hyma.

The classical element in Renaissance culture has also suffered from the attacks of the national and racial schools of northern historians. Early in this century Carl Neumann attempted to prove by the example of Byzantium that classical antiquity could not stimulate a new intellectual life, and asserted the revolutionary thesis that the vigor of Renaissance culture was a natural flowering of the one vital force in medieval civilization, namely *Deutsches Barbarentum.* Since then the Germanic thesis has been carried to extreme of claiming direct Lombard or Gothic descent for all the geniuses of the Italian Renaissance from Dante to Michelangelo. More commonly, however, the recent German historians have been willing to admit the Italian national character of the Renaissance in Italy, but have insisted on the spontaneous and independent development of German culture. In much the same way, the French art historian Louis Courajod and the Fleming Fierens Gevaert proclaimed not only the independent development of French and Burgundian art but also its priority to the Italian, thus reversing the stream of influence across the Alps. In the field of literature and learning, too, recent French historians have been at pains to demonstrate the continuity of development from medieval France through the Renaissance. In doing so they have tended either to minimize the influence of the classics and stress that of the medieval French vernacular literature or to claim the revival of antiquity for the twelfth and thirteenth centuries when France still held the cultural hegemony of western Europe.

The rehabilitation of medieval culture, however, owes most to the scholarly work of recent medievalists who cannot be accused either of undue Romanticism or of national or racial bias; and it is from them that has come the most serious attack upon the conception of the Renaissance as a sudden, dazzling revival of classical learning, rational thought, and free individualism. Elsewhere I have called this movement "The Revolt of the Medievalists." Charles Homer Haskins, Franz von Bezold, and others demonstrated the extent of the classical revival of the twelfth century. H. O. Taylor insisted on the continuity of both the classical and the Christian traditions. Helen Waddell in her charming book on the wandering scholars has demonstrated a feeling for the beauties of nature and the joys of this world among medieval poets influenced by classical models. Étienne Gilson, the champion of scholastic philosophy, carried his defense of medieval thought still further and asserted the absolute superiority of the Schoolmen over the humanists in both the recovery of antiquity and rational thought, and Jacques Maritain has called Scholasticism the true humanism. Lynn Thorndike and George Sarton have asserted a somewhat similar thesis in relation to science, tending to see in humanism a decline of systematic ratiocination for which the aesthetic interests of the humanists were an insufficient compensation; and James Westfall Thompson has discovered a more extensive lay education in the Middle Ages than had generally been supposed. Art historians, too, have contributed, perhaps more than their share, to the reversal of value judgments about medieval and Renaissance culture. Finally, in a book by no means free from special pleading, the francophile Swedish historian, Johan Nordström, has translated all the characteristics of the Burckhardtian Renaissance back into the twelfth and thirteenth centuries. This tendency to discover the Renaissance in the Middle Ages has also been accompanied by a parallel tendency to find much of the Middle Ages in the Renaissance and to view the latter period, in Huizinga's phrase, as the "waning of the Middle Ages" rather than as what Hume called "the dawn of civility and science."

One major result of all this has been a new emphasis on the continuity of historical development. Burckhardt's Italian Renaissance has thus been deprived of the unique character which differentiated it so clearly from the preceding period and from the contemporary culture of the northern countries. It has also been deprived of much of its internal integration by the substitution of a dynamic conception for a relatively static portrayal of the spirit of the age.

The recognition of historical continuity is always, I think, a healthy tendency, and one that was particularly necessary in the interpretation of the Renaissance because of the deeply rooted tradition of its complete differentiation from and superiority over everything medieval. But, granting the corrective value of the recent tendency, is it not possible that the historians who are influenced by it are in danger of discrediting unduly much that was worthwhile in Burckhardt's conception and, above all, of losing sight of the very real differences between the prevailing tone of Renaissance civilization and that of the twelfth and thirteenth centuries? To carry the criticism of Burckhardt's Renaissance to the point of abandoning the Renaissance as a period altogether is, I think, unnecessary and deplorable. The term "Renaissance" itself may be open to objection. It has unfortunate connections. But there is as yet no other recognized term for a period which, I think, requires recognition.

I have been happy to note in the last decade or so a swing of the pendulum back toward appreciation of the originality of Renaissance culture. Some extremely important contributions to this tendency have been made by the historians of music, notably, Heinrich Besseler, Gustave Reese, Albert Einstein, and Edward Lowinsky. The history of music in the Middle Ages and the Renaissance has been until recently a much neglected field, but one capable of furnishing valuable illustrations of the changes in cultural tone through these two ages. Among art historians, Erwin Panofsky has done much to rehabilitate the concept of the Renaissance, as Ernst Cassirer and P. O. Kristeller have done for the history of philosophy and Garrett Mattingly for that of diplomacy.

It should be understood, of course, that recognition of the Renaissance as a period in history does not imply that it was completely different from what preceded and what followed it. Even in a dynamic view of history, periodization may prove a very useful instrument if properly handled. The gradual changes brought about by a continuous historical development may be in large part changes in degree, but when they have progressed far enough they become for all practical purposes changes in kind. To follow a good humanist precedent and argue from the analogy of the human body, the gradual growth of man from childhood to maturity is an unbroken process, yet there is a recognizable difference between the man and the child he has been. Perhaps the analogy, as applied to the Middle Ages and the Renaissance, is unfortunate in that it suggests a value judgment that might be regarded as invidious. However that may be, it is my contention that by about the beginning of the fourteenth century in Italy and somewhat later in the North those elements in society which had set the tone of medieval culture had perceptibly lost their dominant position and thereafter gradually gave way to more recently developed forces. These, while active in the earlier period, had not been the determining factors in the creation of medieval culture, but were to be the most influential in shaping the culture of the Renaissance.

That somewhat involved statement brings me to the hazardous question of what were the fundamental differences between medieval and Renaissance civilization, and to the approach to the problem which I have found most generally satisfactory. It is an approach suggested by the work of the recent economic historians who have called attention to the dynamic influence of the revival of trade, urban life, and money economy in the midst of the agrarian feudal society of the High Middle Ages. Unfortunately, economic historians have seldom spared much thought for the development of intellectual and aesthetic culture, having been content to leave that to the specialists, while, on the other hand, the historians whose special interest was religion, philosophy, literature, science, or art have all too frequently striven to explain the developments in these fields without correlating them with changes in the economic, social, and political structure of society. In the past few years, however, historians have become increasingly aware of the necessity of including all forms of human activity in any general synthesis, an awareness illustrated by Myron Gilmore's recent volume on *The World of Humanism*. Further, there has been a growing tendency to find the original motive forces of historical development in basic alterations of the economic, political, and social system, which in time exert a limiting and directing influence upon intellectual interests, religious attitudes, and cultural forms. As applied to the Renaissance, this tendency has been evident in the work of several historians, notably, Edward P. Cheyney, Ferdinand Schevill, Eugenio Garin, Hans Baron, and some of the contributors to the *Propyläen Weltgeschichte*.

To state my point as briefly as possible, and therefore more dogmatically than I could wish: let us begin with the axiomatic premise that the two essential elements in medieval civilization were the feudal system and the universal church. The latter represented an older tradition than feudalism, but in its external structure and in many of its ideals and ways of thought it had been forced to adapt itself to the conditions of feudal society. And feudalism in turn was shaped by the necessity of adapting all forms of social and political life to the limitations of an agrarian and relatively moneyless economy. Into this agrarian feudal society the revival of commerce and industry, accompanied by the growth of towns and money economy, introduced a new and alien element. The first effect of this was to stimulate the existing medieval civilization, freeing it from the economic, social, and cultural restrictions that an almost exclusive dependence upon agriculture had imposed upon it, and making possible a rapid development in every branch of social and cultural activity. That the twelfth and thirteenth centuries were marked by the growth of a very vigorous culture no longer needs to be asserted. They witnessed the recovery of much ancient learning, the creation of scholastic philosophy, the rise of vernacular literatures and of Gothic art, perhaps on the whole a greater advance than was achieved in the two following centuries. Nevertheless, it seems to me that, despite new elements and despite rapid development, the civilization of these two centuries remained in form and spirit predominantly feudal and ecclesiastical.

But medieval civilization, founded as it was upon a basis of land tenure and agriculture, could not continue indefinitely to absorb an expanding urban society and money economy without losing its essential character, without gradually changing into something recognizably different. The changes were most obvious in the political sphere, as feudalism gave way before the rise of city-states or centralized territorial states under princes who were learning to utilize the power of money. The effect upon the church was almost equally great. Its universal authority was shaken by the growing power of the national states, while its internal organization was transformed by the evolution of a monetary fiscal system which had, for a time, disastrous effects upon its moral character and prestige. Meanwhile, within the cities the growth of capital was bringing significant changes in the whole character of urban economic and social organizations, of which not the least significant was the appearance of a growing class of urban laymen who had the leisure and means to secure a liberal education and to take an active part in every form of intellectual and aesthetic culture.

Taking all these factors together, the result was an essential change in the character of European civilization. The feudal and ecclesiastical elements though still strong, no longer dominated, and they were themselves more or less transformed by the changing conditions. The culture of the period we call the Renaissance was predominantly and increasingly the product of the cities, created in major part by urban laymen whose social environment, personal habits, and professional interests were different from those of the feudal and clerical aristocracy who had largely dominated the culture of the Middle Ages. These urban laymen, and with them the churchmen who were recruited from their midst as the medieval clergy had been recruited from the landed classes, did not break suddenly or completely with their inherited traditions, but they introduced new materials and restated the old in ways that reflected a different manner of life. The Renaissance, it seems to me, was essentially an age of transition, containing much that was still medieval, much that was recognizably modern, and, also, much that, because of the mixture of medieval and modern elements, was peculiar to itself and was responsible for its contradictions and contrasts and its amazing vitality.

This interpretation of the Renaissance leaves many of the old controversial points unanswered, though a partial answer to most of them is implied in it. It may be as well not to attempt to answer all questions with a single formula. There was certainly enough variety in the changing culture of western Europe during both the

Middle Ages and the Renaissance to provide historians with material
to keep them happily engaged in controversy for some time to come.
All that can be claimed for the approach I have suggested is that
it seems to offer the broadest basis for periodization, that it points
to the most fundamental differences between the civilization of the
Renaissance and the Middle Ages, while recognizing the dynamic
character of both. At the same time, by suggesting a broad theory
of causation in the gradual transformation of the economic and social
structure of western Europe, it tends to reduce the controversial
questions regarding the primary influence of the classical revival, of
the Italian genius, Germanic blood, medieval French culture, or
Franciscan mysticism to a secondary, if not irrelevant, status. Finally,
such an approach to the problem might make it possible to take what
was genuinely illuminating in Burckhardt, without the exaggerations
of the classical-rational-Hegelian tradition, and also without the
necessity of attacking the Renaissance per se in attacking Burckhardtian orthodoxy.

Suggestions for Additional Reading

The historiography of the problem of the Renaissance is complex and the literature on the varying concepts of the Renaissance is very extensive. Fortunately, there is available an excellent survey of the literature in Wallace K. Ferguson's *The Renaissance in Historical Thought: Five Centuries of Interpretation* (Boston, 1948). This work is a comprehensive and detailed survey of the concept of the Renaissance as it existed in the minds of the writers of successive epochs beginning with the Italian humanists themselves. Burckhardt's significant essay is discussed in chapter 7 and the remaining half of the book is devoted to an analysis of the more recent writings on the subject of the Renaissance and how they support, modify, or disagree with Burckhardt's synthesis.

Bibliographical surveys of the literature dealing with the concept of the Renaissance can also be found in H. S. Nordholt, *Het Beeld der Renaissance: Een Historiografische Studie* (Amsterdam, 1948) and in H. Baeyens, *Begrip en Probleem van der Renaissance* (Louvain, 1952). See also A. Buck, *Zum Begriff und Problem der Renaissance* (Darmstadt, 1969). An excellent bibliography on the Italian Renaissance, cited as a "short guide," occupies forty-seven pages in the paperback edition of Federico Chabod's, *Machiavelli and the Renaissance* (New York, 1965). This bibliography is preceded by a chapter on "The Concept of the Renaissance."

Jacob Burckhardt's work, *The Civilization of the Renaissance in Italy,* should be read in its entirety. Only in this way can this masterful essay be truly appreciated. A number of editions are available, but it must be noted that in many editions the text and notes have been augmented by another German historian. The translation of S. G. C. Middlemore is recommended.

Within the general Burckhardtian tradition but contributing details and additional knowledge to the history of the literature and art of the Renaissance are Francesco de Sanctis's *Storia della letteratura italiana,* 2 vols. (Naples, 1870–71; Eng. trans. New York, 1931), Phillipe Monnier's *Le Quattrocento, Essai sur l'histoire littéraire du XVᵉ siècle italien,* 2 vols. (Paris, 1900 and 1924), Ludwig Geiger's *Renaissance und Humanismus in Italien und Deutschland* (Berlin, 1882), Eugène Muentz's *Histoire de l'art pendant la Renaissance,* 3 vols. (Paris, 1889–95), and Max Dvořák's *Geschichte der italienischen Kunst im Zeitalter der Renaissance,* 2 vols. (Munich, 1927–28).

Hans Baron, introduced to the reader in earlier pages, has long been engaged in showing the interrelations of ideas and the evolution of the social, political, and economic institutions of Renaissance Florence. Besides numerous German articles, the following may be read with profit: "The Historical Background of the Florentine Renaissance," *History,* n.s., 22 (1938); "A Sociological Interpretation of the Early Renaissance in Florence," *South Atlantic Quarterly* 38 (1939); and "Articulation and Unity in the Italian Renaissance and in the Modern West," *Annual Report, American Historical Association* 3 (1942). The views of his articles can best be learned from his chapter in the *New Cambridge Modern History,* vol. 1 (Cambridge, 1957); his *Humanistic and Political Literature in Florence and Venice at the Beginning of the Quattrocento: Studies in Criticism and Chronology* (Cambridge, Mass., 1955); and his *The Crisis of the Early Italian Renaissance: Civic Humanism and Republican Liberty in an Age of Classicism and Tyranny,* 2 vols. (Princeton, 1955; rev. ed., 1966). The Burckhardtian thesis of a union of the "Revival of Antiquity" and the awakening of the Italian national spirit is stressed, with the latter being interpreted as Florentine in origin and character. Leonardo Bruni is his model for the new "civic humanism" which results from the crisis in Florentine history of the early Quattrocento. For a discussion of Baron's views, see W. K. Ferguson, "The Interpretation of Italian Humanism: The Contribution of Hans Baron" and Hans Baron, "Moot Problems of Renaissance Interpretations: An Answer to Wallace K. Ferguson" in the *Journal of the History of Ideas* 19 (1958).

In addition to Alfred von Martin's *Sociology of the Renaissance* (London, 1944), socioeconomic explanations of Renaissance culture are also found in Edgar Zilsel's "The Sociological Roots of Science," *The American Journal of Sociology* 47 (1942); in Ferdinand Schevill's *History of Florence from the Founding of the City through the Renaissance* (New York, 1936); and in F. Caspari's *Humanism and the Social Order in Tudor England* (Chicago, 1954). See also H. Weisinger, "The English Origins of the Sociological Interpretation of the Renaissance," *Journal of the History of Ideas* 11 (1950).

The problem of growing wealth or economic depression during the Renaissance has received considerable recent attention. The chapters by M. M. Postan and R. S. Lopez in the *Cambridge Economic History,* vol. 2 (Cambridge, 1952) depict the Renaissance as a period of stagnation and depression. Later studies are R. S. Lopez and H. A. Miskimin, "The Economic Depression of the Renaissance," *Economic History Review* 14 (1962), and the discussion of the same authors with C. M. Cipolla in "Economic Depression of the Renaissance?" *Economic History Review* 16 (1964).

The question of the medieval or Renaissance origins of modern science has been the subject of considerable debate. The studies praising the scientific spirit of the medieval period and the link between the origins of science and medieval Aristotelianism by Pierre Duhem in his *Le système du monde,* 10 vols. (Paris, 1913–59) were continued by Lynn Thorndike, *A History of Magic and Experimental Sciences,* 6 vols. (New York, 1923–41), and *Science and Thought in the Fifteenth Century* (New York, 1929). George Sarton, who once wrote that "from a scientific point of view, the Renaissance was *not* a renaissance" in his "Science in the Renaissance" in J. W. Thompson, G. Rowley et al., *The Civilization of the Renaissance* (Chicago, 1929), has greatly modified his earlier views in his more recent *The Appreciation of Ancient and Medieval Science during the Renaissance* (Philadelphia, 1955) and *Six Wings: Men of Science in the Renaissance* (Bloomington, Ind., 1957). His monumental *Introduction to the History of Science,* 3 vols. in 5 (Baltimore, 1927–48) reflects his earlier views. See also H. Brown, "The Renaissance and Historians of Science," *Studies in the Renaissance* 7 (1960) and H. Weisinger, "The Idea of Renaissance and the Rise of Science," *Lychnos* 10 (1946–47).

The subjects of humanism and the philosophical thought of the Renaissance have received much attention and study. For a brief review of the analyses of philosophical and humanistic thought, see W. J. Bouwsma, *The Interpretation of Renaissance Humanism* (Washington, 1959). The philosophical contributions of the Renaissance were brilliantly presented by E. Cassirer in his *Individuum und Kosmos in der Philosophie der Renaissance* (Leipzig, 1927; Eng. trans. New York, 1964). L. Olschki gave a very broad and popular base for humanism in his book *The Genius of Italy* (New York, 1949), while the very different histories of humanism by G. Toffanin in his *History of Humanism* (Eng. trans., New York, 1954) and E. Garin in his *Italian Humanism: Philosophy and Civic Life in*

the Renaissance (Eng. trans., New York, 1956) added materially
to the discussion.

The research and writings of P. O. Kristeller on philosophy and
humanism are best known in this country. See especially *The
Philosophy of Marsilio Ficino* (New York, 1943); "Humanism and
Scholasticism in the Italian Renaissance," *Byzantion* 17 (1944–45);
"The Philosophy of Man in the Italian Renaissance," *Italica* 24
(1947); and *The Classics and Renaissance Thought* (Cambridge,
Mass., 1955). Most of Kristeller's articles have been collected in his
Studies in Renaissance Thought and Letters (Rome, 1956) and his
Renaissance Thought, 2 vols. (New York, 1961 and 1965).

On the varying and complicated interpretations of Renaissance
art, see the bibliographies in E. Rosenthal's article "Changing Interpretations of the Renaissance in the History of Art," in *The Renaissance: A Reconsideration of the Theories and Interpretations of the
Age,* ed. T. Helton (Madison, 1964), and E. Panofsky's "Renaissance
and Renascences in Western Art," in *Figura,* vol. 10 (Stockholm,
1960). In his "Renaissance and Renascences," *Kenyon Review* 6
(1944), Panofsky upholds the Renaissance as a style concept. On
the novel elements in Renaissance music, see the entire article by
E. Lowinsky, "Music in the Culture of the Renaissance," *Journal of
the History of Ideas* 15 (1954), portions of which were given earlier,
and "Music of the Renaissance as Viewed by Renaissance Musicians," in *The Renaissance Image of Man and the World,* ed. B.
O'Kelly (Columbus, Ohio, 1966).

Opposition to the thesis of Burckhardt arose from the historians
of the Middle Ages who denied the originality of the Renaissance.
Henry Thode considered St. Francis of Assisi as the moving spirit
and inspiration of the Renaissance movement. The contrast between
the Middle Ages and the Renaissance which the Romanticists had
maintained was rejected by C. H. Haskins in *The Renaissance of
the Twelfth Century* (Cambridge, Mass., 1927) and in his *Studies in
Medieval Culture* (Oxford, 1929). E. M. Sanford, in her article "The
Twelfth Century—Renaissance or Proto-Renaissance?" *Speculum*
26 (1951), considers that century a unique achievement and not a
rival of nor anticipating the later Italian Renaissance. See also C. W.
Hollister, *The Twelfth-Century Renaissance* (New York, 1969); W. A.
Nitze, "The So-Called Twelfth Century Renaissance," *Speculum* 23

(1948); and U. T. Holmes, "The Idea of a Twelfth Century Renaissance," *Speculum* 26 (1951).

Friedrich von Bezold and Fedor Schneider wrote about the continuation of the classical tradition in medieval humanism, as did H. Liebeschütz in his *Mediaeval Humanism in the Life and Writings of John of Salisbury* (London, 1950) and E. K. Rand, "The Classics in the Thirteenth Century," *Speculum* 4 (1929). J. J. Walsh in his *The Thirteenth, the Greatest of Centuries* (New York, 1907) claimed many modern elements could be found in the Age of Faith. See also J. R. Strayer, *On the Medieval Origins of the Modern State* (Princeton, 1970). Humanism was found even before the thirteenth century by D. Knowles in his "The Humanism of the Twelfth Century," *Studies: An Irish Quarterly Review* 30 (1941) and in his *The Historian and Character and Other Essays* (Cambridge, 1963).

J. W. Thompson revealed the extent of medieval lay education in his *The Literacy of the Laity in the Middle Ages* (Berkeley, 1939). D. Bush pointed out the medievalism and the Christianity of Renaissance humanism in his *Mythology and the Renaissance Tradition in English Poetry* (Minneapolis, 1932) and in his *The Renaissance and English Humanism* (Toronto, 1939 and 1956). R. Weiss showed the strength of the medieval tradition in English humanism in his *Humanism in England during the Fifteenth Century* (Oxford, 1941).

A large number of books and articles deal specifically with the problem of the Renaissance. Reviews of interpretative trends or studies of particular criteria can be found in the following English articles: R. H. Fife, "The Renaissance in the Changing World," *The Germanic Review* 9 (1939); E. F. Jacob, "The Fifteenth Century: Some Recent Interpretations," *Bulletin of the John Rylands Library* 14 (1930); N. Nelson, "Individualism as a Criterion of the Renaissance," *The Journal of English and Germanic Philology* 32 (1933); K. M. Setton, "Some Recent Views of the Renaissance," *Report of the Annual Meeting of the Canadian Historical Association* (1947); A. S. Turberville and E. F. Jacob, "Changing Views of the Renaissance," *History*, n.s., 16 (1931–32); W. W. J. Wilkinson, "The Meaning of the Renaissance," *Thought* 16 (1941); Johan Huizinga, "The Problem of the Renaissance," in his *Men and Ideas, History, the Middle Ages, the Renaissance* (New York, 1959); A. Campana, "The Origin of the Word 'Humanist,'" *Journal of the Warburg and*

Courtauld Institutes 9 (1946); B. L. Ullman, "Renaissance—The Word and the Underlying Concept," *Studies in Philology* 49 (1952), and in his *Studies in the Italian Renaissance* (Rome, 1955); and E. H. Wilkins, "On the Nature and Extent of the Italian Renaissance," *Italica* 27 (1950).

The following studies by H. Weisinger examine the theories of the Renaissance found in the writings of the humanists: "Renaissance Theories of the Revival of the Fine Arts," *Italica* 20 (1943); "The Self-Awareness of the Renaissance as a Criterion of the Renaissance," *Papers of the Michigan Academy of Science, Arts, and Literature* 29 (1944); "Who Began the Revival of Learning? The Renaissance Point of View," *Ibid.* 30 (1945); "The Renaissance Theory of the Reaction against the Middle Ages as a Cause of the Renaissance," *Speculum* 20 (1945); and "Renaissance Accounts of the Revival of Learning," *Studies in Philology* 45 (1948).

Books containing collections of articles and essays on the problem of the Renaissance are *The Renaissance: A Reconsideration of the Theories and Interpretations of the Age,* ed. Tinsley Helton (Madison, 1961 and 1964), with articles by G. Mattingly, P. O. Kristeller, E. Rosenthal, E. Rosen, B. Weinberg, and H. Levin; *The Renaissance: Six Essays* (New York, 1962), is a reprint with some revision of *The Renaissance: A Symposium* (New York, 1952) with articles by W. K. Ferguson, R. Lopez, G. Sarton, R. Bainton, L. Bradner, and E. Panofsky; and *The Renaissance Debate,* ed. Denys Hay (New York, 1965), with a number of short selections from Renaissance and more modern writers.

4 5 6 7 8 9 10